Bryn Mawr
Radcliffe
Sarah Lawrence

Smith

Vassar

Wellesley

$87.60 ring
109.99 ear
$197.79

The Fabulous Bouvier Sisters

Sam Kashner and
Nancy Schoenberger

HARPER

An Imprint of HarperCollins*Publishers*

THE

FABULOUS

BOUVIER

SISTERS

The Tragic and Glamorous Lives

of Jackie and Lee

"Ithaka" from C. P. Cavafy: *Collected Poems*, revised edition translated by Edmund Keeley and Philip Sherrard, ed. by George Savidis. Translation copyright © 1975, 1992 by Edmund Keeley and Philip Sherrard. Reprinted by permission of Princeton University Press.

Excerpt from section I, "Shoes" from "Hospital 1" from *Collected Poems* by Robert Lowell. Copyright © 2003 by Harriet Lowell and Sheridan Lowell. Reprinted by permission of Farrar, Straus and Giroux.

Excerpted from "The Last Day" in *George Seferis: Collected Poems, 1924–1955*, Revised Edition, translated, edited and introduced by Edmund Keeley and Philip Sherrard. Princeton University Press, 1995.

FIRST EDITION

Designed by Fritz Metsch

Library of Congress Cataloging-in-Publication Data has been applied for.

ISBN 978-0-06-236498-2

18 19 20 21 22   LSC   10 9 8 7 6 5 4 3 2 1

ITHAKA

As you set out for Ithaka
hope your road is a long one,
full of adventure, full of discovery.
Laistrygonians, Cyclops,
angry Poseidon—don't be afraid of them:
. . .
—you won't encounter them
unless you bring them along inside your soul,
unless your soul sets them up in front of you.

Hope your road is a long one.
May there be many summer mornings when,
with what pleasure, what joy,
you enter harbors you're seeing for the first time;
may you stop at Phoenician trading stations
to buy fine things,
mother of pearl and coral, amber and ebony,
sensual perfume of every kind—
as many sensual perfumes as you can;
and may you visit many Egyptian cities
to learn and go on learning from their scholars.

Keep Ithaka always in your mind.
Arriving there is what you're destined for.
But don't hurry the journey at all.
Better if it lasts for years,
so you're old by the time you reach the island,
wealthy with all you've gained on the way,
not expecting Ithaka to make you rich.

Ithaka gave you the marvelous journey.
Without her you wouldn't have set out.
She has nothing left to give you now.

And if you find her poor, Ithaka won't have fooled you.
Wise as you will have become, so full of experience,
you'll have understood by then what these Ithakas mean.

—C. P. CAVAFY

They walk the one life offered
from the many chosen.

—ROBERT LOWELL

CONTENTS

The Fabulous Bouvier Sisters

PROLOGUE

"Girls Who Have Everything Are Not Supposed to Do Anything"

Never praise a sister to a sister.

—RUDYARD KIPLING

*J*acqueline Kennedy, the greatly admired former First Lady, was diagnosed with non-Hodgkin's lymphoma at the age of sixty-four. The illness spread rapidly through her body, and Jackie opted to die at home, in her spacious apartment at 1040 Fifth Avenue in Manhattan. Lee Radziwill rushed to Jackie's side when she learned of her sister's illness. For a brief time, their long, complicated relationship seemed to melt away and they were just sisters, as close as they had been in their youth. Jackie refused invasive treatment, and the cancer spread to her liver, spinal cord, and brain. She died at home on May 19, 1994—ironically on her father "Black Jack" Bouvier's birthday—surrounded by her family. Her son, John Kennedy Jr., announced her death to the world, commenting that she died at home, "on her own terms."

Lee wept.

But when Jackie's thirty-eight-page will was read, Lee discovered that substantial cash bequests were left to family members (including Lee's two adult children), friends, and employees—but nothing to her. Not even a memento. Jackie's last words to her sister, "for whom I have great affection," were:

I have made no provision in this my Will for my sister, Lee B. Radziwill, for whom I have great affection, because I have

already done so during my lifetime. I do wish, however, to remember her children, and thus I direct my Executors to set aside
the amount of five hundred thousand dollars ($500,000) for each
child surviving me of my sister, Lee B. Radziwill . . .

She left her one-sixth share of Hammersmith Farm to her
stepbrother Yusha, to whom Jackie had remained close throughout her life.

After reading about Jackie's will, Gore Vidal recalled that she
once told him in Hyannis Port, "I've kept a book. With names."
He thought she was joking about this enemies list, but thought
otherwise after learning about Lee being cut out of the will. By
way of explanation he said, "Her life in the world had been a good
deal harder than she ever let on."

Lee was deeply hurt; the public humiliation was like a slap in
the face. Jackie had certainly been well aware that Lee struggled
to have a semblance of Jackie's riches, often having to sell treasured homes and apartments and paintings in order to maintain
the lifestyle that she and Jackie had been born to. So the question
remains, twenty-four years following Jackie's death: After Jackie
and Lee had been close friends, confidantes, and coconspirators
during the most formative years of their lives, why was Lee so
completely left out of her sister's will?

*

THEY WERE ALIKE in so many ways. In an era that clung to conventional roles for women despite new opportunities ushered in
with the second wave of feminism, both women were raised to
marry well, look to men for financial support, and always present
an impeccable appearance to the world.

Both women had a keen eye for beauty in all its forms—fashion,
design, painting, music, dance, sculpture, poetry—and both were
talented artists (Lee drew elegant botanical sketches, and Jackie

wrote poetry, painted, and drew delightful caricatures). Both loved couture and both would be criticized for spending fortunes on their wardrobes. Both created a series of beautiful, beloved homes that would become refuges from harsh fates that often shadowed their lives. Both loved prerevolutionary Russian culture, and both loved the blinding sunlight, calm seas, and ancient olive groves of Greece. Both loved the siren call of the Atlantic, sharing sweet, early memories of swimming with their father, Jack Vernou Bouvier, at his familial seaside retreat in East Hampton known as Lasata (a Native American word for "place of peace"). Both adored their rakish father and missed him terribly when their parents separated in 1935.

But they were different in important ways. One loved to stand out; one sought to fit in. One was outgoing, flirtatious, and fun-loving; the other was bookish and intellectual, with a deep thirst for knowledge. Although both sisters claimed they wanted to work and be self-supporting, one embraced modernism and feminism, and one remained deeply traditional, adapting herself to fit into societally accepted roles for women. Both were animal lovers: one particularly loved dogs; the other loved horses. One often found herself struggling for funds; the other attracted vast riches. One needed to shine on the public stage; one resisted fame and clung to the shreds of her privacy.

The great irony of their lives is that fate handed shy, introverted Jackie a role on the world stage—for much of her adult lifetime she was arguably the most famous and admired woman in the world—and Lee, who longed to shine, was handed the lesser role of lady-in-waiting. "Being Jacqueline Kennedy's sister," their Bouvier cousin John H. Davis explained, "involved crosses and laurels no other Bouvier but she would have to bear."

But Lee rebelled against the role of lady-in-waiting. She was the first of the two sisters to make "a sharp break with the milieu in which she was raised" when she proposed to her first husband, Michael Canfield, settled in London, and later became the first

Bouvier to hold an aristocratic title, as Davis has noted. She has always known who she is, but has been frustrated in finding ways to express herself on the world stage; she needed to battle those who would keep her in a conventional—and secondary—role. Jackie, on the other hand, did not truly become herself until she was in her forties, after her first husband John F. Kennedy's assassination and her second husband Aristotle Onassis's death. Her inner life and her outward actions finally came together, and her originality and perspicacity were given a chance to fully bloom.

Their story is also one of paradise lost and the struggle to regain it, because at the center of their core, they both yearned for the bliss of their earliest childhood, spent with their parents at Lasata, swimming in the sun-dappled waves off the Hamptons in the arms of their beloved father.

The filmmakers Albert and David Maysles, whom Lee had hired in the 1970s to make a documentary about her and Jackie's early years summering among the sand dunes and hedgerows of the Hamptons, remembered a special moment during filming. Albert Maysles recalled:

> One of the most memorable things that we shot was in the cemetery. Lee was walking around the graves in a very sad mood and she was telling me about her family. All of a sudden, she heard the sound of a train whistle in the distance. That haunting sound transfixed her. It must have brought her back to her childhood and the memory of her father's week-end arrivals on that same train. As the cry of the train came roaring through, there was a captivated look on her face that I had never seen before. It was not a public look—I don't think it has ever been captured by a photographer or a paparazzi. It was a private moment that got inside her soul, and it was beautiful. If I weren't filming, I would have been moved to tears . . . something of great beauty came across in that moment, in the cemetery of all places, surrounded by death.

1

LEE RADZIWILL IN NEW YORK

My sister spoke a rather lovely and convincing French, but I got to live a more French life.
— LEE RADZIWILL

I love walking on the angry shore,
To watch the angry sea;
Where summer people were before,
But now there's only me.
— JACQUELINE LEE BOUVIER

Lee's designer's eye was much in evidence the first time we met Princess Radziwill in 2014 in her Manhattan apartment on East 72nd Street, not far from where her sister had lived at 1040 Fifth Avenue. It was a sunny day in spring and Lee's floor-through apartment was bathed in light. "It's my first priority," she said. "I've never had a place that didn't have fantastic light." We emerged from a small elevator and were greeted at the door by Therese, her longtime lady's maid, and ushered into a living room where light poured in from three tall, graceful windows. She was waiting for us on a fawn-colored sofa, impeccably slim, smoking a Vogue cigarette and drinking a Diet Coke, simply but elegantly dressed in black slacks, her champagne-colored hair immaculately upswept into a regal coif.

Therese had arranged a lunch of chilled cucumber soup and an avocado-and-watercress salad, served on a folding table in front of the large fireplace, where an impressive over-the-mantel mirror gleamed back at us. It lived up to her reputation for serving exquisite meals that subtly matched her décor, such as serving borscht to coincide with the color of her dining room walls. Meeting Lee for the first time, we had the uncanny sense of looking into her wide-eyed, sensuous face and seeing two women: Jackie's face is so famous that it's hard not to see it reflected in Lee's, as if Lee has somehow come to embody both women. Whippet thin, Lee's features are more refined than her sister's, her coloring lighter, her lightly tanned skin a shade of honey. Truman Capote famously described her eyes as "gold-brown like a glass of brandy . . . in front of firelight."

We were struck by the Eastern influences in the graceful room, such as the kneeling camel objet d'art in front of the trio of windows, inspired perhaps by her celebrated trip to India and Pakistan with Jackie in March of 1962. Books, an arrangement of orchids, botanical drawings—the beautiful objects are all carefully *placed*. There's not a hint of clutter; Lee is one who took to heart Coco Chanel's famous remark "Elegance is refusal."

"The lack of clutter, the choices of things to put on the wall," *Vogue* contributing editor André Leon Talley commented, "it's all done with care and love of that *objet*, a sense of editing—editing her clothes and editing her friends and editing the menus for dinner. And she edits people. She edits herself. She edits her wardrobe. She edits her life." One thing Lee has edited most carefully has been her relationship with her sister and the Kennedys, and their impact upon her life.

It's been twenty-four years since the death of her celebrated sister, Jacqueline Bouvier Kennedy Onassis, who had become an international icon of grace, style, and beauty. In her long, slow escape from the Kennedys and the Kennedy mystique—and from her sister's long shadow—Lee has retreated ever more into her own exile. Like Napoleon's flight from Waterloo to Paris and Elba, Lee has gone from the Hamptons to Virginia and New Hampshire, to London, finally alighting in New York and Paris, where she divides her time. She summers in the South of France (like Jackie, Lee has always been attracted to French culture). "I had a very romantic imagination as a young child," she mused over her salad. "And France, Europe, French history—things European took hold of my imagination early on." Lee hardly touched her meal, a habit that went back to Miss Porter's School for girls, where she began seriously dieting as a young teenager. As Talley once said about Lee, "You never see her eating any great plates of food. The soup dances on the spoon, but it rarely ends up in her mouth."

In the weeks after John F. Kennedy's assassination in 1963, the historian William Manchester described Jacqueline Kennedy as "a great tragic actress." But it was Lee who had a brief fling with acting, though now she seems more like an elegant but haunted White Russian in exile, from a noble and wealthy family whose demands, and whose tragedies, have inadvertently shaped her fate. If her muse was beauty, it was history that claimed her.

The late writer, intellectual, and professional contrarian Gore Vidal, whose mother, Nina, was once married to the Bouvier sisters' stepfather Hugh Auchincloss, described Jackie and Lee's relationship as "S & M, with Jackie doing the S and Lee doing the M." A catty overstatement, perhaps—and it's no wonder that there was no love lost between Lee and Gore Vidal—but it's no secret that the two sisters, once so close, had by the end of Jackie's life become estranged. We noticed that when talking about Jackie, Lee always refers to her as "my sister," never by name.

Lee once wrote that she always felt that Jackie was the reasonable one, and she the impetuous romantic: "There are people whose lives are almost destined to be shaped by the impulses of their hearts, rather than by reason . . . The desires of youth, for Jackie, were held in check by a certain faintheartedness."

Surprisingly, Lee spoke openly about her sister, though we had been cautioned by Talley, "It's the subject you never bring up. I mean, there's an unspoken rule that if you're friends with Lee, you don't talk about her sister at all."

Talley first met Lee in 1975 when he was working for Andy Warhol's *Interview* magazine. He recalled that "the first thing she said to me was, 'Oh, I love your suit. It reminds me of my father.'" Talley answered that he'd copied it from a photograph of Jack Bouvier dressed in a beautiful single-breasted, one-button suit with Edwardian cuffs and shiny shoes, standing beside Jackie with her pony. "Style," Bouvier once said, "is not a function of how rich you are or even who you are. Style is more a habit of mind that puts quality before quantity, noble struggle before mere achievement, honor before opulence. It's what you are . . . It's what makes you a Bouvier."

Growing up, both girls had adored their father, so it's likely that the seeds of Jackie and Lee's later estrangement were planted early in life, when it became clear that Jackie was their father's favorite, in part because she was the firstborn, was named after him, and she "actually looked almost exactly like him, which was a source of great pride to [him]," Lee said. Their father used to lavish praise on his two pretty daughters, which came to be known in their household as "Vitamin P." But Lee also noted that Jackie received more praise from their father—and more criticism.

After their parents' divorce, the two girls found a new life with Hugh D. Auchincloss and his family at Merrywood, a stately Georgian house and terraced gardens overlooking the Potomac Palisades in McLean, Virginia. They summered at Hammersmith Farm, Auchincloss's sprawling, wooded estate in Newport, Rhode Island, which was also a working farm. The displaced girls were welcomed by their stepfather and delighted in the farm's menagerie of animals, but they still felt like poor relations. The fact that they were the products of divorce—rare in that world, at that time—and were practicing Catholics in a large Episcopalian household added to their sense of being "other," not quite at home.

"We certainly weren't Catholics like the Kennedys," Lee once wrote, "but we went to church every Sunday in New York with my grandfather Bouvier" and, three times a week, to a convent, "Helpers of the Holy Souls, so we were meant to be grounded in the Catholic faith."

There was another point of contention that became apparent when the two women were grown and making their mark on the world. Both women would be admired for their style and beauty, but many believe that it was Lee who had the more discerning eye and love of beautiful things—fashion, flowers, fabrics, color, design. Her interests in fashion, the Italian Renaissance, and Russian dance all predated Jackie's, who would earn international attention for her tastes and interests—some of them entirely guided by Lee, such as her early interest in French couture.

To this day, Lee still wants to be written about apart from her sister. Would she have been famous without her? She never wanted to be the footnote in Jackie's story. As early as 1963, the journalist Barbara Walters described interviewing Lee on camera for the *Today* show, noting how Lee objected to being introduced as Jackie's sister: "'Forgive me,' Lee interrupted, "but would you please make no reference to my sister and not refer to me as 'Princess'?" And later Lee told her, "If you've no objection, I'd prefer to be addressed simply as 'Lee Radziwill' for the purposes of this interview." Walters concluded:

Whereas Jacqueline Kennedy, at least since her marriage, has always seemed to know what she wants most out of life—to be a wife and mother—her little sister has had no such conviction. On the contrary, ever since her debutante days, Lee has lived the life of a woman in search of identity . . . She is a woman who is trying to wear many hats, some of which are considerably more becoming than others.

Her cousin John Davis believed, "If her sister had not been Jacqueline Kennedy, Lee would most certainly have attained a distinction unrelated to any other person's renown." But for Lee, has it been a search for identity, or a longing to be recognized for her gifts and talents, for her style and beauty, for her intelligence, social acumen, and poise?

2

JACKS AND PEKES
IN PARADISE

*My heroes were Byron, Mowgli, Robin Hood, Little Lord
Fauntleroy's grandfather, and Scarlett O'Hara.*
— JACKIE

Living in a fairy tale can be hell—don't people know that?
— LEE

o be with him when we were children meant joy, excitement and love," Lee wrote about her father, Black Jack Bouvier III, a stockbroker with a seat on Wall Street, known for his dark good looks, elegant style, and roguish behavior. Lee still refers to him as "dashing." In her ravishing coffee-table book titled *Happy Times*, published in 2000, Lee wrote, "JBV, my father, was special. The Black Prince, or the Black Orchid as he was also known, had enormous style and charm . . . He brought gaiety to everything we did together."

An investment banker and a ladies' man, Jack Bouvier bore so close a resemblance to Clark Gable that he was sometimes besieged by autograph seekers. Gore Vidal described him as "a charming alcoholic gentleman with whom Cole Porter had had a 'flirtation,' whatever that might mean, since according to legend, Black Jack was as notorious and as busy a womanizer as an alcoholic can be."

Although his womanizing, heavy drinking, and diminishing fortune ended up derailing his marriage to Jackie and Lee's mother, Janet, he doted on his two daughters, showing them off at the exclusive Maidstone Club in the Hamptons, making sure his beautiful little girls were well dressed and well noticed, and encouraging them to work hard and "be the best." Despite the divorce, he would remain an important figure throughout their lives.

Lee's earliest memories are radiant with pleasure: unaware of the tensions in their parents' marriage, she and Jackie spent their summers at the Bouvier family estate on Further Lane in East Hampton. Lasata was owned by Jack Bouvier's father, "Major" John V. Bouvier Jr., and it boasted a tennis court, orchards, a stable and riding ring—even an Italianate fountain brimming with goldfish—on its fifteen beautifully landscaped acres. On idyllic summer days, "Grampy Jack" Bouvier would take his grand-daughters for rides in his maroon Stutz, and the family would attend the local horse shows, where Janet and her firstborn daughter, Jacqueline, would often compete, but it was Lasata's proximity to the sea that Lee treasured most.

Her father "taught me to trust the sea and to share his love for it," Lee remembers. "I can still hear him calling out to us, 'Come on! Swim out to the last barrel! Now get under those waves so you won't get somersaulted and torn to pieces! Here comes a beauty— ride this one in! Hold my hand, hang on to my shoulders. Let's go!' Being with my father during those early summers, having him to ourselves for days on end, was a joy."

The beautiful Bouvier girls—Jacqueline Lee and Caroline Lee— were bred to dazzle. Jackie was born on July 28, 1929, at South-ampton Hospital on Long Island. Lee arrived there three and a half years later on March 3, 1933. In contrast to her dark-haired, athletic sister, Lee was light-haired, chubby, mischievous, and loved to be the center of attention. She also had a strong adventurous streak. Years later, she recalled that, feeling miserable one day in the family's New York apartment,

> I took my mother's high heels and my dog, a Bouvier des Flandres, and walked across the Triborough Bridge, saying I'm going to escape, I'm going to get out of here! I realized I couldn't go much further, and I didn't know where I was going in any case. And so I turned back, and, of course, when I got home, as usual, I was punished.

Caroline Lee Bouvier would always be known as Lee, her mother's maiden name. The Bouviers were living in an eleven-room duplex at 740 Park Avenue, leased to them rent-free by Janet's father, who had made a fortune in real estate, because Jack Bouvier was experiencing financial insecurities and could not be counted upon to maintain the family as they were accustomed to being maintained. It added to the tensions in that household, as Janet's father later felt that Bouvier had only married his daughter to shore up his financial status, which had been left shaky by the Wall Street crash of 1929—the year of Jackie's birth.

Differences between the two girls would shape the women to come: Jackie had a first-class brain, intellectual curiosity, a fascination with history, and an inherent shyness. In the first half of her life, she would mostly follow in the path that Janet had laid out for her two daughters: observe decorum, dress beautifully but conservatively, and marry a rich husband (or two). Jackie would become the ultimate symbol of prefeminist, demure womanhood, and would be greatly admired for that. Lee would rebel, having several affairs and trying time and again to forge a career and an identity for herself apart from her sister's. Whereas Jackie would become universally admired—practically deified, especially just following the assassination of John F. Kennedy—Lee would often be swatted down, the object of criticism and sometimes ridicule, having to be rescued on more than one occasion by her far more successful sister. Yet Lee continued, always, on her path of adventurous self-discovery, sans her mother's high heels.

From an early age, Jackie won annual prizes on her beloved horse, Danseuse, encouraged by Janet, an avid and prizewinning equestrienne. But Lee—usually so adventurous—was frightened of horses after an early mishap. "I was thrown one day, three times in a row; chipped my front tooth, broke some ribs, had a hoofprint on my stomach," she recalled. "And every time, my father made me get back on."

As young girls, they called each other "Jacks" and "Pekes." Lee adored her older sister, but it was often difficult living up to her already long list of accomplishments, beginning with winning equestrienne prizes when Lee was still a toddler, earning top grades at the Chapin School for girls on East End Avenue in Manhattan, and again at Miss Porter's School in Farmington, Connecticut, and being named Debutante of the Year years before Lee attended a single debutante ball. Sisters are usually competitive—it just goes with the territory—but it was hard living up to Jackie's spectacular successes. Lee realized early on that her adored father "favored Jackie . . . That was very clear to me, but I didn't resent it, because I understood he had reason to . . . she was not only named after him—or at least as close as you could get a girl's name to a boy's—but she actually looked almost exactly like him, which was a source of great pride to my father."

Early on, they carved out their separate realms: Jackie, like her mother, loved riding and competing. Lee adored swimming in the ocean. Truman Capote, with whom she would have a long but ultimately disastrous friendship, nicknamed her "Ondine" in tribute to her mermaid soul. Jackie also loved books, and at nap time when she was supposed to be sleeping, she would creep over to the windowsill and curl up with a book. Afterward, she would dust off the soles of her feet so the family's nurse wouldn't know that she had been out of bed. She recalled:

> I read a lot when I was little, much of which was too old for me. There were Chekhov and Shaw in the room where I had to take naps and I never slept but sat on the windowsill reading . . . My heroes were Byron, Mowgli, Robin Hood, Little Lord Fauntleroy's grandfather, and Scarlett O'Hara.

Jackie's love of books and delight in writing poetry also endeared her to her literary grandfather, Grampy Jack Bouvier, who was a classical scholar proud of his erudition. He disdained his son for his complete lack of interest in language and literature, so Grampy's fondness for Jackie made Black Jack Bouvier all the prouder of her. In a way, Jackie and Lee were raised by snobs—their paternal grandfather did not wear his learning lightly, and Janet Lee Bouvier was always highly conscious of her social standing, elaborating her family's dubious connection to the Southern aristocratic lineage of Robert E. Lee. Their father was refreshingly free of these judgmental traits, adding to his attraction for both girls. When he was around, he doted on the girls, and they loved being with him.

Jackie also later wrote that as a child, she "hated dolls, loved horses and dogs, and had skinned knees and braces on my teeth for what must have seemed an interminable length of time to my family." John Davis observed that "despite her outer conformity . . . from an early age Jackie displayed an originality, a perspicacity, that set her apart from her other cousins . . . She often said things that were wise beyond her years."

Both women would ultimately be admired for their style, but many considered Lee the beauty of the family, outshining her older sister. (Oscar Wilde defined "taste" as the love of beauty, and Lee had that quality to an immense degree.) What developed was a relationship between the two sisters that was extremely close yet threaded with rivalry, jealousy, and competition. Yet it was probably the most important relationship of their lives. "I think you always have some sibling feelings," Lee once wrote about her sister, "but I felt more devotion than anything else. As a small child I think I was probably as annoying as any younger sister. I was knocked out by a croquet mallet [by Jackie] for two days—that sort of thing. So we had plenty of those sibling rows and fights." Lee apparently took a bit of revenge against her older sister, recalling that "although we occasionally fought fiercely, that came to an end when I finally triumphed by pushing her down the stairs. From that moment on, she realized I could stand up to her, and the childhood fights were over."

If Jackie was her father's favorite, Lee, by some accounts, was her mother's. A longtime Kennedy friend who knew the sisters when they were in their late teens admitted that she "found that household to be really unhealthy. Their mother clearly favored Lee." And if Jack Bouvier was especially close to Jackie, "he wasn't around very much, or for very long, so that didn't equal out, really."

Like many parents of that era, Janet pigeonholed her children, labeling Jackie as "the intellectual one" and Lee as the one who "will have twelve children and live in a rose-covered cottage." Of course, in Lee's case, "this certainly did not turn out to be true," as she later observed, but it raises the question of how little their mother knew or understood her daughters. She was especially hard on Jackie. Petite, feminine Lee more closely resembled her mother. Janet, always the impeccably turned-out (if muted) fashion plate, was highly critical of Jackie's appearance. As Barbara Leaming described in *Mrs. Kennedy*:

> She pointed with disgust to Jackie's big, masculine hands and feet, her broad shoulders and wide hips. Her favorite target was her daughter's kinky hair, which was highlighted by a low hairline,

also inherited from [her father]. No matter what Jackie did with her hair, Janet's criticism of its texture and unruliness persisted. With reference to both her hair and her clothes, Janet accused her of sloppiness and compared her unfavorably with Lee.

Part of Janet's displeasure was that as her marriage unraveled, she increasingly disliked Jackie's physical resemblance to her father, just as she resented Jackie and Lee's affection for Black Jack Bouvier. Their cousin Mimi Cecil remembered that when she and her siblings would see him at the beach, they would "just run into his arms. You couldn't help it with Uncle Jack. He was wonderful to his daughters in giving them treats that they didn't get at home with their mother . . ."

Among the treats Jack Bouvier provided were "daring excursions to casinos, racetracks, and boxing matches," warning them that "all men are rats" and that they should "play hard to get and never be easy." Lee especially loved her father's sense of style, later describing his beautiful suits with jaunty boutonnieres.

Janet, by contrast, was the disciplinarian of the house. She was high-strung and quick to anger. She always made sure her girls were perfectly turned out, sharply criticizing them for any sloppiness in their appearance. Jackie's childhood friend Solange Herter described Janet as "overbearingly proper and not very warm."

Nonetheless, theirs was often an enchanted childhood. Years later, Jackie recalled an early memory that she treasured throughout her life:

I'll never forget the night my mother and father both came into my bedroom all dressed up to go out. I can still smell the scent my mother wore and feel the softness of her fur coat as she leaned over to kiss me good night. In such an excited voice she said, "Darling, your father and I are going dancing tonight at the Central Park Casino to hear Eddy Duchin." I don't know why the moment has stayed with me all these years. Perhaps because it was one of the few times I remember seeing my parents together. It was so romantic. So hopeful.

There were other lovely memories as well. The girls were encouraged to create holiday gifts—usually drawings and poems. Lee remembers how much her mother loved the annual Christmas plays the girls put on for their parents, and sometimes Janet would weep with maternal joy.

Janet and Black Jack Bouvier divorced in 1940 after messy public accusations of infidelity that became tabloid fodder (much to the family's humiliation, the *New York Daily Mirror* ran the story "Mrs. Bouvier Sheds 'Love Commuter'" with photos of Bouvier's lovers), which cast a pall over the two girls, as if divorce itself were not shameful enough in the 1940s. So early on, the sisters were not strangers to the scent of scandal.

After her parents' divorce—rare in high society in 1940s America and rarer still (and looked down upon) in Catholic families—Jackie became even more introspective. A family friend at the time, Aileen Bowdoin Train, recalled that Jackie "was much more private than any other person I've ever known. She was always standing back watching the scene, and, sort of, recording it in her mind. Looking at people, seeing how they acted toward one another, she was a born observer." She might have felt culpable, as children of divorce often do, especially as there had been a tug-of-war between Janet and Jack for their elder daughter's affection.

Jackie found solace in her books and in riding Danseuse, which her Bouvier grandfather boarded for her in Central Park now that divorced Janet had decamped with her girls to 1 Gracie Square. Jackie would later confide in the pianist Peter Duchin, son of the bandleader Eddy Duchin, that she never felt completely at home in the haute society she had been born into:

You know, Peter, we both live and do very well in this world of Wasps and old money and society. It's all supposed to be so safe and continuous. But you and I are not really of it. Maybe because I'm Catholic and because my parents were divorced when I was young—a terribly radical thing at the time—I've always felt an outsider in that world.

Lee reacted by becoming nearly anorexic, shedding her baby fat and causing her mother concern. Years later, Lee recalled how the excoriating insults traded between her parents affected her. "I was like a tuning fork, then and now," she explained. "My sister wasn't, so much. She could send bad news to the basement and lock it up. She was like a sphinx in that way."

Perhaps as a result of their parents' bitter divorce, the two sisters became even closer. "I looked up to her, counted on her and admired her," Lee later wrote. When Jackie left home to attend school at Miss Porter's, Lee felt bereft.

Janet's divorce and remarriage to the unprepossessing but extremely wealthy investment banker Hugh D. Auchincloss was exactly what she had been trained to do by her wealthy, social-climbing father, Major James Thomas Aloysius Lee (who conceived the apocryphal connection to General Robert E. Lee): Janet had married brilliantly. Whereas Jack Bouvier's fortune had declined after a series of bad investments and through his father's failed stewardship of the Bouvier riches, Hugh D. Auchincloss—called "Uncle Hughdie" by Jackie and Lee—was of older, richer, and more established stock. Bouvier was the Catholic great-grandson of a French carpenter who had worked for Napoleon's brother. But the Auchinclosses—Scottish Presbyterians—were old money, nourished by Standard Oil, going back generations. Some in the Auchincloss clan looked down on the Bouviers as *arrivistes*.

Suddenly thrust into a family of three stepsiblings (Hugh, known as "Yusha," Thomas, and Nina), with two more children to come from that union (Janet and James), Jackie and Lee were no longer the center of Janet's fierce attention. Gore Vidal described his former stepfather as "a magnum of chloroform," but "Hughdie" proved to be a devoted, steady husband and father. Lee in particular was enchanted by Hammersmith Farm: "To arrive there, as a child of 8, was just a fairy tale," she reminisced. "It was good for my imagination. It was such a wonderful place." She was delighted when her stepfather named two Guernsey calves Jacqueline and Caroline after his new stepdaughters.

Nonetheless, the two girls were aware that they were the poor relations in the family, as their stepsister, Nina, and stepbrothers, Yusha and Tommy, each had their own trust fund, whereas Jackie and Lee had only a small allowance from their father, who was on a financial downward spiral. "They were like little orphans," said the writer and socialite Helen Chavchavadze, who had been in the same class as Lee at Miss Porter's. "Jackie and Lee were very fused, the way sisters are when they haven't had much security."

There was much to love about Merrywood, but it wasn't always easy being there. John F. Kennedy once chastised Gore Vidal for his uncharacteristically cheerful description of the Auchincloss family, which he wrote about for *Look* magazine: "What's this golden season shit you're telling, Gore? It was *The Little Foxes*." In fact, in Vidal's memoir *Palimpsest*, he reveals his intense dislike of his stepfather. He and Jackie both found their patrician, avuncular, well-meaning stepfather a thrilling bore, though Jackie remained fond of him. Not Gore—"My lifelong passion for bores began with Hughdie," he wrote in *Palimpsest*.

As described in Sally Bedell Smith's *Grace and Power: The Private World of the Kennedy White House*, however, Auchincloss was actually a serious bibliophile, a nineteenth-century club man who took refuge in reading. It was in his library at Merrywood that Jackie steeped herself in stories of America's founders, especially George Washington, whose "human qualities" she came to appreciate, according to her stepbrother Hugh D. (Yusha) Auchincloss III.

But there was the inescapable fact of the two girls' divided loyalties. "I dreaded Christmas," Lee wrote years later, "because it was always kind of bittersweet. We spent it at Merrywood, but then we had to rush to New York to see our father, and he was spending Christmas alone. Except for us, he was really kind of abandoned."

Unlike Janet, Bouvier never remarried.

The usual warfare flourished between the divorced parents, as the girls relished their time with their black sheep father, who was now cast out of paradise and living in a small, sunless four-room apartment at 125 East 74th Street, a far cry from the lavish Park Avenue duplex that had been lent to them by Janet's father. When they visited, Bouvier would serve his girls lunch on a folding card table in front of the fireplace, as the apartment's dining room was turned into a tiny bedroom for his daughters to use. (To this day, Lee sometimes serves intimate dinners in the same fashion, on an exquisitely set folding table in front of the fireplace.)

When Jack's father sold the East Hampton estate, where the Bouvier girls had spent early carefree summers riding, learning to play tennis, eating triple-decker ice cream cones, and swimming at the Maidstone Club and in the Atlantic Ocean, Bouvier was reduced to summering in a small rented cottage blocks from the beach. But the girls didn't mind so much—they were still delighted to spend time with their father.

Jackie was the first to attend Miss Porter's School in Connecticut, followed by Lee three years later. Both entered as sophomores, with Lee arriving a year after Jackie graduated. "We were like el-lipses, separated by three years," is how Lee characterized it.

Neither girl really wanted to attend the all-girls preparatory high school, but Jackie made a cold peace with being there. Her grades were good, and she was a natural athlete and horsewoman. Always bookish, she became an editor of the school newspaper, *Salmagundy*, for which she wrote and drew a comic series called *Frenzied Freda*. Physically, Jackie was still in chrysalis—not yet a hit with the young men she met at mixers, as she was re-served, and usually taller than the boys her age. She was slim, flat-chested, large-boned. Her main interest was her horse, and she couldn't wait to visit the stable where Danseuse was boarded.

Years later, Lee confessed how much she hated being at Miss Porter's: "I always hated school, but I really hated Miss Porter's. Very *rah rah rah* and their teams must win! I was terrible at sports, and I was always the last to be chosen for a team, which was so embarrassing and made me feel pathetic."

Despite Jackie's reputation as a shy bookworm, however, "it may surprise you [that] my sister was something of a rebel, early on," Lee recalled. Surprising, too, that the future First Lady was a bit of a ringleader and a tomboy at Chapin. "She was full of the devil," recalled a former classmate. Jackie's lifelong friend Nancy Tuckerman described her at Chapin's as "naughty as everything; she would disrupt whatever she could." On "dreaded" bird walks, Jackie would yell and scare the birds out of the trees; she would drink from public water fountains (a big no-no); she would mock classmates and teachers alike. "I think she had the best sense of humor and of the ridiculous throughout her life," Tuckerman said, but she could be manipulative and bossy. Jackie once told her friend, who would later become her personal secretary in the White House and whom she called "Tucky," to walk under a horse "for good luck." It was a dangerous stunt, but Nancy, naïve about horses, did it. Jackie was good at getting people to do her bidding, and she often "sent Lee off to do her dirty work," Tuckerman recalled.

Another classmate, Sally Smith Cross, remembered Jackie as a pretty girl with "thick brown braids bouncing as she ran to the center of 'The Roof' for a game of corner kickball. I can also see her being chastised and sent to Miss [Ethel Gray] Stringfellow's office for having challenged the inexperienced teacher of Modern Dance . . . she was a very able student and also a ringleader, whose stuffed zebra, Flapjack, became our class mascot." There was something impishly perverse about her; Lee recalled that during the Second World War, Jackie persuaded her Swiss governess to teach her German, which upset Janet.

With Jackie away at school, eleven-year-old Lee was lonely. Decades later, she recalled how she was once left alone with the servants "at this enormous house of my mother and stepfather in McLean, Virginia," while they were on a deep-sea fishing trip in Chile. She decided that the thing to do was to adopt an orphan to take Jackie's place.

> All I did was play in the woods with my dogs day after day. And so I and a very fat cook called Nellie, who was my only friend, decided I couldn't stand it any longer. I looked up in a Yellow Classified Pages "orphanages," took my pathetic allowance, called a taxi.

Lee marched into the nearest Catholic orphanage and announced to the Mother Superior, "I've come to adopt an orphan, and I have a lovely place where she would be terribly happy— horses and dogs and walks, and she would really love it!"

The "absolutely stunned" Mother Superior told her she was just too young to adopt anyone. Lee returned home, disappointed. When Janet and Hughdie returned a week later, Lee recalled, "I just got such hell for this—'how you could upset me, how you could torture me the way you have? We were so worried about you!'

"I couldn't figure out quite why that was, as they were in Chile on a motorboat."

At Miss Porter's, if Jackie was tomboyish and self-possessed, Lee appeared frailer and more feminine, not interested in horses or athletics. But she often found herself—not Jackie—the center of attention from the boys in their Eton jackets brought in for socials from prep schools like Buckley and St. Bernard's.

While each was at Miss Porter's in her turn, they would visit their aunt Annie Burr Lewis, Hugh Auchincloss's sister, who would serve them tea in the afternoons. Her husband, Wilmarth Sheldon "Lefty" Lewis (a nickname straight out of Damon Runyon, oddly), was a bibliophile and an authority on Horace Walpole, the English art historian and man of letters. Lewis was famous for editing twenty-six of fifty volumes of Walpole's correspondence ("Could you imagine, twenty-six volumes!" Lee commented). Even then, Aunt Annie noticed how different the girls were: Lee preferred her tea without milk, while Jackie put the milk in first; Lee turned down her aunt's chocolate cake, but Jackie—for a skinny girl—really enjoyed her aunt's rich chocolate layer cake and scones and sandwiches with the crusts cut off. Jackie fell in love with her aunt and uncle's library—he had a great collection of antiquarian books—which were of little interest to Lee at the time.

Lee, curiously, was fascinated by Catholicism and its iconography—she filled her bedroom with various crosses and Russian icons, which probably reflected her nascent interest in décor, objets d'art, and Russian culture rather than Catholicism. Perhaps she was also inspired by the ceremonies of the Catholic Church; she would be drawn to and flourish in dramatics at Miss Porter's. If Jackie preferred being left alone with a book,

Lee bloomed in the spotlight. She enjoyed, as she still does, being fussed over. "Flattery—my great flaw!" she recently admitted.

At Miss Porter's, people thought Lee the prettier of the two sisters; she had a more feminine, curvier body, which she made more svelte by dieting. Lee didn't enjoy food the way Jackie did, but she did take Jackie's adolescent advice to smoke cigarettes to keep the weight off. As teenagers, both girls smoked (Jackie would be a heavy smoker her entire life, though she was never photographed with a cigarette). Concerned at how thin Lee had become, Janet threatened to send her to a weight-gain camp, and only got her daughter to eat by promising to let her redecorate her room.

Lee believed in frivolity: "Showing off was part of my character," she said. Whereas Jackie won praise for excelling in French and history and English, Lee shined outside of the classroom. If Jackie "wanted to learn all the arts," Lee remembered, she herself wanted to learn the art of being popular. "I behaved as though the whole world should know me," Lee recalled. In contrast, Jackie "would have liked to act on the spur of the moment, but she didn't know how. The desires of youth, for my sister, were held in check by a certain faintheartedness."

Despite their closeness, a certain jockeying for attention continued between the two girls. Jackie excelled in Farmington, but at her first coming-out party, at the Newport Clambake Club in August of 1947, Lee found a way to steal Jackie's thunder by showing up in a frothy pink strapless dress sprinkled with rhinestones that set tongues wagging. Jackie had worn a chic white off-the-shoulder tulle gown, but Lee's dress—which she had designed herself, working with a local seamstress—got all the attention. Janet was furious, but Jackie didn't seem to mind, and in fact appropriated that dress for her debutante ball, where she was named Debutante of the Year by the influential gossip columnist and social arbiter Igor Cassini, who wrote under the nom de plume Cholly Knickerbocker. He was the brother of the fashion designer

Oleg Cassini, who would later play an important role in Jackie's life. Thus began a pattern of Jackie sometimes appropriating Lee's sense of style and earning praise for it.

It's a good thing that both sisters triumphed at their coming-out parties, because, as Gore Vidal later noted, "There was never much money for either girl."

Certainly, Hughdie's fortune—when he had it—was insufficient to launch two ambitious girls in society. As Vidal wrote, "Janet (just described by *Newsweek* as 'an icy social climber, trying to disguise her Irish [sic] roots') had no money until she reconciled, late in life, with her father, who had objected—I wonder why—to her marriage with Jack Bouvier. So Jackie, constantly presented as a wealthy debutante of the highest society was, like me, a poor connection of the Auchinclosses."

Jackie's Bouvier cousins were surprised to see how much she dazzled at debutante balls and soirees, given how shy and difficult to talk to she had been as a girl. At a dinner dance given at the Newport Clambake Club the summer of 1947, hosted by the Auchinclosses and the Grosvenors (parents of Jackie's friend Rose Grosvenor), her cousins were astonished by how the formerly withdrawn Jackie captivated the guests.

At eighteen and fifteen years of age, each sister was developing her own style of dress—Jackie was more like Janet in her preference for casual, conservative, extremely well-made clothes. Janet dressed in simple but exquisitely tailored suits, or skirts and twinsets worn with a strand of pearls, but all in beige and browns, so that one wag described her as looking like a mushroom. "She was never seen without her perfect white kid gloves," her youngest child, Jamie Auchincloss, recalled. Lee, now slimmer and sleeker than her older sister, had far more flair. She loved color and a more dramatic style.

A childhood friend of Jackie's, Sylvia Whitehouse Blake, noticed that "Jackie didn't care a whit for fashion in those days. She and I ran around in shorts and sneakers all summer. The only time we dressed up was during Tennis Week, Newport's social highlight. But even then we weren't exactly your typical *Vogue* fashion plates." Nonetheless, another one of Jackie's friends was struck by her unadorned beauty: "First of all, her beauty was incredible. She didn't wear any makeup—she didn't have to! I mean, to me she was breathtaking!" Jackie would later describe her beauty routine when she was a college student at Vassar:

Wash your face with hot water and a rough wash cloth and really rub, with upward strokes on the cheeks and forehead . . . Rinse with cold water: the shock will stimulate circulation and leave it tingling. With the same upward motions massage in a rich cream before retiring. Do this for about two minutes and wipe off what is left so that you won't find it on your pillow the next morning.

She used Dorothy Gray's Special Dry Skin mixture, later switching to the expensive high-end brand Erno Laszlo. Years later, after ascending to the White House, she would add a peroxide rinse for her teeth to remove the nicotine stains resulting from her two-pack-a-day smoking habit.

Lee, remembered Sylvia Whitehouse Blake, "was shorter than Jackie but more rounded, with a classically attractive, heart-shaped face and tiny, delicate features. She never left the house unless dressed for Ascot."

Jackie saw how boys flocked to Lee. While Jackie kept her nose buried in a book when she wasn't riding Danseuse, now boarded at Miss Porter's, Lee triumphed in the school play, the George S. Kaufman–Moss Hart madcap comedy *You Can't Take It with You.* It seemed as if Lee was the one destined for fame—she loved the

limelight—and although each girl in her turn was named Debutante of the Year by Cholly Knickerbocker, *Life* magazine devoted
a whole page to Lee's coming out, eclipsing Jackie's.

One of several things they had in common, though, was their
soft, whispery way of speaking. Lee's voice was slightly huskier;
Jackie's had the breathy little-girl quality of Marilyn Monroe's,
which belied her sharp intelligence. Their own mother sometimes
couldn't tell them apart over the telephone. They also shared a
kind of halting style of speech, as if their words were divided into
lines of verse. One of Lee's phone messages sounded like:

Sam . . . this is Lee Rad-zi-vill . . . Would you call me . . .
please? I forgot to tell you . . .
about Truman . . .
and my fur coat.
Thank you . . . Lee

Despite their differences, the two sisters were often thick as
thieves growing up. As teenagers, they would make the rounds
of their favorite restaurants in New York when they visited their
father in Manhattan. Years later, they were once asked to leave
Elaine's, the popular Upper East Side restaurant, after sitting and
talking and smoking for hours in one of the front banquettes,
where everyone could see them, ordering nothing but ice water.

Jack Bouvier felt he was losing his daughters the closer they
became to the Auchinclosses. The estrangement was also painful for Jackie and especially for Lee, who felt torn between the
wealth, security, and status their stepfather afforded them and
their love for their cast-off father, now living in reduced circumstances. He tried to maintain his role of affectionate and generous
father—it was Jack Bouvier who paid for Jackie's Vassar education, and he was pleased that Vassar, in Poughkeepsie, New York,

was closer to Manhattan than it was to McLean, Virginia. She could visit her father on weekends, and he could more easily visit. On his visits to the Seven Sisters college, Jackie "would have the glory of showing him off in the main dining room, enjoying the way the girls would gawk at him as if he were a movie star," as her cousin Davis recalled.

Jackie made frequent visits to her father's New York apartment to take advantage of dates and social events in the city, which sometimes made Bouvier feel as if she were just visiting for convenience's sake. He groused to his sisters that his daughter only wrote or phoned "when she needed her allowance" of fifty dollars a month, and that Jackie would turn up a half hour before a social engagement and rush off on the train early the next morning. He never withheld Jackie's or Lee's allowance—and he paid for both their college educations and gave them generous checks on special occasions—but he was hurt by what he perceived as their neglect of him. But no matter what Bouvier managed to do for his beloved daughters, Janet Auchincloss—with her second husband's wealth—could outdo him. Davis remembered:

> When Janet would schedule dental appointments for Jacqueline in Washington (which Jack would subsequently be asked to pay for), Jack would immediately interpret the action as a way of getting Jackie to come to Virginia, and he would angrily counterattack by insisting she have her teeth fixed in Manhattan: he would not pay for any more treatments in Washington, D.C. And so it would go in countless other matters.

Though he also complained that Lee only called him from Miss Porter's when she was in need of funds, he did in fact spend more time with her, especially when Jackie left for France in her junior year. Lee spent two summer weeks with him in East Hampton, in his small, rented cottage, which she enjoyed nonetheless because it meant time spent with her father. And in the fall, Bouvier traveled to Farmington to see his younger daughter perform in *You Can't Take It with You*. He was so delighted by Lee's performance that he returned to New York full of grandiose plans for her future as an actress.

3

AMERICANS IN PARIS

We are not the Brontë sisters.

—LEE

I flatter myself on being able at times to walk out of the
house looking like a poor man's Paris copy . . .

—JACKIE

What could be more wonderful than to be affluent, pretty young girls in Paris in 1951, in immaculate, wrist-length white gloves? Rather surprisingly, after months of coaxing, Janet agreed to let eighteen-year-old Lee travel to Europe in the summer of 1951 with twenty-two-year-old Jackie.

Three years earlier, Jackie had spent her junior year abroad in Paris, which she once referred to as "the happiest year of [my] life." While abroad, she'd studied French at the University of Grenoble and French literature and history at the Sorbonne. "I have an absolute mania now about learning to speak French perfectly," she wrote to her mother. "We never speak a word of English in this apartment and I don't see many Americans." She also noted that in the cafés that year, all the American girls in Paris were drinking Picon-citrons, and many of her college compatriots were still wearing the girlish, ankle-length white socks of the era—but not Jackie.

Jackie's letters home fired Lee's imagination. In August of 1949, she wrote to her younger sister:

I just can't tell you what it is like to come down from the moun-
tains of Grenoble to this flat, blazing plain where seven-eighths
of all you see is hot blue sky . . .

Last Sunday we all went to Sassenage, a village on the plain
near Grenoble. We visited the grottoes and waded in underground
rivers—and explored the town and sang songs and danced in a
lovely little restaurant under rustling trees by a brook with a
waterfall . . . We missed the last tram and had to walk back to
Grenoble (all the way back)—about five miles!

Lee longed to go abroad as Jackie had done. Now a freshman
at Sarah Lawrence, she was bored by Bronxville, except for her
lively social life. What reading she did was not on the curriculum:
"It was Fitzgerald's novels—*The Beautiful and Damned, Tender Is
the Night*—those Riviera novels with their doomed characters,"
she recalled. "When my sister spent her year abroad, and wrote
back these exciting, almost fevered letters, I just couldn't wait to
go! I thought I was going to live at Versailles! It was that kind of
thing. Of course, the reality [was] much different. But it was still
a swoon-worthy notion."

Janet "was extremely apprehensive about letting her daughters go alone on such a venture," Lee later wrote, "in spite of the
fact that Jackie had already lived in Paris for a year. But then
Jackie had been well chaperoned and supposedly studying hard
under rigid conditions. This trip would be just us and the Hillman
Minx," the car they used to tootle around in Europe, from Cannes
to Cap d'Antibes.

The trip was offered as Lee's belated high school graduation
present, but it was offered to Jackie partly out of guilt: Jackie had
won *Vogue*'s sixteenth annual Prix de Paris award, which was
to send her to France for six months to work in the Paris office,
then to the States to work for *Vogue* for six months in New York.
Her prizewinning essay—actually the answers to six questions

posed by *Vogue* editors—are remarkably assured and thoughtful, reflecting her deep engagement with the arts and a serious intellect, seldom displayed among the usual crop of debutantes in 1950s-era America.

When asked to name "People I Wish I Had Known" from the arts, literature, or "other milieus," Jackie chose Charles Baudelaire, Oscar Wilde, and Serge Diaghilev. She wrote:

> It is because I love the works of these three men that I wish I had known them. If I could be a sort of Overall Art Director of the Twentieth Century, watching everything from a chair hanging in space, it is their theories of art that I would apply to my period, their poems that would have music and ballets composed to.

She cited lines from Baudelaire's sonnet "Correspondances," praising the poet's synesthesia: "[Perfumes] green as prairies, sweet as the music of oboes, and others, corrupted, rich and triumphant." She appreciated the sensual imagery in Wilde's poetry as well, quoting "the musk and gold heat that emanates from a vase of flowers" in "The Music Room." But more tellingly, given the role she would play in a then unimagined future, she praises Diaghilev, the Russian impresario of dance, for his ability to bring together Rimsky-Korsakov's music, Bakst's and Benois's theatrical sets, Fokine's choreography, and Nijinsky's brilliant dancing:

> Serge Diaghilev dealt not with the interaction of the senses but with an interaction of the arts, an interaction of the cultures of East and West. Though not an artist himself he possessed what is rarer than artistic genius in any one field, the sensitivity to take the best of each man and incorporate it into a masterpiece all the more precious because it lives only in the minds of those who have seen it and disintegrates as soon as he is gone . . . [He is] an alchemist unique in art history.

She herself would become adept at "an interaction of the arts" in her future role as First Lady, a role for which she had prepared herself in her wide exposure to the performing arts.

In her six-part essay, Jackie also proved herself adept in describing a typical college girl's beauty routine, inventing an advertising campaign for perfume, and advising *Vogue* to educate women about men's fashion. "You can never slip into too dismal an abyss of untidiness if once every seven days you will pull yourself up short and cope with ragged ends," she cautioned in answer to the command "Make out a plan of beauty care suitable for a college girl."

After displaying her erudition and artistic sensibility in the first part of the essay, her "beauty plan" shows her to be a more typical, down-to-earth American girl, advising her classmates that they can

> avoid smudged nails daubed on the New York Central from a bottle of polish that has spilled in your pocketbook, strange unwanted waves in your hair because you have washed it at midnight and gone to bed too tired to wait for it to dry, stubbly legs with razor cuts, and a legion of other horrors . . .

She also gives a telling description of herself, chafing a bit at her mother's eagle-eyed attention to always looking one's best:

> I am tall, 5'7", with brown hair, a square face, and eyes so unfortunately far apart that it takes three weeks to have a pair of glasses made with a bridge wide enough to fit over my nose. I do not have a sensational figure but can look slim if I pick the right clothes. I flatter myself on being able at times to walk out of the house looking like a poor man's Paris copy, but often my mother will run up to inform me that my left stocking seam is crooked

or the right-hand top coat button is about to fall off. This, I realize, is the Unforgiveable Sin.

In an answer to the question of how she might display a perfume in a *Vogue* advertisement, Jackie again displays her sophistication and artistic sensibility. She asks, "Why not quote some of the poetry [perfume] has inspired?" Making an analogy between perfume and fine wine, she expressed her own poetic capacity and an already refined sensibility when she wrote:

> Both are liquids that act upon the closely related senses of taste and smell to produce an intoxicating effect. Wine has an even stronger appeal in literature . . . why not pilfer some of its drawing power . . . ? . . . The layout . . . would show some strewn flower petals, a thin-stemmed crystal wineglass with the blurred suggestion of a women (a long neck, an earring—her hand), pouring perfume out of a Diorama bottle into the glass.

Her six-part essay—and an original short story that inspired one of the judges to comment, "She is already a writer . . ."—won her the coveted prize.

Jackie had begun a love affair with all things French, even before living in Paris. The summer before junior year, she had been given the present of a European tour with two friends. Visiting museums and practicing her French had been thrilling, a preparation for her junior year abroad.

Jackie had majored in French in college, but since Vassar did not offer any opportunities to study abroad, she applied and was accepted in Smith College's Junior Year in Paris program.

Jack Bouvier was delighted at Jackie's upcoming trip to Europe, although he would miss her visits to see him in Manhattan. But at least Jackie would get a break from having to choose between spending holidays and weekends in Merrywood or with her father on East 74th Street.

Before sailing, Jackie and thirty-four other Paris-bound French majors had attended a luncheon in their honor with gossip columnist Hedda Hopper and had been toasted by the French consul in New York. On board the *De Grasse*, which departed from New York Harbor on August 23, 1949, the group was asked to sing Edith Piaf's popular "La vie en rose." Jackie was singled out to sing one of the verses on the final night of their ocean crossing. She did so—she knew all the French verses. As Alice Kaplan has noted in *Dreaming in French*, France would become the place where Jackie "could become [her]self, or protect [her]self from what [she] didn't want to become . . ."—i.e., a prim product of Janet's all-too-proper upbringing. Kaplan writes that Jackie was one

> whose fate now depended on her own wits . . . since her father had lost his fortune and she could not rely on an inheritance from her stepfather. The Vassar girl and toast of high society had a sense of her worth but little security. She was on a quest in Paris . . .

Jackie's infatuation with France derived, in part, from the fiction that her father's family of Bouviers had been French aristocrats. Not true—the Bouviers had been Provençal shopkeepers in France, and Jackie's great-grandparents Michel Bouvier and Louise Vernou had met as French immigrants in Philadelphia. Indeed, the very name "Bouvier" derived from the word "*boeuf*" (beef) and signified cattle herders. Jackie and Lee's ancestors on her father's side were, in essence, French cowboys, though from the French Revolution to the Bouviers' emigration to America, they became shopkeepers. Her great-grandfather became a highly successful cabinetmaker in Philadelphia, improving his social status through marriage and becoming a wealthy land speculator. But the Bouviers exalting their past was no more of a fabrication than

Janet Lee Auchincloss's clinging to the idea that she descended from Southern aristocracy and not immigrant Irish stock—like that other wealthy and influential family, the Kennedys.

Her French heritage captivated Jackie in ways that did not shape her sister. She preferred to pronounce her name in a French manner—"Jack-*leen*"—and frequently used French words and expressions, such as naming her horse Danseuse. But it was Auchincloss's wealth and prominence, not Bouvier's, that showered Jackie with invitations to socially prominent families in Paris during her year abroad.

Smith's program was intellectually rigorous in preparation for a career in teaching French, and everyone was expected to speak only French for the duration. Their itinerary began in the provinces, in Grenoble, where the students studied French grammar before heading to Paris.

When Jackie moved to Paris to study at the Sorbonne that October, she lived at 76 Avenue Mozart in the 16th arrondissement with a French family: the comtesse de Renty and her two daughters, Claude and Ghislaine, and Ghislaine's four-year-old son, Christian. Janet had made the connection to the de Rentys through a Franco-American family she'd met in Newport. Jackie got the largest bedroom, though she shared the apartment with two other study-abroad students, including a friend of Jackie's from New York, Susan Coward. There was ample space—"four bedrooms, two parlors, a dining room, and a kitchen with the traditional wrought iron 'cage' beneath the window for keeping food fresh . . . a back staircase for the servants, exiting onto the inner courtyard" in Alice Kaplan's description—but there was only one toilet and one bathtub for the apartment's seven inhabitants. That meant only one bath a week for the three boarders, unless they were willing to visit the public baths.

Four years after the Liberation, the memory and the effects of war were still palpable. Sugar and coffee were rationed, and coal was scarce, so the apartment was frigid in winter, and Jackie wrote that she was "swaddled in sweaters and woolen stockings, doing homework in graph-paper *cahiers.*" For the countess, depredations of the war were still etched in memory. She and her husband had been part of a nationalist wing of the French Resistance known as the Alliance, founded by a former member of the Vichy government. Its recruits were mostly from the upper classes. Little experienced in espionage, they were arrested and deported more often than other Resistance fighters. The de Rentys were deported a week before the liberation of Paris on August 22, 1944, and the count was sent to Dora, a German slave-labor camp, where he was put to work digging the construction site for Wernher von Braun's underground missile factory. He only lasted four months. The countess survived him at Ravensbrück, one of the women's camps, and when she returned to Paris, now a widow, she needed to rent out rooms to survive. Nonetheless, according to her daughter Claude, the comtesse de Renty enjoyed the role of housing young American students and introducing them to the best of French culture that had survived the war, inviting Jackie to accompany her to the Sèvres porcelain museum and to the Louvre. "Jackie knew what had happened to my parents," recalled Claude, "but did not ask any questions. At that time, nobody talked about it." As Kaplan observed, Jackie was secretive: "Perhaps that secrecy, born of her own private sorrows, blended well with a family that had so much to forget."

Jackie's quest to discover herself and mature beyond Janet's reach was tested by an experience in February of 1950, six months after she arrived in France. A friend and classmate, Martha Rusk, invited Jackie to accompany her on a trip to Austria and Germany just before New Year's, and was surprised when Jackie accepted, mostly because it involved traveling third class by rail. That didn't faze Jackie—it was all part of the great adventure of exploring Europe, and being on her own. As she later wrote in a letter home:

It's so much more fun traveling second and third class and sitting up all night in trains, as you really get to know people and hear their stories. When I traveled before it was all too luxurious and we didn't see anything.

They spent a few days in Vienna before heading to Munich, where much of the city, like Vienna, was in bombed-out ruins. In Munich, they were only a ten-minute trolley ride away from Dachau, the first Nazi concentration camp, where medical experiments were carried out among prisoners. More than 41,000 people had been murdered there, either worked to death or destroyed by disease and malnutrition; others were gassed or cremated in ovens. When the American GIs arrived, they found 5,400 corpses within the camp. Over 15,000 had been buried by the Nazis in a mass grave.

By the time Jackie and Martha visited the camp, Dachau had been dedicated and sanitized, preserved as a memorial site. The two young Americans wandered through a series of empty, whitewashed rooms, in eerie silence. They were accompanied by a young GI they'd met on the trolley, who was equally stunned by what he saw and learned there. Back in Munich, Jackie and Martha tried to forget their Dachau visit by spending New Year's Eve at a nightclub with several friends.

Though Jackie might have tried to hide her sense of horror, and never wrote directly about it, she talked about the experience with her stepbrother Yusha Auchincloss. Yusha later wrote that she had been "deeply affected by what she saw there and never forgot it."

She was appalled and outraged at what the Nazis did, but she did not condemn the Germans as a race. She was a very emotional person, but she would try to repress emotions, and after seeing the camp, she managed still to never speak of all the Germans in

a derogatory way. She always saw the Nazis as distinct from the
German people . . . [but] she never forgot what she saw.

If anything, the trip and what she learned there deepened
a gravitas that she already possessed; it was one of the key features of her personality she did not share with Lee. Her sojourn
in France had matured her and had gone far in showing her who
she really was. She later wrote that her travels taught her not to
be ashamed of her thirst for knowledge, which she had previously
sought to hide. Now Jackie was ready to resume her life in America, but with an enduring love for Europe.

After returning to the States, instead of completing her studies at Vassar, Jackie spent her senior year as a student at George
Washington University, in DC, now majoring in French literature
and taking classes in creative writing and journalism. One of her
writing professors at GWU, Muriel McClanahan, recalled her as
"beautiful, and she could write like a million. She didn't need to
take my class."

She lived with her mother and stepfather at Merrywood while
finishing her undergraduate degree—which might have been
part of the deal she'd made with Janet to allow her to take her
junior year abroad. One of her classmates at GWU was the avant-
garde musician and composer David Amram, who remembered
being struck by Jackie's "dignity" and "bearing." He recalled
playing music for her at a mutual friend's house, music from the
Khyber Pass on the border of Pakistan and Afghanistan, which
Jackie very much enjoyed. "She always had that 'world view,'"
Amram recalled.

Her next trip to Europe, taken with Lee, would be very different in style and mood.

*

STUDY ABROAD HAD been a life-enhancing sojourn for Janet's dark-haired daughter, but to allow her to return for six months as the recipient of *Vogue*'s Prix de Paris?

Janet ordered Jackie to turn down the prize.

Perhaps Janet sensed that her daughter's love affair with all things French revealed a preference for her father and his French ancestry, as opposed to her own Irish heritage. But it's more likely that Janet wanted to ensure that Jackie would marry and not waste her time pursuing a career in journalism—in Paris! Both girls were being groomed to make good matches, in an era where a good marriage and a respectable husband were the summit of what most women—even privileged girls—could expect. At the time, the average age of a married or engaged woman was twenty, and Jackie was twenty-two, with no real prospects. (It was feminine, flirty Lee who had all the beaux!)

At the urging of both Janet and Jack Bouvier, afraid that they would lose their elder daughter to the sophistications of Paris, Jackie turned down the Prix de Paris. She wrote to the judges that she had already spent her junior year in Paris and that her mother felt "terrifically strongly about 'keeping me in the home.'"

So Lee and Jackie's summer sojourn was meant to be, for Jackie at least, a kind of consolation prize. Perhaps Janet would have changed her mind about allowing either daughter to go, had she heard that Jackie had lost her virginity on her first trip to France. An unsubstantiated rumor suggested that this took place in a pension lift on Paris's Left Bank, to John Marquand Jr., an early contributor to the *Paris Review*.

*

LEE WAS THRILLED at the prospect of traveling to Europe with her big sister. She later wrote, "I couldn't imagine anything that could be more fun than a trip with Jackie, since we were both absolutely psychic about laughter and had the same sense of the ridiculous." She "longed to see everything [Jackie] had been writing me about" in her letters home during her earlier year abroad. With Jackie as Lee's chaperone, and armed with their stepfather's letters of introduction to ambassadors and doyennes throughout Europe, the two young women made their way into the greater world.

The sisters left for Europe well prepared for their adventure: armed with a portfolio of papers "tucked into our dainty purses," as Lee described it, including vaccination certificates; traveler's checks; a letter of credit; letters to American Express in London, Paris, Madrid, Nice, Rome, and Lucerne; a letter to Chase Bank, Paris; international driving licenses; an AAA membership card; a card "for legal representation in case of accident"; and seven extra passport pictures. On June 7, 1951, at 9:45 a.m., "after pleading and pestering and praying for a year," passport No. 218793 (Jacqueline Lee Bouvier) and No. 545527 (Caroline Lee Bouvier) embarked to Europe.

It was a splendid adventure.

Luckily for posterity, the two young women kept a playful scrapbook and journal of their travels, written by Lee and illustrated with insouciant drawings and poems by Jackie, and later published in 2005 as *One Special Summer*. They created it to present to their mother as a thank-you gesture for letting them go on this trip. Their adventures, poems, and reassuring letters to Janet ("We DO sew on all our buttons and wear gloves and never go out in big cities except in what we would wear to church in Newport on Sundays") are sprinkled with tourist snapshots, showing the girls in St. Mark's Square dressed—horrors!—in slacks and sandals (Jackie) and short shorts and ankle straps (Lee).

"Look at us," Lee later remarked, poring over those snapshots. "How did those countries let us in? We look like two criminals arriving off the boat."

Among their adventures in Europe: the sisters sneak into first-class dinner dances aboard the ship; Jackie takes art lessons from a rather lecherous teacher in Venice; Lee suffers a wardrobe malfunction at a gala reception (her underwear slips down while she's chatting with an ambassador); Lee takes singing lessons from Signora Gilda Dalla Rizza, "Queen of all the sopranos in Italy."

Known as Puccini's favorite soprano for her creation of the role of Magda in *La rondine* in 1917, Signora Dalla Rizza had retired from the stage in 1939 and taught at Conservatorio Benedetto Marcello in Venice. However, she did give private lessons, and one of them was with Lee Bouvier, who was more impressed by Signora Dalla Rizza's enormous bosom than by her vocal technique.

"We went to her house on the Grand Canal," Lee wrote in *One Special Summer*, "and were ushered into this salon where we sat shaking, while the house shuddered and thundered with her singing scales in another room" in her trademark guttural and nasal style. "On the piano was a picture of Toscanini with a long dedication to her—also, one from Puccini—she was the first to sing 'Madama Butterfly' . . . and portraits on the walls of her in different costumes." When the diva finally entered, she couldn't speak any English and very little French, and as neither Lee nor Jackie knew any Italian, Jackie went to work thumbing through her Italian grammar book in an attempt to communicate.

Lee was asked to sing a few arias, but Lee was too terrified to even open her mouth. Jackie, on the sofa behind the signora, attempted to stifle a fit of hysterical laughter. Lee was then asked to simply sing a scale, which Lee was still too frightened to manage—her voice cracked halfway through. Jackie continued to giggle, and suggested that Lee sing something from a popular musical comedy of the day, *Call Me Madam* (which was Irving Berlin's last successful musical, written in 1950 as a send-up of Perle Mesta, the famous Washington hostess whom President Truman had appointed as ambassador to Luxembourg).

Instead—out of desperation—Lee launched into "Aba Daba Honeymoon," a novelty song popularized by Debbie Reynolds in a movie called *Two Weeks with Love*. (The song would later be reprised at the end of the decade in a Three Stooges picture, *Have Rocket, Will Travel*. Thomas Pynchon once called it "the nadir of all American expression.")

Lee had hoped that its refrain—"Aba daba daba daba daba daba dab, said the chimpie to the monk"—might sound vaguely Italian to the diva, and if she sang it fast, "it might even sound like coloratura. I ended with a screech, like a cat being run over." The diva was not amused, and the two young women left Venice in a hurry.

Years later, Lee said that yes, she'd grown up wanting to paint and to act and to write, but she had really wanted to *sing*. "There's something celestial about a beautiful voice," she believed. Her sister liked to make fun of Lee's singing lessons, putting her hands over her ears when Lee practiced her scales.

Not surprisingly—given their good looks, good manners, and irrepressible youth—the Bouvier girls were a tremendous social success in Europe. The bon vivant Reinaldo Herrera—husband of the couturier Carolina Herrera and scion of a wealthy Venezuelan family—first met Lee at a dinner party Vincent Astor hosted in the 1950s. Looking back on the trajectory of the sisters' lives, he recently commented, "These two girls, with all the innocence of America and the generosity of America, go over [to Europe] and they're amazed that they're a success! And they're amazed that all these people in Paris and everywhere kept being their friends, until the bitter end." One of his acquaintances, he recalled, "was in love with both of them. Until the day he died, he talked with awe about the Bouvier girls."

Their most impressive encounter was meeting one of Lee's heroes, the Renaissance art historian Bernard Berenson. Lee had begun a correspondence with Berenson when she was just fifteen. She later said that the only way she got through Miss Porter's was her love of her art history class, taught by her favorite teacher, Sarah McLennan ("I lived for her class and was transported by the subject"). Lee wrote to Berenson about her European tour and was thrilled to be invited to meet him.

A slight figure at eighty-six, with an immaculately trimmed white beard, Berenson did not disappoint. He walked toward them out of the woods of his beautiful estate, the Villa I Tatti, outside of Settignano near Florence, like a figure out of Dante. Upon meeting the two enchanted girls, he immediately began talking to them about love. "Never follow your senses," he advised. "Marry someone who will constantly stimulate you, and you, him."

But Lee's first question to their eminent host and sage had nothing to do with romance or art. Instead, she blurted out, "Why did Mummy divorce Daddy?"

At seventeen, she was still looking for answers to the upheavals of her early life. If Berenson had an answer, he didn't say. Instead, the art historian served them tea, and proceeded to define all experience as either "life enhancing" or "life diminishing," warning them not to "waste your life with diminishing people who aren't stimulating, and if you find it's often you are with unstimulating people, it must be because you yourself are not stimulating." Lee never forgot that—even today, when attending a cocktail party or reception, she always seeks out the most interesting person in the room.

Berenson also spoke of "a house of life. Art is not *real* life, but an *ideal* life," he told the two impressionable young women, and for Lee, those were the words she carried away with her. "That is how I have tried to live," she said years later. "I hear his words in my head to this day."

While the two proper girls sipped their tea in Berenson's beautiful Italian garden, his collection of fragile seventeenth-century teacups reminded Lee of one of her childhood fantasies: "My sister was the White Queen" she later recalled, "and I was her handmaiden, her lady-in-waiting, bringing her tea in tiny cups."

"Come back soon, darlings, and see me soon" were Berenson's parting words to the starstruck debutantes. A final piece of advice Berenson gave the two girls, however, had nothing to do with art history: "American girls should marry American boys. They wear better." But he also said, "The only way to exist happily is to love your work."

Gore Vidal later noted that "Italy had been sealed off not only by war but by Fascism." Among the few Westerners who knew Italy well at that time were "mad Ezra Pound, gentle Max Beerbohm," and Bernard Berenson.

Jackie, like Lee, was deeply impressed by their afternoon with Berenson; she had discovered a mentor that day whose words and sensitivity marked her, even though it was Lee, of course, who had begun the correspondence and secured the invitation to visit him. Lee's fascination with art history, and especially Italian Renaissance and, later, nineteenth-century Russian art, predated Jackie's. This was a pattern that would follow the two women throughout their lives: Jackie often took her aesthetic interests and style, in décor and in couture, from her younger sister, and earned international acclaim for her discernment, while Lee increasingly resented it.

There was an unfortunate coda to their special summer, which happened during their last week abroad, following the enchanted visit to I Tatti. They were staying at Marlia, a villa on a vast, parklike estate that had once belonged to Napoleon's sister, the Duchess of Lucca, Elisa Bonaparte Baciocchi. The current chatelaines were the Count and Countess Pecci-Blunt, and the Bouvier girls were made welcome by letters of introduction from Hugh Auchincloss. The countess, Anna Pecci-Blunt, was known for her brilliance and social prominence. It was there that the two well-brought-up young women made a faux pas heard round the world, like something out of Edith Wharton's *Age of Innocence*: they left the villa without bidding their hostess good-bye.

They had an early-morning flight back to America, and the girls felt it would be inconsiderate to wake the countess. "We were just being polite," Lee later recalled, but when the countess awoke and found them gone, she considered their exit the height of rudeness. The word quickly went out that those American girls had no manners! A fellow guest at Marlia observed, "It marked them for several years to come."

"We were accomplices," Lee recalled about their special summer, "but only for a short time." On returning home, Janet Auchincloss was delighted with the booklet of poems and drawings that Jackie and Lee had put together for their mother. Jackie's illustrations are funny and pleasing ("You can see how much Jackie was influenced by [Saul] Steinberg," Lee observed). Her poems, too, are witty and charming, including one that uses as a refrain images of Lee being corralled by a series of doting swains that suggest that Jackie really was looking out for her younger sister: "Yes, she's taking the air / with Monsieur Moliere" and "Oh she's behind the trees / With the Duc de Guise":

> *I did minuets*
> *I drank champagne*
> *looking for Lee*
> *always in vain*
> Mais vous n'avez pas vu ma petite soeur?
> Elle est si jeune—j'ai un peu peur.

"That book was so much fun," Lee said, looking back. "Filled with enthusiasm, but it was such an organized trip. We had to call our mother all the time."

As for the two sisters, they would not travel together again for another twelve years, and by then Lee would be accompanying the First Lady of the United States of America.

Years later, the young woman who became Lee's daughter-in-law, Carole DiFalco Radziwill, reflected on the difficulties Lee had being the younger sister of the White Queen.

"I think it was hard to be overshadowed by her sister," she said, "when you feel like you have something to say and you just know no one is ever going to be interested, whereas your sister is beloved on the world stage. Most siblings have stuff between them, but how about, 'The world likes you best'? You can't fight that."

Which is exactly what Lee—and Jackie—set out to do.

4

LONDON CALLING

If you went on a date with Marilyn Monroe,
what would you talk about?
— JACKIE, AS THE "INQUIRING CAMERAGIRL"

A daughter in my mother's house, or a mistress in my own?
— LEE

Back home in the States, Jackie took a job in January of 1952 as an "Inquiring Cameragirl" for the *Washington Times-Herald* for twenty-five dollars a week. Again, her well-connected stepfather asked Arthur Krock, then the Washington bureau chief of the *New York Times*, to help land her a position, which he did, as a receptionist to the editor of the *Washington Times-Herald*, Frank Waldrop. But Jackie had far loftier ambitions than being a receptionist; she really wanted to write.

Waldrop recalled Jackie telling him, "I want to be in the newspaper business."

"Are you serious?" he asked. "Do you want to make a career, or just hang around until you get married? Because I don't have time to fool around with this."

"No," she answered. "I really want to write. I'm serious about making a career of writing."

If he wasn't impressed by her ability to read and speak French, her tony education, her beautiful manners and obvious intelligence, Waldrop was impressed with her directness. He recalled:

She was a bright young woman. She could see around corners. She had gone to Krock. She wasn't wasting time. She was just getting right into things. She had sense enough to do that.

Jackie saw the job of writing the Inquiring Cameragirl column as a way into journalism. It involved asking questions and taking photographs of various Washingtonians from all walks of life—construction workers, hospital staff, hotel clerks, truck drivers—and young politicians. In developing the photographs, Jackie discovered an interest in photography, and in approaching strangers with her camera and her provocative questions, she found a way to overcome her innate shyness.

Her questions ranged from playful to penetrating, reflecting the concerns of the day, including the evolving awareness of how women's traditional roles were being challenged in contemporary culture. For example:

> *Do you think bikini bathing suits are immoral?*
> *Do you consider yourself normal?*
> *You look important. Are you?*
> *What prominent person's death affected you most?*
> *Do the rich enjoy life more than the poor?*
> *Do you think a wife should let her husband think he's smarter*
>   *than she is?*
> *What do you think women desire most?*
> *When did you discover that women are not the weaker sex?*

She once asked a circus clown if he "was really hiding a broken heart," and attendees at an American Psychological Association convention, "How do you think you're maladjusted?"

Increasingly, her questions showed a deepening interest in politics, and she wanted to know what it was like to cover the White House press conferences. Her Inquiring Cameragirl questions reflected this new interest: "Which first lady would you have liked to have been?" she asked, and "Would you support a woman for president of the United States?" "Should a candidate's wife campaign with her husband?" "Do a candidate's looks influence your vote?" She even cheekily asked, "Do you think Mamie Eisenhower's bangs will become a nationwide fashion?" (They didn't.)

Jackie managed to sneak into the Republican headquarters on election night after Eisenhower and Nixon's victory, and soon after interviewed Pat Nixon. She devoted her column to the 1953 Eisenhower inauguration, interviewing two of Mamie Eisenhower's nieces, Ellen and Mamie Moore. She illustrated it with a fetching cartoon she drew of one of the girls, Mamie, alongside the new president. When the story and sketch ran in the *Times-Herald*, the girls' mother was angry, urging Waldrop to "do something to make that brash cameragirl, whoever she is, know her place." But Arthur Krock at the *New York Times* loved it and brought it to the attention of Bess Armstrong, who covered First Ladies for the *Times*, and who suggested that Jackie write and illustrate a children's book about the history of the White House.

Jackie loved the idea, but didn't follow through. She also became interested in the Octagon House, which had been the temporary home for James Madison and his wife, Dolley, after the White House was seriously damaged by fire during the War of 1812. She was well ahead of her time in seeing that the relatively new format of historical documentaries could go beyond print journalism, and she wrote a script for a television documentary on the subject, portraying it as Dolley Madison's haunted house:

> . . . Little boys and girls dared each other to run up the steps, then ran back to the sidewalk squealing with delight and horror . . . There are days when you can smell lilacs . . . They say [on] those days that Dolley Madison is "around . . ."

Jackie managed to find a television station interested in her script, but the station went out of business before her project could be realized.

Jackie loved being independent and self-supporting, though "she was always a little short of money," recalled Waldrop. "She always had to be careful how she spent . . . She would always be looked after by her stepfather, but he had his own children. She certainly wasn't going to get anything substantial from her father [Bouvier]. She worked, and she earned a living."

Jackie wasn't quick to rush into a marriage, relishing her escape from Janet's eagle eye and sometimes stifling social milieu. By the time she was nineteen, Jackie knew that she "didn't want to marry any of the young men I grew up with—not because of them but because of their life . . ." Nonetheless, Jackie became engaged to a New York stockbroker named John G. W. Husted Jr., a friend of Hugh Auchincloss, who had already brought her so many important connections in her young life. The *Times-Herald* announced their engagement on January 21, 1952, the wedding to take place six months hence.

Perhaps Jackie wasn't as independent as she felt herself to be, accepting a proposal from a Wall Street broker close to and approved by her family. And in a pattern that both sisters would follow, square-jawed investment banker Husted bore a passing resemblance to Black Jack Bouvier.

*

LEE HAD PERSUADED her parents to send her to Rome the summer after her first trip abroad, where she continued her singing lessons. On her return, she dropped out of Sarah Lawrence after just three terms. The journalist Barbara Walters, who had been a student at Sarah Lawrence at the same time as Lee, remembered her as

a beautifully dressed, shy girl—inclined to bite her fingernails and spend every weekend away from college. She was no great student, even in her favorite subjects (psychology and design), and a notable nonparticipant in extracurricular activities. Her friend, even at the time, was her sister, although there were understandable signs of rivalry.

Walters recalled when Jackie visited the campus and decided to show a portfolio of her drawings to one of Lee's favorite professors. Jackie was a talented but undeveloped artist, and she was no doubt pleased when the art history professor spent nearly an hour going over her portfolio. But Lee wasn't. "I wish you would someday spend half as much time on me!" she complained.

For Lee, more important things than finishing college were in the offing: after a summer in Italy, she took a job as a special assistant to Diana Vreeland at *Harper's Bazaar.* More exciting (because this was 1953 and the surest way to leave the confines of Janet's household), there was a wedding in the offing: despite the *Times-Herald* announcement of Jackie's engagement, Lee was going to beat her older sister to the altar.

Lee apparently did not share her sister's early conviction to make a career for herself before marrying. For Lee, it was by way of marriage that she would transcend the realm of Janet's considerable influence on her young life. That spring, at the age of twenty, Lee married Michael Temple Canfield, a shy, handsome twenty-seven-year-old publishing scion whom she had known and dated occasionally since she was fifteen.

Michael was the adopted son of Cass Canfield, the wealthy and distinguished publisher of Harper & Row (which would become the Kennedys' publishing house), but he was rumored to be the illegitimate son of Prince George, Duke of Kent, and Kiki Whitney Preston, an American adventuress who first met the duke in Kenya, where she allegedly introduced him to cocaine. As a result of this thrilling rumor, young Michael adopted rather dapper English airs and dress, and—at six foot three inches, blond and imperially slim—he did cut an elegant figure. (Gore Vidal described him as an "uncommonly charming and decent youth . . . someone out of place in our wild world of bloody tooth and claw.")

Canfield knew both girls, and he once took them on a rowboat ride in Central Park. He watched the two sisters whispering together in the back of the boat, in deep, serious conversation, and finally asked them what they were talking about.

"Gloves," they replied.

*

ON THAT RAINY day in early spring—April 18, 1953—Hugh Auchincloss hosted the wedding reception at his stately Merrywood home, and Bouvier—still chastened by and envious of his successor's wealth—gave away the bride. It was his first visit to Auchincloss country, and after being given a tour of its rolling lawns, its grand Georgian house, the Potomac shimmering in the distance, Bouvier bitterly felt the difference in their status. He was proud of how beautiful Lee looked, but it was a sober reminder of how much he had lost.

Auchincloss had slight misgivings about Lee's marriage to Michael Canfield, not because of Lee's youth (twenty was a normal age for young women to marry in the 1950s), but because "he'll never be able to afford her," he confided, prophetically, to a friend.

Lee later said that one reason she married young was that she couldn't wait to be on her own and set up house. The couple moved into a tiny penthouse apartment in New York, which Lee delighted in decorating, but soon thereafter the couple decamped to London. Sent abroad to work in Harper & Row's London office, Canfield was instead persuaded by Lee to take a position as secretary to the ambassador to England, which quickly won the young American expats entrée to the best of London society.

By marrying first, Lee upstaged her older sister, at least in the eyes of the Auchinclosses. To punctuate that fact, she tossed Jackie her bridal bouquet just before leaving Merrywood for her honeymoon. Jackie had already broken off her engagement to John Husted, which had never been a passionate love match on her part, but rather something that had seemed suitable.

Within a month after catching Lee's bouquet, Jackie became engaged to the most eligible bachelor in America, the dashing young senator from Massachusetts, John F. Kennedy. Not only was he extremely handsome, witty, and intelligent, but also, as a Kennedy scion, he was very, very rich. And Canfield was not.

*

THEY HAD BEEN seeing each other for about a year, introduced by Jack's friend Charles Bartlett at a Washington, DC, dinner. Young Jack Kennedy was struck by Jackie's intelligence and her somber beauty. Leaning over the asparagus in Bartlett's dining room, he invited Jackie out on their first date.

Jackie found ways to get and keep Kennedy's attention during the yearlong courtship that followed, and to sound him out on the subject of marriage, with playfully provocative questions she posed in the *Times-Herald* as its Inquiring Cameragirl: "Could you give any reason why a contented bachelor would want to get married?"; "Should engaged couples reveal their past?"; and—ironically, perhaps, given Kennedy's much publicized romantic exploits—"[Do you agree that] the Irish are deficient in the art of love?" and "If you went on a date with Marilyn Monroe, what would you talk about?"

They were noticed publicly for the first time when twenty-three-year-old Jackie accompanied thirty-five-year-old Kennedy as his date to Dwight Eisenhower's inaugural ball in January 1953. Jackie feared that Kennedy's supporters considered her "a snob from Newport who had bouffant hair and French clothes and hated politics." (And it wasn't just Kennedy's supporters. Once elected, Kennedy worried that the menus in the White House were becoming too French. "What the hell was Potage aux vermicelles?" he peevishly asked. "I just don't want any more persons in this house being too French.") But in fact Jackie's style and knowledge of French were assets to the presidential hopeful. She had already proved invaluable to him, helping him prepare his remarks for his first major speech on the Senate floor, by translating and summarizing nearly a dozen French texts on the French Empire, including Indochina. Jackie's reading aloud from de Gaulle's *Mémoires* helped inform Kennedy's speeches. De Gaulle's "All my life I have had a certain idea of France" became Kennedy's "I have developed an image of America" in his announcement of his candidacy for president in 1960.

The ceremony was held on September 12, 1953, touted in the press as "the wedding of the year." The gala reception, organized by Janet, was at Hammersmith Farm in Newport. Once again, Black Jack Bouvier was invited to escort his daughter down the aisle, but once again he was so abashed by the opulence of the Auchincloss estate that he sulked, half dressed, with a bottle of Scotch in his room at the Hotel Viking and railed against the Auchinclosses.

Here's how Gore Vidal described it:

. . . Black Jack came to Newport, Rhode Island, to give away the bride. He was on his best behavior. But inspired by who knows what furies, Janet decided that although she could not bar him from the church, she could disinvite him from the reception, which, as it turned out, the Kennedys were to take over as a sound-and-light spectacle, celebrating the triumph of the Boston Irish over that old Protestant patriciate which had scorned Jack's father, Joe Kennedy, not because he was Irish and Catholic, as he would have it, but because he was so exuberantly and successfully a crook.

After years of disappointment and decline, Bouvier no longer cut a dashing figure. Sadly for father and daughter, he had gotten too drunk to walk his favorite daughter down the aisle, and the honor fell to Hugh D. Auchincloss, his nemesis.

*

THE YOUNG COUPLE settled in Georgetown while Kennedy flourished as the young senator from Massachusetts. It was a blissful time for them both, but it was marred by two unexpected sorrows: in 1955, two years after their marriage, Jackie suffered a miscarriage. The following year, Jackie gave birth to a daughter she named Arabella, but the infant was stillborn.

*

IN LONDON, LEE was enjoying an extraordinary social whirl in the homes of London's elite, but the marriage was not particularly happy. Not only was Canfield a heavy drinker, but the couple was unsuccessful in their attempts to conceive (Canfield was later discovered to be sterile), though Lee desperately wanted a child. She soon began having affairs, which Michael knew of but did not complain about. The coup de grâce for Canfield came when it became clear that Lee intended to live at a level well beyond her husband's means. When Jackie visited her sister in London and Canfield asked her how he could hold on to Lee, Jackie answered, "Get more money, Michael." When he demurred, pointing out that he already had a modest trust fund and a good salary, Jackie explained, "No, Michael. I mean *real* money."

*

THE 1950s HAD not been kind to Jack Bouvier. He began the decade by selling his seat on the New York Stock Exchange for $90,000 (the same seat, right before the 1929 stock market crash, had sold for $625,000). He retired on a nest egg of $200,000—far less than his father had. He drew up his will and, as his nephew Davis recalled, "became more of a recluse than ever," holing up in his New York apartment with Esther, his housekeeper, now his sole companion.

> A lean, weatherbeaten Swedish woman with a long, creased neck and protruding eyes, Esther cleaned Jack's apartment, cooked his meals, did his laundry . . . loaned him money . . . took care of his shopping, accompanied him on his occasional travels [to Florida and Cuba], and listened to his endless declarations of love for his daughters.

Later in life, Jackie expressed her gratitude for Esther's care of their father by helping to support her in her advanced years. It wasn't lost on Bouvier that at sixty-four, his life was greatly diminished—the financial cost of his divorce, the estrangement of his daughters, his lack of female companionship and of a doting family surrounding him in his twilight years. He blamed Janet for all of it. He lived for his daughters' phone calls and visits— increasingly rare as Jackie was caught up in the demands of her husband's political career, and Lee was living in London.

Bouvier continued to send his daughters small checks (which included a little message to each, written on the check itself, such as "to a beautiful girl on her birthday").

On July 27, 1957, Bouvier was rushed to Lenox Hill Hospital in Manhattan, suffering from severe abdominal pains. His doctor had not informed him that he had cancer of the liver. He was in torment until August 3, when he slipped into a coma and died in Lenox Hill at the age of sixty-six.

Jackie flew in from the Kennedy compound in Hyannis Port, Massachusetts, with Jack Kennedy. As she would on a more famous occasion just six years later, she organized the funeral. Her extended family was impressed by "the decisive, distinctive way she handled everything, from the obituary to the burial." Jackie sent Jack Kennedy to select the casket and deliver the obituary and a photograph to the *New York Times*. She insisted that Jack deliver the text and photo personally to the managing editor, no doubt to ensure respectable space on the obituary pages of the newspaper. She got the photo from one of her father's former girl-friends, which must have been an embarrassing confrontation for the young Washington wife.

For her father's funeral, Jackie insisted on festooning St. Patrick's Cathedral on Fifth Avenue with garlands of summer flowers instead of the usual dark wreathes and waxen lilies. "I want everything to look like a summer garden," she told her Bouvier aunts, "like Lasata in August."

Few people attended besides family—Bouvier's sisters and nephews and his two daughters—but in the last pew sat a row of veiled women. They were Bouvier's former paramours, and they had all come for their last assignation with Black Jack Bouvier.

After the funeral Mass, he was buried in East Hampton in the graveyard of the church where he had married Janet Lee a lifetime ago. At the site of his burial, mourners heard the rattling of the Long Island Rail Road train as it rolled past on its way to the nearby station.

After the funeral, Bouvier's will was read. He left various small bequests for his sisters, nephews, and their children, but the greater part of the estate went to Jackie and Lee to be divided equally: approximately $80,000 apiece after taxes. He also left a painting of Arabian horses by Schreyer to Jackie, and his writing desk to Lee.

For Lee—despite a surprisingly generous bequest—her father's diminished circumstance before his death had evoked a need for the comforting haven of wealth. For both sisters, Black Jack Bouvier would remain in their memories and haunt their imaginations as a deeply romantic, idealized figure.

*

BACK IN LONDON after the funeral, Lee accepted an invitation from *Vogue* to select American fashions for the US pavilion at the Brussels World's Fair, as their "permanent representative" from the fair's opening on April 17 to its close on October 19, 1958. She loved choosing and promoting American couture and jauntily posed for *Vogue* atop a tower of suitcases. Lee had finally begun to find her métier—but the troubles with her marriage persisted and she embarked on a number of discreet, and not so discreet, affairs. One of them, with the émigré Polish aristocrat Stanislas "Stas" Radziwill, would change their lives.

Stas Radziwill, the scion of an ancient Polish family brought to its knees by the German invasion, worked for the Polish underground and escaped to London at the end of World War II. Virtually penniless, he traded on nothing but his charm and his wits, marrying a Swiss heiress and eventually making a fortune in real estate. He was bighearted, larger than life, sometime imperious, and cut a recognizable figure in London, living beyond his means and swanning around town in a big Cadillac. By the time Lee met him, he was married to his second wife, the heiress Grace Maria Kolin.

Lee first met Stas (who was nearly twenty years older than she) in 1952 at a shooting party in the English countryside, at the home of Lady Lambton. The dashing Pole was passionate about shooting and was an excellent shot—a pursuit that Lee did not share ("I hated to see those birds fall from the sky"). Stas was there with his second wife, Grace, and Jackie was there as well, on a visit to London to see her sister. She surprised Lee with a flirtatious gambit when she turned to Radziwill and said, "Stas, you have such beautiful lips." (Perhaps Jackie was signaling to Lee that Stas was a worthy prospect.)

. . .

While John Kennedy's star was rising, he had set his sights on the presidency, Canfield's drinking had accelerated and his stint at the American embassy was about to end. The marriage was essentially over when Lee began her romance with Stas. James Symington, the son of Democratic senator Stuart Symington of Missouri, was an attaché at the embassy at the time, and he recalled a dinner party he gave for the Canfields, the Radziwills, and Lord and Lady Dudley.

"It was on March 26, 1957—I remember the date because it was a birthday party for my son, who had just turned two. The invitation read that he would be asleep, but I would be hosting in his place. I remember Lee as a pretty girl—I remember she looked great!" Symington had known Canfield since they were both students at St. Bernard's School in Manhattan. "He worked for the ambassador in London before me; when Jock Whitney took over the embassy, I became his secretary," he recalled. "I guess you know that after their divorces, Lee married Radziwill, Grace married Lord Dudley, and Michael married Lady Dudley. It was quite a trio!"

Seven years after their first meeting, Lee Bouvier Canfield became Princess Lee Radziwill. When Radziwill had become a British citizen, he'd been required to officially give up his princely title, but he managed to cling to it, as did Lee. For Lee, it was a prize she was not going to give away.

John Davis later wrote:

When Lee married Prince Radziwill in March 1959, she was a childless, relatively impecunious divorcee living in a by no means opulent apartment in London, who had been occupying her time with various fashion assignments such as running the fashion show at the American Pavillion at the Brussels World's Fair of 1958. Within two-and-a-half years of her marriage, she had become one of the great ladies of the Western World.

If Canfield's connections through the American embassy had thrust Lee into the highest echelons of London society, her marriage to Stas allowed her to flourish in a much grander style, not to mention granting her the dubious title of princess, which she used, albeit illegitimately. Though Stas wasn't nearly as rich as his brother-in-law, his success allowed Lee to live a life that even Jackie would envy: a three-story Georgian house at 4 Buckingham Place (a charming house not far from Buckingham Palace, though in a relatively modest neighborhood), and a sprawling weekend country home outside of Henley-on-Thames in Oxfordshire, just an hour's drive from London.

Called Turville Grange, it was a stately Queen Anne brick-facade "bakehouse" built in the seventeenth century on fifty acres, facing Turville Heath. The lavish gardens behind the manse overlooked the Chiltern Valley. The estate was so vast it included a large guesthouse, a cobblestone courtyard, a stable with a dovecote, and an herb garden. The Radziwills had a staff that would make any Edwardian household proud: a cook, a butler, two maids, and a nanny for their children. In the middle of the courtyard, like something out of an Elizabethan ballad, was a mighty beech tree surrounded by a bench used for mounting horses. A large kitchen garden and a rose garden lined by espaliered pear trees completed the landscape. Stas designed an elegant, indoor swimming pool (which Lee disliked).

Lee's longtime friend Leslie Caron, the celebrated French actress and dancer, saw that Stas delighted in pleasing his stylish wife, allowing her to lavishly redecorate both of their homes and providing Lee with holidays in leased or borrowed Italian and Portuguese villas. Caron thought that he treated her like a child bride, like Nora in Henrik Ibsen's *A Doll's House*, and she felt that, like Nora, Lee "wanted to try out her wings and be independent in the same way."

Of the city and country residences, Lee felt most at home

in Turville Grange, which she described as "a house of flowers. When you entered, it had a smell of straw rugs and burning
fires, mixed with the scent of sweet flowers." It was their *"Month
in the Country* house," Lee recalled—it was Chekhov and Turgenev, two Russian writers Lee admired. They filled the place
with their menagerie—including three horses and a pony, a cat
named Pussy Willow, and five dogs. "Lee was creating a personal,
earthly paradise of her own taste and expression," said her friend
André Leon Talley. In some ways, it was Lee's answer to Merrywood and Hammersmith Farm, and their duration there was
probably the happiest time of their marriage.

Lee turned to the designer Renzo Mongiardino to decorate
both houses. "My living room is like a bowling alley, can you
come fix it?" she wrote to the Italian designer. Mongiardino was
an architect who worked as both an interior designer and a theatrical set designer. He frequently collaborated with the opera and
film director Franco Zeffirelli, notably on Zeffirelli's production
of *The Taming of the Shrew* in 1967, for which he was nominated
for an Academy Award for Best Art Direction, and on *Romeo and
Juliet* in 1968. He was nominated again in 1973 for art direction
on Zeffirelli's *Brother Sun, Sister Moon.* He also designed sets for
a production of *The Nutcracker* choreographed by Rudolf Nureyev
and for several operas in Milan, Venice, and London. As an interior decorator, he was in high demand among the grandest families in Europe, naming among his clients Aristotle Onassis; the
Italian industrialist Giovanni Agnelli and his wife, Marella; Gianni Versace; Edmond and Lily Safra; the Rothschilds; and the
Hearsts—and Lee and Stas Radziwill, not quite in that echelon,
but edging closer.

Though grounded in the modern movement, Mongiardino
took his designs further, juxtaposing the ordinary with objet
d'art, employing rich, textured fabrics and sculptured panels, using trompe l'oeil to superb effect. He inserted fakes among the

antiques, guided by his sense of proportion and harmony. Thus "authenticity" took a back seat to dramatic effect. After all, he was trained as a set designer, so design had to set a mood, make an impact, be memorable and beautiful, but not necessarily historically accurate. Lee chose him for all of the above, and because their tastes resonated with each other. She wanted an opulent, rich, and layered look. She was inspired by a cushion Renzo had designed that she spotted in an *Elle* magazine photo spread, and knew immediately she wanted him to design her two homes. "His eye was extraordinary," Lee later said, "and I learned so much from him."

With Mongiardino, Lee's two homes were transformed into sumptuous, inviting, enchanted retreats. For the house at 4 Buckingham Place, Mongiardino designed the living room and bedroom with a rich display of tapestries, giving them a nineteenth-century, old-world atmosphere. Cecil Beaton, the favorite photographer of the royal family and a celebrated theatrical designer, photographed the living room for *Vogue* in 1966.

Inviting the designer to turn his eyes toward the Turville country house, she apologized that it was "no palazzo," just a project "to amuse him." She supplied four yards of eighteenth-century fabric, which Renzo "copied . . . for the living room exquisitely— even better than the original." The dining room had a Russian theme (Lee dubbed it "the Turgenev dining room"), achieved by pasting richly colored Sicilian scarves—hand-painted by the designer Lila de Nobili—to the walls; it, too, was photographed for *Vogue* in 1971.

Lee certainly enjoyed the perks of her London house, but her heart was in the country. "We had wonderful gardens," she later wrote,

a fantastic kitchen garden and a huge pink-walled vegetable garden . . . We had a marvelous chef; we had a full household.

We were an hour and a half from London, so it was very easy. Stas insisted on building an indoor swimming pool, which was hideous, but he enjoyed it.

For Lee, turning to a theatrical designer to transform her houses seemed fitting, as she was drawn to the arts of invention and dramatic self-presentation. She had found escape from the domestic tensions of her childhood homes in fantasy and a love of beauty. Lee confided that she always preferred the nineteenth century to her own, in love with its music and painting. "I love all the dramatic composers—Debussy, Scriabin, Mahler, Ravel—and painters like David and Delacroix. They had such power and vitality, and such warmth." As the London designer and decorator Nicky Haslam observed, in her theatrical flair, Lee had "not *safe* good taste." In the dramatic Mongiardino, she'd found her ideal designer.

Born August 4, 1959, five months after her marriage to Stas, her first child and only son, Antony, arrived. She chose to give birth in Lausanne, Switzerland, because they were known for having the best obstetricians in the world, and because it was easier there to put out the story that Antony (later changed to Anthony) was three months premature. Despite a difficult birth, he was a robust, black-haired, healthy boy, and Lee adored him. By marrying first and having a child barely two years after Jackie bore Caroline, Lee was keeping pace with her older sister. But more important, Lee was happy.

The early years of her marriage to Stas were blissful. "Stas was crazy about Lee," friends of the couple observed, and "immensely proud of Lee . . . They had a mutual respect and admiration for each other which was rather exciting for both of them." Besides the great satisfaction of completely redecorating her town and country houses, she and Stas took frequent trips to Europe and to the States. She took up horseback riding at Windsor and joined Stas on weekend shooting parties, living the life of landed aristocracy, with a tilt toward the bohemian crowd represented by Lee's friend Cecil Beaton. Lee even occasionally took her pet dog, a pug named Thomas, for high tea at the Ritz in London. They entertained extravagantly, hosting candlelit dinners at 4 Buckingham Place. Stas used salty language and told bawdy stories, and he liked to tease Lee by saying, "Shit! The little girl is very, very small . . . It is fantastic how much she costs to dress!" For her part, Lee teased Stas about his Polish accent and broken English, doing spot-on imitations.

Once the decorating of her two houses was complete, Lee continued to search out eighteenth- and nineteenth-century French and Italian drawings. She still searched for creative outlets, and wrote an unpublished article with the revealing title "The Anxiety to Distinguish Oneself." She gave it to the Harvard professor, economist, and Kennedy friend John Kenneth Galbraith to edit, and he changed it so much that Lee ended up "throwing it away." But the anxiety remained, only to be relieved for a time when Rudolf Nureyev entered the picture. She fell mightily for the world-renowned Russian dancer, undermining her marriage to Stas.

*

IT DIDN'T MATTER that Nureyev, though bisexual, was primarily gay. After all, Truman Capote would fall in love with Lee—for her grace, her beauty, her intelligence, her star power. Lee found herself powerfully drawn to the ruggedly beautiful dancer. Many women were attracted to his sensuality, his exuberance, his glamour. Another worshipper was Princess Margaret, who commented after attending the London premiere of his production of *The Nutcracker* in February of 1968, "He was more beautiful than I can describe, with his flared nostrils, huge eyes, and high cheekbones." Mick Jagger and Marianne Faithfull, Jagger's then paramour, were also devotees; Faithfull admitted that they were "obsessed" with Nureyev.

Since his dramatic defection to the West on June 16, 1961, in Paris, Nureyev was regarded as a rock star, a tempestuous and supremely gifted artist, attracting the adoration of thousands of balletomanes. Lee adored him, but Jackie had seen him first.

In April of 1963, when London's Royal Ballet took up residence at Carnegie Hall for their New York season, Jackie Kennedy (as well as Princess Grace of Monaco and Greta Garbo) joined the ranks of Nureyev worshippers. She attended Nureyev's New York premiere and was deeply impressed by his performance with the celebrated dancer Margot Fonteyn, who at forty-two years of age had seen her career reignited by her partnership with the twenty-three-year-old Russian in *Giselle*. The principal ballerina described that evening as "one of the strongest artistic experiences of my life . . . there were 40 curtain calls . . . Seeing [them] made up for having missed Nijinsky and Chaliapin."

At another performance, Jackie asked to go backstage to meet Nureyev, but the dancer's manager, the impresario Sol Hurok, discouraged her, and Nureyev reportedly left "fuming." But not long after, Jackie invited Nureyev and Fonteyn to the White House for tea, beginning a thirty-year friendship between the "two sixties icons, he, ballet's most famous prince, and she, the queen of Camelot," in the words of Nureyev's biographer Diane Solway. His brilliant presence ignited Jackie's interest in tsarist Russian culture, which she would return to later in life.

Like her sister, Lee found in Rudolf Nureyev the apotheosis of artistry and a kind of peacock beauty that mirrored her own lean, high-cheekboned face; in photographs, they could have been twin descendants of the Tatars. Throughout her life, Lee found herself drawn to artists deeply devoted to their work—Truman Capote, the designer Renzo Mongiardino, and, of course, Nureyev, who possessed another quality that spoke to her. "I have the greatest sympathy for those who end in despair," she once said, and perhaps in Nureyev she sensed the wisp of impending doom.

Lee first met the Russian dancer when she and Stas saw him dance with the Royal Ballet in London. Joan Thring, the Australian manager who organized many of Nureyev's world tours, recalled that Lee had phoned her in March of 1966 to say that she wanted to do something for the dancer on his fast-approaching birthday, on March 17. She asked if she could throw a party for Nureyev, and after that, Joan Thring said, "she never let go."

Lee and Stas threw a lavish party for Nureyev on his twenty-eighth birthday, and Lee invited many of his fellow dancers, though the appeal was somewhat lost on Stas, who referred to the celebrated Russian simply as "Lee's friend, the dancer."

The following year, Lee invited Nureyev to stay with them at their London house and at Turville Grange, as the Russian dancer did not yet have a permanent home. At first, Nureyev was suspicious of Lee's hospitality—he was by temperament a self-protective man. Lee described him as being like "a very alert animal: on guard and afraid of being caught or trapped." Lee started showing up at his classes and rehearsals, deepening his suspicion, but he was finally won over, Lee believes, by seeing "the way we lived, the way I did things." Nureyev did indeed love the exotic nineteenth-century atmosphere of Lee's two homes, and in fact he followed her lead in hiring Renzo Mongiardino to design the sets of the next ballet he choreographed. He'd particularly admired Lee's dining room, with its antique leather walls, taken from Mongiardino's set for Zeffirelli's *The Taming of the Shrew*. "It was heavy and dark," Lee recalled, "and Rudolf adored it. He'd never heard of Renzo before, but he was also so curious and receptive."

Nureyev stayed with the Radziwills for seven months, bonding over their love of Oriental design and rich fabrics. Lee described a typical day:

He had lunch at four or five o'clock in the afternoon before a performance, and after a performance it took him hours to wind down. We used to go [window shop] antiquing about 11 and walked and walked until 2 in the morning. And Rudolf would inevitably become thrilled about some extremely dark, heavy piece of furniture. And the next day I would have to go and find out what it was.

Nureyev eventually owned a home called Villa Arcady in the hills above Monte Carlo, in the town of La Turbie, Monaco. Lee loved it: the music continuously wafting throughout the house, its nineteenth-century feel, its wrought iron gates, white stucco walls, and heavy furniture. (Cecil Beaton believed that Nureyev liked substantial, grand-sized furniture and heavy iron pieces so that they could never be stolen, which he described as a vestige of his peasant upbringing.)

Lee recalled, "When I first knew [Rudolf], the only language he spoke, apart from Russian and Tatar, was English—poorly— but then I always found Slavic English with no prepositions more expressive and far more provocative than English spoken as expected!" Of course, that was what Stas's English sounded like, and it was part of Nureyev's immense appeal. "Part of his charm," recalled one of his friends, "was to get women to fawn all over him. Gay or straight, he flirted like crazy." Nureyev "enjoyed a special rapport with women," writes Solway, though "his interest in them was primarily social or aesthetic, not sexual."

Rudolf was drawn to Lee, whom he described as ". . . not just a socialite. She attracts people of substance." Nonetheless, one of his friends, the ballerina Lynn Seymour, observed that he "had female lovers, whom he'd get fascinated with for a while," and Lee was one of them—one who was incredibly persistent. "Lee kept pushing and Rudolf finally just gave in," one of Lee's friends reportedly said.

Nureyev was also enjoying a friendship with Jackie, and they would often shop together on Fifth Avenue when he was in New

York. He managed to balance his friendship with both sisters, but the two women competed for his attention. Lee was often spotted dancing with Nureyev late into the night at nightclubs in Monte Carlo and London. Though he flaunted both friendships, the dancer was much closer to Lee. "I believe my sister was—you'd have to use the word 'jealousy' to describe how she felt about how close we were at one time," Lee later reminisced.

During his visits with Lee at Turville Grange, the two were often alone together, with Stas away in London. In fact, Nureyev rarely saw Stas. Joan Thring was convinced that Lee had succeeded in bedding Nureyev, just based on the intimate way they wandered the grounds of Turville Grange at dusk. Lee knew Nureyev was "99-and-a-half percent homosexual" and that she would have to take the initiative if they were going to be intimate. Apparently, she did. In fact, Nureyev claimed that Lee was one of two women he had gotten pregnant. He confided in the *Observer*'s ballet critic Maude Gosling (who wrote with her husband, Nigel, under the pseudonym Alexander Bland) that he had impregnated Lee, adding, "And what do you think she did? She destroyed my baby."

Decades later, Lee refuted this allegation, attributing it to Nureyev's confusion in the late 1980s when he was dying from AIDS. "Perhaps he was upset that he would die without an heir," she mused.

Despite whatever bitter feelings—or delusions—Nureyev nursed at the end, their friendship was genuine and it lasted throughout his life. He treasured an extraordinary objet d'art Lee had given him: a gold, jewel-studded, double-headed eagle, which he secreted away in the cavernous fireplace of his Monte Carlo home. He was always afraid of being robbed, but perhaps its secret place was also an indication of how Nureyev had to keep hidden his deeper feelings for Lee. When asked about this, her only answer was an enigmatic smile worthy of Mary Astor in *The Maltese Falcon*. "I only ever wanted him to myself," she said. "Always."

5

BOUVIER STYLE:
THE WHITE HOUSE YEARS

I seem so mercilessly exposed and don't know how to cope with it.
— JACKIE

Good night my darling Jacks — the bravest and noblest of all. L.
— LEE

L ee was only twenty-seven when John Kennedy won the presidency and her sister moved into the White House, ascending to the title of First Lady. Stas had proved a great help to the Kennedy-Johnson ticket by campaigning in Polish communities in the Midwest, warmly speaking to the crowds in their native language, which was difficult for him as he suffered from stage fright.

Kennedy was grateful to Stas and hugely enjoyed his company. They were both charismatic men-about-town who relished their wealth and the company of beautiful women. Jackie also adored her new brother-in-law: his solidity, dark complexion, and penchant for women and wine, so like their father's, made him irresistible to both sisters. Jack and Jackie cherished his visits to the White House, where he would play backgammon with the president, helping him to relax, and bring back deep gossip from London for the president to enjoy. Lee recalled that "Jack Kennedy loved gossip, but not nearly as much as my sister." Jackie, remembers Lee, once asked a guest of the White House what he knew about *"le scandale,"* the breakup of Elizabeth Taylor and

Eddie Fisher's marriage by Richard Burton during the making of *Cleopatra*. "Do you think she'll run off with him?" Jackie had eagerly inquired.

In the heady days after the Democratic National Convention in Los Angeles that had nominated Jack Kennedy for president, Stas and Lee vacationed with the Kennedys and the Arthur Schlesingers, who drove down from Cambridge to the Kennedy compound at Hyannis, on Cape Cod. They all spent a blissful afternoon on the Kennedy boat. Arthur M. Schlesinger Jr., a Pulitzer Prize–winning historian, Harvard professor, and Jack's special assistant, would eventually be, at forty-three, one of the old men of the Kennedy administration. He recalled that outing:

> We brought along several hand-cases of empty coke and tonic bottles; these were to be targets for rifle shooting. After we got out an appropriate distance, the boat stopped, and Jack tossed the bottles overboard. Several of them sank straight away. Others floated for a moment. And Jack and Radziwill shot at them. Jack is plainly an excellent shot. All this was carried out agreeably, with much banter and laughter.

After shooting, the boating party dove from the boat and swam in the icy waters of the Atlantic, then warmed themselves with Bloody Marys and "an excellent lunch . . . cigars and conversation," returning to port before 5 p.m. Schlesinger had never seen "Jack in better form. He was warm, funny, quick, intelligent, and spontaneous."

How wonderful for Jackie and Lee that their husbands relished each other's company, bringing the sisters even closer in the early, exuberant days just before the election, and in the two and a half years to come. At the time, both were pregnant, both expecting in November.

. . .

If Jackie was cautiously hopeful, Lee had mixed feelings about her second pregnancy. She conceived just six months after Anthony's birth, although she had not wanted to become pregnant again so soon. The birth of her second child would be more difficult than Anthony's had been. On August 18, 1960, on a short visit to New York City from Hyannis Port, she was rushed to New York Hospital and gave birth to Anna Christina Radziwill, who was three months premature. Tina was frail and kept in an incubator for several months, and Lee found herself in the grip of paralyzing postpartum depression. While Stas campaigned for Jack Kennedy, Jackie comforted her sister, but Lee was so distraught and so anxious that Stas felt she would recover better at home, in London. They flew back, leaving Tina in the hospital, to be sent for by the children's nurse.

When the tiny infant finally arrived in London in the arms of her nurse, Lee and Stas met them at Heathrow, and with great satisfaction brought Tina home to 4 Buckingham Place. Finally holding her newborn, Lee reportedly said, "This is really the most wonderful Christmas present I have ever had."

The Kennedys were disappointed when Lee and Stas had to miss his inauguration as the thirty-fifth president on January 20, 1961. Mother and infant were still too weak to fly to Washington. Jack called London twice during the festivities to see how they were faring. He especially missed having Stas there, who had such a calming effect on the young president. Jackie, too, was left weakened by the birth of her son, John Kennedy Jr., born November 25, 1960, and had to take frequent rests between inaugural activities.

At home in London, Lee's recovery from depression was slow and fitful. Angry at Stas for wanting a second child so soon after Anthony's birth, and blaming her husband for her breakdown and for Tina's frailty, she resolved to bar her bedroom door against her

husband. From then on, Stas would find sexual fulfillment outside of their marriage, as would Lee. It was hardest on Stas, who
genuinely loved Lee, but as an old-world European aristocrat, he
considered such an arrangement the norm. He accepted it, but the
glorious days of their marriage were over.

*

AFTER NOT SEEING Jackie for the four months since the election,
Lee was well enough to fly to Washington, where she was thrilled
to see her sister, who met her at Washington's National Airport.
Both arrived looking fit and tanned—Lee from a vacation in Ja-
maica and Jackie from having spent over a week in Palm Beach,
Florida.

Jackie had flown back on a commercial airline, along with two
Secret Service agents, taking up five seats in first class, and had
passed the time by reading a biography of the French mistress of
Philippe d'Orléans, Madame de Genlis—one of both sisters' enduring interests.

Despite some renewed feelings of competition, Jackie's two and
a half years in the White House brought the sisters closer together.
Somewhat overwhelmed by her new status and responsibilities,
Jackie relied on Lee, knowing she could relax with her sister and
exchange confidences. They became the whispering sisters once
again, speaking often in transatlantic calls and exchanging flur-
ries of letters. Lee and Stas made frequent visits to the White
House, where Lee would occupy the Queen's Bedroom with Stas
staying in the Lincoln Bedroom.

Lee loved her visits to the White House, and her role in advising Jackie in matters of couture. At Jackie's request, she often arrived with photographs of Paris showrooms and ateliers. Lee and
Stas's visits were a welcome respite for Jackie, who complained to
Gore Vidal that as First Lady, she was "never alone. You sit in a
room and try to write a letter and someone comes in." She made

it her priority to hold cultural gatherings with writers she admired, such as Tennessee Williams and William Faulkner, but what she really needed was "to spend an evening with just a few people. I'm terrible at crowds, and everyone gets so precious in the White House, they'd all clam up." Lee gave her that necessary feeling of normalcy and intimacy that the demands of being First Lady seemed to prohibit.

When the Radziwills were in town, they were the center of a social whirl—a White House reception for Latin American diplomats, a performance of the Comédie-Française, a party thrown by the French ambassador. They also traveled to one of Jackie's favorite spots, an estate the Kennedys owned in Middleburg, Virginia—horse country—where Jackie often rode and Jack played golf and shot skeet. Jackie loved having Lee and Stas with her. They traveled to New York City for a four-day trip where they dined with Lee's former boss at *Harper's Bazaar,* Diana Vreeland. Driven around in a black limousine bearing the plate "JK102," Lee and Jackie scoured antique shops and art galleries. They attended a performance of the New York City Ballet, escorted by Adlai Stevenson, then Kennedy's ambassador to the United Nations. They stayed at the Kennedys' duplex apartment on the top two floors of the Carlyle Hotel, decorated with Louis Quinze furniture and paintings ranging from African-American artist Romare Bearden to the American-born Impressionist painter Mary Cassatt. (The owner of the Carlyle made sure to find out what book the president was currently reading and would have his staff run out and purchase the book, leaving it opened to the page the president was currently on. There could have been no more attentive staff than that!)

On one such visit to New York, Jackie and Lee summoned the fashion designer Oleg Cassini to this elegant setting, asking him to bring his latest creations. The sisters admired the dresses, which Cassini draped over the Louis Quinze furniture. For Jackie—who made the trip with ten suitcases of clothes—it was a welcome hiatus from the pressures of her life as First Lady. For Lee, it was a chance to share the glamour and privilege that the role of First Lady afforded them both.

On March 15, 1961, Jackie organized her first dinner dance at the White House, which she made in honor of Lee and Stas. Jackie's first social secretary, Letitia "Tish" Baldrige, who had known Jackie since Miss Porter's and Vassar and who helped organize the gala, recalled that there were certain requirements for the guest list. Beauty was one of them.

"The guests all had to be beautiful," Baldrige later recalled. "[Jackie] said it was for Jack's sake, but it was for her sake as well." Lee was the same way: they often commented on how attractive— or unattractive—a person was. It always mattered to them. Jackie would often seat the "single beauties" next to her husband, in part to please him, but possibly to choose his paramours, as Jackie was by now aware of his proclivities. One of those beauties, the socialite turned writer Helen Chavchavadze, believed that "Jackie was in charge of choosing his playmates. It was very French."

It was the first of only five dinner dances in the Kennedys' thousand days in the White House, and it was a tremendous success, lasting till three in the morning. Both sisters dazzled, Jackie in a white sheath gown and Lee nearly upstaging her in red brocade (as she sometimes had during their debutante days). The seventy guests included the Aga Khan, the Carlyle Hotel muralist and children's book author Ludwig Bemelmans, and—on John Kennedy's arms—the comely Pinchot sisters, Tony (who was married to Ben Bradlee, then editor of *Newsweek* and later executive editor of the *Washington Post*) and Mary Meyer (who would later become one of Kennedy's paramours and would be murdered under mysterious circumstances). Jack had made unsuccessful passes at Tony, but as she later said, "I think it surprised him I would not succumb. If I hadn't been married maybe I would have." Because they were Jackie's social equals—and both were married—they were not the women Jackie had in mind for her husband's dalliances.

Festivities began in the East Room for cocktails. The State Dining Room was set up with nine round tables sumptuously adorned with yellow linen and baskets of spring flowers. Champagne flowed, and the menu consisted of mostly French cuisine—*saumon mousseline normande, poulet à l'estragon*, mushrooms *aux fines herbes, casserole marie-blanche*. Dancing to Lester Lanin's orchestra in the Blue Room rounded out the evening. The entire gala had a slightly naughty air because, in part, it took place during Lent, and theirs was certainly one of the few Catholic households observing Lent with champagne, feasting, and dance.

It was a glorious and gracious way for the Kennedys to thank Stas for helping the president with the Polish-American vote, and it was Jackie's way of including Lee in her sudden, unexpected social prominence and astonishing level of privilege. It ushered in a period of shared pleasure, grand adventures, moral support, and intimacy between the two sisters, not felt since their delightful tour of Europe ten years earlier.

"I have boxes of letters from Jackie," Lee said. "Most are from '60 on—I have her life then, imploring me to come over, what pleased Jack or didn't please him, what would make him happy, and a lot about our children and trying to keep them together and seeing each other every summer. Those letters showed great anxiety to keep us together and the children together as often as possible. We did spend those first three Christmases in the '60s in Palm Beach together with our children and a large part of every summer as well."

London in winter was rainy and often dreary, so Lee especially looked forward to spending Christmases with Jackie and their children at Jayne and Charlie Wrightsman's oceanfront estate in

Palm Beach, a kind of winter White House not far from a vacation home owned by the Kennedy family.

Jayne Wrightsman was the second wife of Charles Wrightsman, the president of Standard Oil from 1932 to 1953. Besides their Palm Beach estate, the Wrightsmans lived at 820 Fifth Avenue. Jayne would become known as a legendary art collector, completely self-trained after buying an art history book that inspired her. She was especially interested in French furniture—a passion she shared with both Jackie and Lee—so her Palm Beach home combined the airy and damp-friendly feel of a beach house with museum-quality French furniture, a collection that eventually made its way to New York's Metropolitan Museum of Art.

Their Palm Beach vacations were idyllic. Anthony would join his cousin Caroline, just two years older, to loll and frolic on the beach, trailed by their younger siblings, frail little Tina and "John-John," just three months apart. It was heavenly for the children to re-create the blissful fun that Jackie and Lee had found as children, playing in the surf, coming home with sand in their bathing suits, feeling the daytime sun on their faces and the cool evening breezes off the ocean. Jackie and Lee would find themselves lost in long conversations as they watched over their brood. On Christmas Eve, the children would dress as Joseph, Mary, and the Wise Men for an annual Christmas play.

"It was wonderful to be together again," Lee recalled, while Stas and Jack Kennedy played backgammon or golfed, or the two families took advantage of good weather to sail on the Kennedy yacht, named the *Honey Fitz* after Jack's grandfather. They'd all learned to ignore the Secret Service agents who trailed the *Honey Fitz* in a raft of smaller boats.

*

JACKIE HAD PROMISED Kennedy that as First Lady she would only wear American couture, so Cassini technically fit the bill, albeit with a strong European flair that pleased Mrs. Kennedy. And she already had a history with the Cassinis: Oleg's brother, Igor, wrote the pseudonymous Cholly Knickerbocker column that had named Jackie Debutante of the Year in 1947. (He gave Lee the same honor three years later.) Oleg Cassini took an active role in shaping Jackie's public image, advising her to adopt the persona of a movie star, telling her that "she needed a story, a scenario, as First Lady."

Cassini was also impressed by Lee's chic fashion sense and sangfroid: "She wore an elegant mask," he recalled. "I could imagine both her and her sister at the Court of Louis XV. Destiny had separated them. It was Jackie who became the historic figure, and Lee the society woman, but their roles could have been reversed."

At first, Lee relished her association with the newly minted glamour of the Kennedy White House, happy to play lady-in-waiting. Not having to please an electorate, Lee was more daring, and more European, in her taste, wearing the French designer André Courrèges and smuggling Givenchy dresses into the White House. As early as 1960, Lee landed on the International Best-Dressed List for the first time, and stayed there for many years. Oleg Cassini aside, Jackie called Lee daily—sometimes hourly—for fashion advice when Lee was in London.

"Lee was the first to be dressed in a Paris couture house, and not Jackie," André Leon Talley explained. "It was Lee who took Jackie to have those clothes made at Givenchy. Once Lee became Princess Radziwill, she had a way of life that was very, very different from her sister's. You would never be able to find a picture of the First Lady curled up in a caftan, or find her in a bikini."

"Lee has an extraordinary amount of original style," agreed the designer Ralph Rucci, who became close to Lee in 2000. "I think her sister, the First Lady, had a great deal of influence, but with less courage to develop her own style. Lee has always been an original. Mrs. Vreeland said that Jacqueline Kennedy released style in this nation. Well, she had a great deal of assistance, and she had the best tutors. But Lee is the original."

Talley noted that Lee forged an original style that was part French, but really very classically American. "There's a lot of French influence on Lee's style," he said. "She loves Paris, but she is, for me, a true American in her sense of style. I mean, she's as American as a sweater—the most perfect, expensive cashmere twinset, but she's not as American as apple pie, certainly not frozen apple pie! She's truly a Bouvier, and the Bouvier style had a very important impact on the image of American women. It made a big, big, big mark."

*

IN MAY OF 1961, Jack Kennedy headed for Vienna for the summit with the combative Russian premier, Nikita Khrushchev. There was much riding on this meeting during the Cold War years, and it would prove a testing of the young president's mettle. But before he headed to Vienna, the first stop on the president's inaugural European trip was Paris, where he would introduce Jackie to an adoring French public.

Right before Air Force One left from Idlewild Airport in New York, a disheveled figure with a German-Jewish accent climbed aboard for a private consultation with the president. He then left the plane, but soon after, he and his wife boarded an Air France jet chartered for them, and they flew to Paris. Once there, they were driven to the Hôtel Napoléon, where they checked in.

Dr. Max Jacobson had arrived in Paris.

During the 1960 campaign, the president's Yale friend Charles "Chuck" Spalding had introduced Kennedy to the notorious doctor through Stas Radziwill.

"I picked up Jacobson from Radziwill," Spalding later told the investigative journalist Seymour Hersh. "I'd see Stash [sic] jumping around town and went to see Max. I guess it was speed, or whatever he gave us." Soon after, Spalding paid a visit to the Kennedys. "I was hopping around," he recalled. "They said, 'Jesus! Where do you get all this energy?' After seeing Max, you could jump over a fence."

Jacobson, known as "Dr. Feelgood" and "Miracle Max," administered shots of a concoction he made up in his lab, which turned his fingernails black. He called his elixir "miracle tissue regenerator"; it was a bouillabaisse of "amphetamines, animal hormones, bone marrow, enzymes, human placenta, painkillers, steroids, and multi-vitamins." His practice hovered at the edge of respectability, but his injections, not surprisingly, gave his patients jolts of energy and clarity. The downside was that the amphetamine-laced tonics could lead to addiction, grandiosity, and even psychosis, but in the 1960s, this was still unknown territory. That such a fringe doctor would be ministering to the president was suspect, and dangerous, and thus he was often consulted surreptitiously. Kennedy suffered with chronic back pain as a result of an old war injury, as well as the exhaustion of campaigning and governing, so the injections gave him blissful—if short-lived—bouts of being energized and pain-free. When Bobby Kennedy suggested that one of his aides have the injections analyzed, Kennedy famously told him, "I don't care if it's horse piss. It works."

"Miracle Max" visited the White House more than thirty times to administer his magical injections, as well as making visits to Palm Beach and Hyannis Port, to inject not only Kennedy but Jackie as well. He'd often leave his drugs and hypodermic needles behind for self-injection. He would never send the Kennedys a bill for his services, feeling too indebted to the US for its intervention in World War II, when Jacobson and his family escaped the Nazis and were given sanctuary.

Jacobson's other patients included an astonishing roll call of celebrities, from government to Hollywood to the arts: Lauren

Bacall, Ingrid Bergman, Leonard Bernstein, Humphrey Bogart, Yul Brynner, Maria Callas, Truman Capote, Oleg Cassini, Montgomery Clift, Rosemary Clooney, Marlene Dietrich, Eddie Fisher, Judy Garland, Alan Jay Lerner, Mickey Mantle, Marilyn Monroe, Zero Mostel, Elvis Presley, Anthony Quinn, Paul Robeson, Nelson Rockefeller, Elizabeth Taylor, Billy Wilder, and Tennessee Williams. Also caught in the net was *Life* photographer Mark Shaw, who was a favorite of the Kennedys. Of these, Zero Mostel died of amphetamine-related heart failure; Truman Capote, Montgomery Clift, Judy Garland, Marilyn Monroe, Elvis Presley, and Elizabeth Taylor all had struggles with prescription drug abuse. Mark Shaw died at the age of forty-seven of acute intravenous amphetamine poisoning. Lee recalled seeing the elegant British actress Margaret Leighton (who appeared in the film adaptation of Gore Vidal's play *The Best Man*) pounding on Dr. Jacobson's door in New York, desperate for a fix.

But the biggest victim of his elixirs, perhaps, was Dr. Jacobson himself. Increasingly dependent upon his own miracle shots, he ended up working around the clock, seeing up to thirty patients a day. In 1968 he attracted the attention of federal authorities for amphetamine misuse and lost his license to practice medicine seven years later. He died in 1979, at the age of seventy-nine, which meant that he lived a lot longer than many of his clients.

Curiously enough, Lee managed to escape the pull of Dr. Jacobson's miracle elixir. "He was an awful man," she said years later. "And physically dirty." She was not going to be injected by a man with blackened fingernails. To her credit, if not her foresight, Lee wouldn't let him near her.

*

BESIDES DR. JACOBSON, Lee also accompanied the Kennedys to Paris.

Lee, relegated to riding with the entourage, followed the president and First Lady's limousine as the motorcade traveled from

Orly Airport into the city. An estimated five hundred thousand Parisians thronged the streets to greet the glamorous president and his beautiful wife. Lee heard their chants of "Viva Zhack-ee" and "Kenne-dee" fill the air. Later, in exchanges with French journalists, Jackie spoke French for forty minutes, further delighting the Parisians.

In a meeting with General Charles de Gaulle of France, Kennedy made inroads against de Gaulle's anti-American stance, impressing the aging politician and former leader of the Free French. But if he was impressed by the young American president's intelligence and geopolitical savvy, he was even more enchanted by Jackie, delighted to speak French with her over luncheon at the Élysée Palace, home of the French president.

Arthur Schlesinger recalled that visit in his 1965 history, *A Thousand Days: John F. Kennedy in the White House*:

Jacqueline sat by the General and engaged him in animated conversation in French, about French history—Louis XVI, and the Duc d'Angoulême, and the dynastic complexities of the later Bourbons—until de Gaulle leaned across the table and told JFK that his wife knew more French history than most French women.

Schlesinger was one of the first historians to recognize her keen intelligence, giving full credit to Jackie's valuable contributions to the nation as First Lady.

Later, according to Gore Vidal, Jackie wrote a thank-you letter to de Gaulle and was pleased when he promptly answered her, "while Jack's letter to the general had gone unanswered."

Jackie was given a royal tour of Paris in a brilliant return to the city she loved but had not seen since her summer tour with Lee. What made it even more wonderful was that her docent was the writer and freedom fighter André Malraux, then de Gaulle's minister of culture, a figure she'd admired since being introduced to his work while a student at Vassar. She had read Malraux's most famous novel, *La Condition Humaine*, winner of the 1933 Prix Goncourt, and it was he whom she had most wanted to meet. Indeed, Tish Baldrige, who accompanied Jackie along with her personal secretary, an attractive young woman named Pamela Turnure, thought that Jackie had "an intellectual crush" on the French writer, as the two hit it off immediately. Jackie even flirted a little: when Malraux asked her what she did before marrying Jack Kennedy, she answered rather coyly, "*J'ai été pucelle*"—"I was a little virgin." (If true, it discourages belief in the gossip that she'd lost her virginity in a Parisian elevator on her first trip to France.) This was the beginning of a friendship between Jackie and Malraux that would last until his death in 1976.

Schlesinger would write that Jackie was "deeply moved" at Malraux's attendance at the state events welcoming the Kennedys because his two sons, Pierre-Gauthier and Vincent, had been killed in an automobile accident just a few days earlier. She had written a note to Malraux, allowing him to stay home and grieve ("Monsieur Malraux must not feel obligated to keep his promise"), but he graciously attended the state dinner at the Élysée Palace, looking "white and taut," in Schlesinger's description.

The next day, Malraux escorted Jackie, with Lee beside her, to the Jeu de Paume to view the great collection of French Impressionist art. Jackie especially responded to seeing her favorite painting, Manet's *Olympia*, reminiscent as it was of David's famous reclining portrait of the French *saloniste* Madame Récamier. They next toured Malmaison, the home of Empress Josephine, whose French Empire style had always impressed Jackie. She learned that the influential decorator and art restorer Stéphane Boudin had done some of the restoration work, and she made note of that.

For Lee, it must have felt like a repetition of their earlier meeting with the art critic Bernard Berenson, as Malraux focused his attention on Jackie while Lee trailed behind as part of Jackie's entourage. Not only that, Lee had conflicting feelings about the idolatry being heaped upon her sister by the French press, particularly when they praised the First Lady's style, couture, and knowledge of French painting, which had always been Lee's special passions. The historic role that Jackie was now being asked to play seemed to seal Lee's fate as Jackie's sister-in-waiting.

During the official visit, Jackie managed to make a brief escape from the watchful eyes of Tish Baldrige and her thick black notebooks that held the First Lady's social obligations. She slipped out of the Queen's Chamber at the opulently appointed Quai d'Orsay while her husband napped, and pressed one of the Secret Service agents into driving her around Paris, to take in the city she had fallen in love with as a college student. For forty-five minutes, she was free of the trappings of the presidency, happily touring the Parisian sights at dusk.

One hundred fifty invited guests took part in the final state dinner, held in a dazzling, candlelit Hall of Mirrors in Versailles. Jackie wore a stunning Givenchy gown with diamond clips in her hair. Bouvier cousin John Davis wrote in *The Bouviers: Portrait of an American Family* that

> invitations to Versailles that evening were so highly coveted that scores of Americans and Parisians whose sense of self-importance had led them to assume they should have been invited, were forced to leave Paris rather than face the shame of having been excluded.

Schlesinger watched Jackie's triumph from afar, noting later:

> The Parisians cheered the President, but it was now apparent that as much as they liked him, it was his wife whom they

adored. Her softly glowing beauty, her mastery of the language, her passion for the arts, her perfection of style—all were conquering the skeptical city. This was a good deal more than the instinctive French response to a charming woman. It had the air of a startled rediscovery of America as a new society, young and cosmopolitan and sophisticated . . .

On the last day of his visit, Kennedy wittily remarked to the Paris Press Club at the Palais de Chaillot that he was "the man who accompanied Jacqueline Kennedy to Paris, and I have enjoyed it." As Davis has pointed out, not only did the French show their appreciation of the First Lady, Kennedy himself saw her with renewed respect, recognizing what an asset she was to his presidency: "In marrying her he had acquired what the Kennedys generally lacked: elegance, cosmopolitan appeal, and a link with the nation's past."

Not surprisingly, Lee was feeling overwhelmed, overlooked, and underappreciated, so she was happy to encounter a cousin, Michel Bouvier, in a reception line at the Élysée Palace. At last, here was someone who knew her, and who provided a few moments of normalcy to the whirlwind state. visit in which Jackie was hailed as an American queen. She had seen little of Michel since those halcyon days at Lasata, and she was thrilled when his wife, Kathleen, complimented her on her taffeta gown. Kathleen recalled Lee looking "young and happy and beautiful and terribly successful."

Malraux's tragedy wasn't the only one that marred the triumph of the Kennedys' visit. Jackie's popularity stirred an enthusiasm among the French to claim kinship with the graceful and sophisticated First Lady. A pretty young woman of nineteen named Danielle Bouvier, eldest daughter of a family of subsistence farmers who worked a two-acre plot in the small village of La Mirandole, was convinced that she was related to the First

Lady. An American journalist had "discovered" her and her family and, soon after Kennedy's election, sought to authenticate the connection. Danielle had never traveled far from her home, but she was fascinated by all things American, and was "especially fond of rock and roll, chewing gum, and blue jeans," as Davis wrote. Egged on by the American journalist, Danielle started to dress like Jackie and adopted her bouffant hairdo, to much teasing from the townspeople.

"If Jacqueline would only invite me to see her in America," she pined, "my whole life would change." The family wrote to the First Lady, and when they learned about her impending state visit, they made up their minds to travel to Paris to meet her.

Jackie, for her part, had no way of knowing who among the many claimants were actually related to her, so Tish Baldrige and Pam Turnure decided to simply ignore the many requests from French Bouviers for an audience with the First Lady. But, miraculously, two French journalists turned up and told the Bouviers of Mirandole Farm that they had arranged an official visit with the Bouviers of Hammersmith Farm to meet the First Lady and her sister. It was decided that Danielle would be the one to travel to Paris, accompanied by her father. She was, of course, ecstatic. She hurriedly packed her finest dress of white silk in her only suitcase and left with the two journalists. She stopped in the village to buy a gift for her "American cousin"—a mechanical nightingale in a cage.

The day before the Kennedys were due to arrive at Orly, Danielle, her father, and the two journalists set out on their journey to Paris. Two hours and a hundred kilometers into their trip, while making a dangerous curve, their car hit a tree and Danielle was killed in the accident. Everyone else in the car survived. Pulled from the wreckage was a broken birdcage with the toy nightingale. On the gift box the young woman had written, "For my dear cousin Jacqueline from her cousin Danielle." A French archivist later proved that "the Bouviers of Mirandole Farm bore no blood relationship to the First Lady of the United States."

The Kennedys and their entourage—excluding Lee, who had returned to her home in London—hastened to a cold and grim Vienna for a cold and grim summit with Khrushchev, to discuss, among other topics, nuclear disarmament.

Dressed in an elegant and seductive mermaid dress designed by Cassini, Jackie was ogled by the stocky, pugilistic Russian premier at an official dinner at the Schönbrunn Palace. Unlike her meetings with de Gaulle and Malraux, Jackie and Khrushchev had little to say to each other. She tried to talk about Ukrainian history, but he countered by extolling Ukraine under Communism. "Oh, Mr. Chairman, don't bore me with statistics," she replied, eliciting a big laugh from the premier. Searching for another topic of conversation, she remarked that one of the dogs that the Soviets had sent up into space had recently had a litter of puppies. "Why don't you send me one?" she asked. Again Khrushchev laughed. But two months later, the Russian ambassador, Mikhail Menshikov, arrived at the White House "bearing a terrified small dog," as Schlesinger wrote.

Puzzled, Kennedy asked, "How did this dog get here?"

"I'm afraid I asked Khrushchev for it in Vienna," Jackie admitted. "I was just running out of things to say."

The Kennedys ended their state trip in London, where Kennedy met with Prime Minister Harold Macmillan in June of 1961. While there, they were able to attend the christening of Lee's daughter, Tina, at Westminster Cathedral, which had been postponed until the president and First Lady's arrival. The private event was turned into a media circus, with press and photographers crowding around because of Kennedy's presence, but Lee was used to that by now.

The Kennedys stayed with Lee and Stas at 4 Buckingham Place, along with Dr. Jacobson, who lingered to administer his elixir to Jack and Jackie. Lee was unhappy about his visit, but as long as he entered through the garden and avoided meeting her, she allowed him in.

It was not a typical party for the Radziwills. What with Jacobson stealthily entering through the garden, the CIA's London station chief coming in through another entrance, and the men huddled together wringing their hands about how poorly the summit with Khrushchev had gone, there was little gaiety. For the first time in his young presidency, Kennedy had felt the full weight of his office, learning that seventy million Americans could be killed in a nuclear war with the Russians. He told his friend and supporter Joe Alsop, the *Washington Post* columnist, that he "will never back down, never, never, never" in his dealings with the Russian premier.

Gloom hung over the London town house, alleviated somewhat when the president and First Lady, accompanied by Stas and Lee, were guests of Queen Elizabeth at a dinner at Buckingham Palace. It caused a bit of fussing in the English press, because Stas and Lee were officially invited as Prince and Princess Radziwill, a title Stas had been forced to abandon when he expatriated. Stas had often been referred to in the press as Prince Radziwill and Lee as Princess Radziwill, but after Kennedy's election, which elevated the prince's profile, there were now public grumblings when their titles were used. It was a point of contention for both of them. For Stas, whose aristocratic family went back several generations in Poland, using the title reflected his pride in his ancestry. It had been difficult for him to give up this connection to his past, though he often pretended that it didn't matter so very much. But when a stolen silver place setting bearing the Radziwill family crest was presented to the exiled prince by Kennedy's old friend Kirk LeMoyne "Lem" Billings, Stas openly wept.

For Lee, the title reminded her that she had achieved a kind of nobility, like America's de facto queen. After Jackie's spectacular success in Paris she was now being celebrated in the realms that Lee had conquered first: European high society and haute couture. *Time* magazine dubbed Jackie "First Lady of Fashion." Clint Hill, the Secret Service agent assigned to guard the First Lady, felt that she had "become more popular than Elizabeth Taylor, Sophia Loren, and Grace Kelly all put together." Her popularity and style seemed to reach the farthest corners of the globe: Noël Coward noticed on a trip to the Fiji Islands in 1962 that the Fijians "all wear skirts regardless of gender. And as they all go in for 'Jackie' hair-dos, this is apt to cause confusion."

Lee looked on, wondering how her sister had managed to completely eclipse her in so short a time. As First Lady, Jackie had now trumped Lee in the admiring eyes of the world. From then on, Lee would always be referred to as Jackie's younger sister. Davis explained:

> Her sister's accession to the White House promised to magnify a problem Lee had to cope with for some time, the problem simply of being Jackie's sister. Although she was abundantly gifted herself and was quite capable of shining on her own, she had often been obscured by the shadow of her sister's prominence, and now that shadow threatened to eclipse her identity . . . If Lee felt any sibling resentment of her sister's success, however, she was brave and intelligent enough not to show it.

But she would long remember Prince Philip's remark to her during the private dinner given by the queen: "You're just like me—you have to walk three steps behind."

*

KENNEDY LEFT FOR Washington right after the royal dinner at Buckingham Palace, but Jackie stayed on in London to be with her sister. They shopped, dined out with Lee's friends, and when they left a private tour of an antique show at Grosvenor House, they found themselves surrounded by a gaggle of screaming teenage fans.

The next morning, the two sisters left for a two-day trip to Greece, guests of the Greek prime minister, Constantine Karamanlis. But after the opulence of the Élysée Palace, Versailles, the Schönbrunn Palace, and Buckingham Palace, Karamanlis realized that his small Athens apartment wouldn't do, so he enlisted shipping tycoon Markos Nomikos to lend them his sumptuous villa at Kavouri and the use of his 125-foot yacht, the *Northwind*, to cruise the Greek islands.

Tish Baldrige accompanied them, and though she was just thirty-four, she played the role of Jackie's taskmistress, chaperone, and chief organizer. The job of getting the villa ready for its exalted guests fell to her, as did coming up with their Greek itinerary and keeping the sisters on track. Organizing Jackie was a challenge, as Jackie wanted to do what she pleased, when it pleased her.

The sisters blossomed in the sun-washed seascapes of Greece, sunbathing and swimming and sightseeing among ancient ruined temples. At first they adhered to Baldrige's schedule, but behind her back they conspired to rebel against her and go their own way. Greece itself seemed to liberate them. Lee later described it as "a beautiful part of the world, covered with almond and lemon trees, set in a satin sea, with a magnificent coastline . . . silent with heat." Finally, the sisters had a taste of real freedom. Being in Greece felt luxurious, elemental, and it harkened back to their sweet early memories of sun and sea at Lasata. They wandered into a pear orchard where a Greek farmer, not knowing who they were, gifted them with fresh warm pears fattened in the sun. Jackie described Greece, rather prophetically, as "a miracle . . . My dream is to have a house here to spend vacations with my children."

The sisters drew closer as they relished their two days of pleasure, and they reverted to their former wisecracking, mischief-making ways as Jacks and Pekes.

Baldrige was annoyed. "There was whispering behind my back and conspiratorial giggling," she later complained. She was so exasperated that she turned to Kennedy for help, which only earned her the sobriquet of "chief tattler." Jackie had always had a rebellious streak, mostly hidden beneath her shyness and her demeanor of a good, properly brought up girl. Lee—who also nurtured rebellion in her heart—encouraged and abetted Jackie in undermining Tish Baldrige's strict schedule. Baldrige put it down to "a momentary lapse of selfishness going back to her school days"—they had been students together at Miss Porter's—"of doing what she wanted, being independent, and stamping her foot."

As she had in Paris, one night Jackie slipped free of her minders, this time to go nightclubbing. At one such venue, she and Lee danced the *kalamatianos*, the exuberant ancient Greek folk dance in which all the dancers hold hands in a circle while the two lead dancers hold each end of a handkerchief.

Back in the States, the press was taking note, giving Jackie a hard time with headlines designed to embarrass the new administration. The *Washington Star* announced, "First Lady Dances Till 1," and *Time* magazine described her as speeding through the Greek countryside "in a Mercedes with young Crown Prince Constantine at the wheel." There was even public clucking about Jackie being photographed in a bathing suit.

Kennedy ordered Jackie back to the White House. He was suffering with excruciating back pain, and he needed her near him, not to mention wanting to quell the unflattering reports. Jackie spoke to her husband every night, commiserating with his back pain, but she refused to cut her holiday short. Her two-day vacation turned into eight. When she finally returned, a "tanned and radiant" Jackie was met by Kennedy's limousine, the president slouched in the back seat, in too much pain to stand. *Newsweek* reported on her homecoming:

> [Jackie] flew into the arms of her husband, waiting for her in his car with his crutches at his side. As photographers clicked away and a crowd of 200 cheered, the First Couple kissed and chatted excitedly until, a trifle embarrassed, the President commanded his driver: "Come on, let's go."

After the European trip, Jackie recognized her influence and power, and found subtle ways to use it, furthering her long-held ambition to celebrate the arts in the White House. The words she had written in her prizewinning essay for *Vogue* twenty years earlier—"If I could be a sort of Overall Art Director of the Twentieth Century, watching everything from a chair hanging in space . . ."—were coming true. She now had the power and ability to be a kind of high arts impresario, in part due to her taste, her erudition, but also her beauty. Especially in midcentury America, before the second wave of feminism took root and flourished, beauty—and the devotion it often inspired—exerted its own kind of power. Columnist Stewart Alsop, Joe's brother, noted, "All the men are in love with Jackie."

As Jackie began to recognize her own allure and purpose, Lee was losing her sense of herself, overwhelmed by the attention paid to her sister. While Jackie scaled the heights of world approval, Lee watched and waited.

*

IT SOON BECAME clear to Lee that her sister's fame would bring them both a fishbowl existence. In the White House, Kennedy had asked Jackie to never speak in public, and never write letters to anyone outside the family. "I write the most beautiful letters to these dreadful journalists, and I show them to Jack, and he says, 'Oh, that's really great. Now, go tear it up,'" she ruefully confided in Gore Vidal. Her enforced reticence, however, simply added to her Garbo-like air of mystery. For both Jackie and Lee, the White House years were a golden time, but one lived like a mechanical nightingale in a gilded cage.

Nonetheless, Jackie felt that those years brought her family closer together. "She had dreaded coming to the White House," Schlesinger observed, "fearing the end of family and privacy. But life for herself and her husband and children was never more intense and more complete. It turned out to be the time of the greatest happiness." And Jackie wanted to be sure Lee shared in that. It was in her power to offer Lee the grand hospitality of the White House, receiving her and Stas like visiting dignitaries, but she was powerless to affect how her sister would react to Jackie's paramount place in the cultural life of America.

*

IN NOVEMBER OF 1961, the Kennedys gave another black-tie dinner dance in honor of Lee, and for the powerful Italian industrialist Giovanni (known as Gianni) Agnelli and his wife, Marella. Agnelli was the extremely wealthy head of the Italian car company Fiat. Lee had been a guest on their yacht many times and would host them in the twelve-room, cliff-side villa they rented in Amalfi in the summer of that year. (Lee, in fact, was rumored to have had an affair with Gianni, a handsome rogue said to have bedded the wives of many men.) Jackie and Jack had first met the Agnellis during trips to the South of France and at the Wrightsmans' home in Palm Beach. And there was another connection:

Franklin Roosevelt Jr., under secretary of commerce in Kennedy's administration, had represented Fiat in America.

Whereas the first dinner dance for Lee and Stas had been elegant and grand, this dinner party was far more raucous. One reason was the popularity of the Twist, the gyrating dance introduced by Chubby Checker. (In order to dance the Twist, you were supposed to imagine putting out a cigarette with your toe while drying your backside with a towel.) Oleg Cassini brought it into the White House from the Peppermint Lounge, and Jackie and Lee were both crazy about it. However, it was considered so suggestive by much of America that Pierre Salinger, Kennedy's press secretary, denied it had ever been danced at the White House. That night champagne glasses overflowed, and guests danced the Twist and partied till 4 a.m. Lyndon Johnson reportedly fell on top of another guest and slid to the floor. Franklin Roosevelt Jr., fooled by the Continental mustache, mistakenly toasted Oleg Cassini, thinking he was Stas Radziwill. This faux pas delighted Kennedy, who doubled over in laughter.

As the evening wore down, a drunken Gore Vidal sidled over to Jackie and steadied himself by resting his arm against her back. Bobby Kennedy—who never liked Vidal—rushed in and pulled Vidal's arm away from Jackie. Vidal followed Bobby out of the Blue Room, snarling, "Never do that again," adding, "I've always thought you were a god-damned impertinent son of a bitch." Vidal then insulted Kennedy's good friend Lem Billings, who was also drunk, and when he spied Jack Kennedy, Vidal barked, "I'd like to wring your brother's neck." Jack asked Schlesinger if he could get Vidal out of the White House before more mayhem ensued.

Schlesinger enlisted George Plimpton, the cofounder of the *Paris Review*, to help him escort Vidal out of the White House and to the Hotel Jefferson. They watched him "lurch into the lobby" of his hotel, and then the two men returned to the White House gala.

After the White House dinner debacle, Jackie resolved never to have Gore Vidal in the White House again, but the entire incident would have serious repercussions for Lee fifteen years later.

*

DESPITE PROLIFERATING RUMORS of Jack Kennedy's affairs and dalliances with other women, Jackie remained a loyal and loving wife. It was fairly expected that men of wealth and influence had mistresses and lovers outside of marriage, and wives were expected to put up with it, to some degree. It was a behavior that Black Jack Bouvier had indulged in, though when it became the subject of public scandal, Janet divorced him. That seems to have been the trade-off for a certain class of American men. Wives were supported magisterially, given social status, and their children were protected, and alpha males kept their dalliances secret.

It was a philosophy that both Jackie and Lee knew and accepted, as daughters and wives. In their teen years, the sisters—and especially Jackie—had been fascinated by famous French courtesans such as Louise de la Vallière and the Marquise de Montespan, both mistresses, at different times, of Louis XIV. They also admired the nineteenth-century Parisian socialite Madame Récamier, famously the subject of Jacques-Louis David's graceful neoclassical portrait of the young beauty reclining on a divan. Instead of playing with dolls, the two sisters collected information and images of celebrated Parisian courtesans.

On one occasion, Jackie was showing a *Paris Match* journalist the private office used by Evelyn Lincoln, President Kennedy's longtime secretary. One of the staff members, the twenty-year-old Priscilla Wear, nicknamed "Fiddle," was also present. She was a coltish, pretty young woman who, like her friend and fellow staffer Jill Cowan, nicknamed "Faddle," was wellborn—and could type! Their presence in the White House seemed to be limited to answering the phones and signing Kennedy's autograph on pictures sent to fans. In making introductions, Jackie glanced at Priscilla and turned to the French reporter, whispering, *"C'est la femme qui couche avec mon mari."* Very sophisticated, very upper class, very French.

Jackie knew the bargain she had entered into, yet she loved her husband and felt she could bring a certain style and class to the People's House. She took her duties as First Lady quite seriously. As Oleg Cassini observed, "Jackie wanted to do Versailles in America." Schlesinger saw the tremendous advantage that Jackie brought to the White House. "There was nobody to touch Jackie using style as a political tool," he observed.

> The things people had once held against her—the unconventional beauty, the un-American elegance, the taste for French clothes and French food—were suddenly no longer liabilities but assets ... she represented all at once not a negation of her country but a possible fulfillment of it, a suggestion that America was not to be trapped forever in the bourgeois ideal, [but could achieve] a dream of civilization and beauty.

Jackie had been a student of the role of First Lady since her early days at the *Washington Times-Herald*. Now, as the nation's First Lady, she was able to use her love of history, her intelligence, her good eye for décor and objets d'art to undertake a much-needed restoration of the People's House.

Discovering on her arrival that the White House no longer reflected its own unique American history, having been redecorated and reimagined by the stream of presidents and their First Ladies before her, she raised the funds to restore the White House to its full glory, and spearheaded the effort to locate the actual furnishings, paintings, sculptures, and objects that had once graced the White House rooms. And when the originals could not be found, she located identical items from each period of history, based on photographic and written records. Mary Todd Lincoln, destitute after the assassination of President Lincoln, had sold the White House furniture to raise funds for her to live on. Chester A. Arthur sold wagons full of historic furnishings, and Dwight and Mamie Eisenhower redecorated the White House to give it a more contemporary look (Jackie later described the effect as looking like the lobby of a Sheraton hotel). Theodore Roosevelt filled the State Dining Room with a moose head and other trophies from his hunting expeditions. (Woodrow Wilson hated them so much that he sat with his back to the taxidermied trophies whenever he dined there.)

Jackie formed the Fine Arts Committee, inviting historians, museum curators, decorators, and socialites to help her to restore the White House so that it truly and accurately reflected the nation's heritage. Charles Montgomery, director of the Winterthur Museum, and collector Henry du Pont chaired a committee to locate authentic antiques from the early 1800s, as so much had been lost in the devastating fire during the War of 1812.

One of the interior decorators invited to join the committee was Dorothy May Kinnicutt, known as Sister Parish (a childhood nickname and her married surname), whose colorful name often gave rise to misinterpretation, as when the *New York Times* announced, "Kennedys Pick Nun to Decorate the White House."

Sister Parish was an old-money WASP whose paternal grandfather had been the novelist Edith Wharton's friend and personal physician. Her clients were mostly of her class, including, besides the Kennedys, Brooke Astor, William and Babe Paley, Betsey and Jock Whitney, and Sarah, the Duchess of York. Jackie first met Sister Parish socially and then invited her to decorate the Georgetown house she lived in with Jack Kennedy when he was still the junior senator from Massachusetts. After Kennedy's election to the presidency in 1960, she asked Parish to redecorate a country house they leased in Virginia, called Glen Ora, before taking up residence in the White House. (Jackie lavished $10,000 on redecorating the country house, infuriating Kennedy, especially as the house was leased and had to be returned to its former style when they left.)

A budget of $50,000 was raised for the entire redecoration project (roughly $350,000 in today's dollars). Jackie wrote to Sister Parish:

> I want our private quarters to be heaven for us naturally, but use as much of [the Eisenhowers'] stuff as possible & buy as little new—as I want to spend lots of my budget below in the public rooms—which people will see & will do you & I proud!

Despite her noble intentions, Jackie ended up spending the entire budget in the first two weeks on the family's private quarters on the second floor, adding a kitchen and a dining room. Luckily, her Fine Arts Committee was adept at convincing collectors to donate many of the period pieces and furniture that, quite often, had once belonged to the White House.

In choosing to work with Sister Parish, Jackie showed her taste for unfussy, inviting, and refreshing décor. The look became known as "American country style," and it was hugely influential, reflected in today's collections by Ralph Lauren and Martha Stewart. As journalist Steven M. L. Aronson wrote in *Architectural Digest* in 1999:

> A Sister Parish room overflowed, to be sure—but buoyantly. It was romantic and whimsical but not sentimental; and, always, it was light—the rug might be Aubusson, the mirror Chippendale and the chandelier Waterford, but she undercut these "brand names" with all manner of charming distractions. Her living rooms *lived* . . .

Jackie also sought advice from Jayne Wrightsman, who had been an early mentor when Jackie first arrived in Washington. Jayne and her friend the wealthy socialite and collector Bunny Mellon were helpful in Jackie's transformation of the White House, though Jackie had to rein in their penchant for French décor. Jackie felt it incumbent to state that the Fine Arts Committee she assembled would make sure that she would not fill the White House "with French furniture, or hang modern pictures all over it and paint it whatever color we like. I don't 'do up' old houses. These things aren't just furniture. They're history."

Nonetheless, when Sister Parish suddenly quit over a disagreement with the First Lady, Jackie was quick to hire French decorator Stéphane Boudin to finish the job. She had been impressed by Boudin's restoration of Empress Josephine's château in Paris on her official trip, and so she found a way to bring in the French influence that most pleased her sensibilities. He would end up designing the Red Room and the Blue Room of the White House, much to Sister Parish's and Henry du Pont's disapproval.

John Walker, then director of the National Gallery of Art, wryly commented:

> . . . because the thought of a Frenchman doing over the White House might possibly cause some question among 100 percent Americans . . . his visits were not publicized. It is not true, as Washington gossip related, that he was carried into the White House wrapped in a rug.

Though Jackie had ample guidance from Jayne Wrightsman, the Fine Arts Committee, Sister Parish, and Stéphane Boudin, it was clear that she—like her sister—had a genius for décor. Even the White House upholsterer, Larry Arata, noted that Jackie had "exquisite taste. She seemed to know a lot about everything whether it was materials, paintings, or anything pertaining to art." In her taste for airy, light-filled, gracefully proportioned rooms, Jackie had much in common with Lee, though Lee went about it in a more baroque, eclectic way, using the theatrical set designer Mongiardino to achieve a similar, but much richer, effect. When it came to redecorating the White House, Jackie let history be her guide, and her goal was absolute authenticity down to the smallest detail. If Lee was after drama, Jackie was after historical accuracy.

All of that is apparent throughout her celebrated and unprecedented White House tour, recorded by CBS on January 15, 1962, in which Jackie presented her transformation of the White House to an avid and appreciative public. The program was directed by Franklin J. Schaffner, who would go on to direct *Patton*, starring George C. Scott, and *Papillon*, with Steve McQueen and Dustin Hoffman. The television commentator Charles Collingwood was an able guide throughout the hour-long broadcast. Jackie—in low-heeled shoes and a red sheath with a hemline falling just below the knees—led him through the various rooms of the White House and commented both knowledgeably and charmingly on the changes and acquisitions in each room.

Pamela Turnure, Jackie's press secretary, was on hand to adjust the microphone that had been concealed beneath Jackie's dress at the small of her back, because CBS "couldn't have a technician fiddling with the First Lady's person," as Collingwood later observed.

Time magazine described the broadcast in admiring tones, expressing, perhaps, a bit of surprise at Jacqueline Kennedy's erudition. Her poise and attractiveness were already well-known, but few had suspected her intelligence and how effortlessly she seemed to have mastered the names of painters, furniture makers, major donors, and the hundreds of historical minutiae that had gone into the extensive redecoration.

In "an expert performance," *Time* reported, and "without

notes or prompting," Jackie "showed a connoisseur's knowledge of every antique and *objet d'art* that came into view . . . She easily rattled off the names of bygone artists and cabinetmakers, displayed an impressive knowledge of intimate White House history." If she was nervous, it didn't show up on camera, but she did smoke between takes, missing the ashtray and dropping ashes on an expensively restored settee. But on camera, she smiled winningly throughout the entire room-by-room tour.

Jackie described how the Green Room "used to be the dining room, and here Jefferson gave his famous dinners and introduced such exotic foods as macaroni, waffles, and ice cream to the United States." She spent extra time showing off Lincoln's bedroom, which had been lovingly restored to its former state, with the addition of a sample of the historic wallpaper from the Petersen House, the rooming house across the street from Ford's Theatre, where Lincoln was rushed after being shot by John Wilkes Booth, and where he died.

What made an equally strong impression on the public, besides the scope and beauty of the restoration and Jackie's unerring knowledge of White House history and décor, was the whispery, childlike voice in which her accomplishments and knowledge were conveyed.

She sounded like Marilyn Monroe. She sounded like a woman who had been reared in the 1930s and '40s who was taught to hide her intelligence and not appear threatening to men. She sounded like a woman uncomfortable with the sudden glare of the spotlight. She sounded like a woman trying to overcome an inherent shyness. As Janet had noted early on, "There's a certain stiffness about Jackie, even shyness . . . It's not that she's frightened of people, but she's not outgoing." Nonetheless, Jackie appeared slightly flirtatious, even girlish, despite her proper equestrienne's posture and careful enunciation of the facts she possessed. It produced an odd, slightly dizzying disconnect: historical erudition, insight, and even wit related in the voice of a shy, careful, beautiful, girl-ish woman.

Norman Mailer would notice it, and he wrote about it in the July 1962 issue of *Esquire*, in an article titled "An Evening with Jackie Kennedy," one of three essays comprising "The American Woman: A New Point of View." (The other two women were Mary McCarthy, profiled by Brock Brower, and singer Brenda Lee, by Sarel Eimerl.) Mailer describes his impressions of Jackie on two different occasions. The first was meeting her at the Kennedy compound in Hyannis, among a gathering of "journalists, cam-eramen, magazine writers, politicians, delegations, friends and neighboring gentry, government intellectuals, family, a prince, some Massachusetts state troopers, and rednecked hard-nosed tourists patrolling outside the fence for a glimpse . . ." Also present were Lee and Stas; Arthur Schlesinger and his wife, Marian; and Pierre Salinger. Jackie among the vast Kennedy entourage struck Mailer as simply, in his condescending description, "a college girl who was nice. Nice and clean and very merry."

Mailer's second impression, based on her performance as White House docent and decorator-in-chief, was that she resembled "a cat, narrow and wild, and her fur was being rubbed every which way." He goes on to blast the tour as pummeling us with facts but giving us "no sense of the past" ("We do not create a better nation by teaching schoolchildren the catalogues of the White House"). He admits to feeling compassion for how hard she tried, how ea-ger she was to please, but goes on to say, "At times, in her eyes, there was a blank, full look which one could recognize," hyper-bolically comparing it to the deadened look of a nineteen-year-old woman of his acquaintance who had slashed her wrists. From this extreme comparison, Mailer goes on to say that "it is to be hoped that Jackie Kennedy will come alive . . . I liked her, I like her still, but she was phony—it was the crudest thing one could say, she was a royal phony."

Perhaps Mailer was put off by her upper-class, boarding school, East Coast accent ("lit-ter-a-ture") and her proper attire and demeanor. In part it was a class bias, with Mailer fulfilling his usual role of being the proverbial bull in a nineteenth-century china shop. In part, it was the default criticism often levied by alpha males against pedestal-topping, unattainable women. But there is a kernel of genuine insight as well, when he writes:

There was something very difficult and very dangerous she was trying from deep within herself to do, dangerous not to her safety but to her soul. She was trying, I suppose, to be a proper First Lady and it was her mistake.

There was no sign of the rebellious ringleader of her days at Miss Porter's, her sometimes sly, mocking wit, her deep engagement with language, literature, and poetry. Mailer had seen that Jackie was trapped in the proper role of First Lady. "Afterward," he wrote about the White House tour, "one could ask what it was one wanted of her, and the answer was that she show herself to us as she is." This was something that Jackie, in 1962, simply could not do.

Despite Mailer's often sour complaints, Jackie's White House tour was widely popular and won an Emmy. It was broadcast on Valentine's Day to 46.5 million viewers, over CBS and NBC, and rebroadcast the following Sunday on ABC, when 10 million people watched the black-and-white hour-long program. Enchanted by her poise, her knowledge, her sweet decorum, America fell in love with Jackie all over again.

6

THE TRAVELING SISTERS

*I*n 1963 Barbara Walters described Lee as Jackie's "glamorous sister and closest friend." Among other benefits, Lee gave Jackie an excuse to take extended stays away from the White House, on family vacations to Palm Beach, London, and the Amalfi Coast. In March of 1962, the White House sent both sisters on a three-week goodwill tour of India and Pakistan, which recaptured the sense of adventure they'd shared on their summer trip to Europe eleven years earlier and their splendid holiday in Greece the previous year. The trip had been suggested and arranged by John Kenneth Galbraith, then Kennedy's ambassador to India and a favorite of Jackie's.

The two sisters began their state visit in Rome, where Jackie had a private audience with Pope John XXIII on March 11, 1962. She was there to intercede on Lee's behalf, asking for an annulment of Lee's marriage to Michael Canfield, as their divorce had not been recognized by the Catholic Church. It was something that Stas, a devout Catholic, had especially wanted, so he and Lee could be married in the eyes of the Church three years after their civil ceremony. Lee had petitioned the Vatican in July of 1961, but the pope had refused to intervene. It took pressure from the Kennedys before he reluctantly agreed to hear Lee's petition, and Jackie met with the pope for a half hour, where the two conversed in French. The next day, the sisters left Rome for India.

However much she loved light, Lee was almost blinded when she stepped off the plane in New Delhi on March 13, 1962, where a crowd of three thousand awaited them. Jawaharlal Nehru, India's prime minister, greeted them warmly, and they were encircled by women in brilliantly hued saris—"a sea of pink, fuchsia, turquoise against the most beautiful blue sky" was how Lee later described her first glimpse of India. Lee was impressed by Nehru, whom she described as "the most fascinating, gentle, and sensual man I ever met." Over a hundred thousand people lined the road cheering as Jackie's motorcade made its way slowly into New Delhi, shouting "Jackie, Jackie, welcome, Mrs. Kennedy!"—an echo of the Paris trip—as Lee sat silently beside her.

Throughout their visit, the two sisters were met by worshipping crowds who called Jackie *"Ameriki Rani"*—"American Queen"— looking upon Princess Lee Radziwill as her lady-in-waiting. Crowds surged around them, causing near riots in Agra, where Jackie was photographed in front of the Taj Mahal wearing a turquoise dress, which, as Galbraith later wrote in his *Ambassador's Journal: A Personal Account of the Kennedy Years*, "could be picked out at any range up to five miles." (Galbraith also wrote that the press paid "far too much attention to the subject of clothes . . . designer, dress, handbag, and so forth." Not surprising, as the two sisters between them had brought sixty-four pieces of luggage.)

At the Maharaja and Maharani of Jaipur's Amber Palace, thousands of children danced and sang to welcome the First Lady. They drove to Amber, a twelfth-century city in the Rajput hills, where they climbed atop one of the liveried royal elephants, among hundreds of photographers.

Jackie and Lee, perhaps realizing that their usual muted beiges would not stand out in India, wore pinks and lavenders throughout their trip, mostly designed by Oleg Cassini, Lee mixing it up with some peach and lemon yellow. In Karachi, Pakistan, they rode a ceremonial camel, where they were perched sidesaddle in sleeveless summer dresses and high heels. At first Jackie was reluctant to climb onto the camel's back, so Lee mounted first and took a seat in front, holding the reins until Jackie ordered, "Hand me the reins, Lee," and she did.

The sisters embraced the local customs. Jackie "threw holi chalk powder, ate wild boar and candies wrapped in pounded silver, watched endless folk dancing and singing." She even made the attempt to stand on her head as Nehru demonstrated yoga postures. They made the grand tour of India's most stunning sights: in Agra, the Taj Mahal flooded with moonlight; in Lahore, the Shalimar Gardens; the historic Khyber Pass bordering Afghanistan, through which Genghis Khan once rode. In Lahore, more than a thousand men marched in their honor, each one holding aloft a burning torch. They took a train ride across the Ganges Plain in a luxurious imperial train that had once belonged to the last viceroy of India. They cruised the Ganges, the sacred river of India, in a barge covered with marigolds. They were met by massive crowds everywhere they went, and were showered with gifts—flowers, saris, books, jewel-encrusted daggers, and carpets too big for them to carry. "At the end of each day, we would collapse with exhaustion and laughter, shaking our heads at the incredible events," Lee would write some fifty-three years later, sitting in her New York apartment graced by artifacts from that long-ago trip.

At a party given for Jackie by the Maharaja of Jaipur at the Amber Palace, Jackie and Lee had the heady pleasure of teaching their royal hosts how to do the Twist. "Do you know the Twist?" Jackie had asked her hosts, and when they said no, the two sisters enthusiastically demonstrated the dance. East meets West.

The very European maharaja and his wife were already good friends of Lee's, yet the focus of attention was always on Jackie, who was aware of how Lee was being overlooked throughout their trip. She tried to "compensate for Lee's so obviously inferior position, being relegated to the back of motorcades, overlooked, and sometimes even left behind," as one Kennedy biographer noted. Jackie was becoming "the most photographed woman in the world," the society photographer Cecil Beaton wrote in his diaries. "She is still the most photogenic person in the world, infinitely more so than her infinitely more beautiful sister, Lee Radziwill." At one point, Jackie was so besieged by autograph seekers that Lee stepped in and signed autographs for her sister, as their plump, rounded handwriting was so much alike.

Nehru was particularly responsive to women, and particularly the Bouvier sisters. Where he had been bored and taciturn in talks with Kennedy earlier that year, he had come to life seated between Jackie and Lee at a state dinner in his honor at the White House. Now in India, at the end of their tour, Nehru and Jackie sat together at the American embassy's garden. Nehru in his white jacket sporting a red rose and Jackie in a red-and-white dress sat on the steps and talked and laughed together, obviously enjoying each other's company. Galbraith believed it enhanced India and America's international relationship, because Nehru was India, and Jackie was America.

At the end of the trip, Jackie confessed to Lee that she much preferred India to Pakistan, which they subsequently visited. Pakistan was "a man's country" in which the women were still in purdah, whereas there were many prominent women in India to whom the men were "agreeable and responsive."

On their wildly successful ambassadorial trip, Jackie had relied on Lee for companionship and refuge. Barbara Walters, who was assigned to accompany the tour as a writer-reporter for the *Today* show, later wrote that Lee was "at her best" as Jackie's companion, "conducting herself with dignity, warmth, and—for the most part—good judgment whenever she travels with the First Lady and shares with her the world spotlight." And Galbraith, who knew both women well, was impressed at how Lee comported herself through the visit. "Lee was wonderful, Lee was very good. She was the ideal sister." Jackie thought so, too. She later said to Joan Braden, who had been Jackie's ghostwriter during the presidential campaign and who accompanied Jackie and Lee on the trip, "I was so proud of her."

Although the outpouring of adulation for Jackie took its toll on Lee, it didn't stop her from inviting Jackie on a lavish family vacation just three months later, in June of 1962, at a cliff-top villa in Conca dei Marini, Italy, near Amalfi in the Bay of Salerno.

*

THE NINE-HUNDRED-YEAR-OLD VILLA, called El Episcopio, was perched 1200 feet above the Bay of Salerno and was reached by climbing three hundred rocky steps from a private beach below. Lee especially loved the Amalfi Coast, another world of sea and light. In addition to Stas and their two children, and Jackie and four-year-old Caroline, Lee invited several friends, including Gianni and Marella Agnelli, to join them.

Lee had gone to great lengths to prepare a fabulous vacation for her sister and niece, as a way of reciprocating the imperial hospitality Jackie had afforded Lee and Stas at the White House over the past two years. She wanted everything to be perfect, which put her nerves on edge to the point that she suddenly fired her cook forty-eight hours before her guests were to arrive, sending out for a French chef to step in at the last minute. She organized local security to supplement that provided by Secret Service agent Clint Hill, who arrived with the First Lady.

It *was* perfect. When Jackie and Caroline arrived in Ravello, they were met by the mayor, dancing children, and a live band in the brightly festooned piazza. The only drawback was a paparazzi riot that thronged the town to photograph the First Lady. But once the guests made their way through the villa's stone arches and wrought iron gate, their two-week vacation was sublime. Taking in the sweeping view of the aquamarine sea and the scent of blossoming lemon and orange trees, Jackie turned to her sister and said, "Oh, Lee, it's just magnificent."

In the evenings, looking down from the villa's terrace, they could see the fishing boats and moored yachts strung with white lights glinting in the Bay of Salerno. Besides the pleasures of the villa, the private beach, the excellent local food, the sun and the sea, they sailed on the Agnellis' eighty-two-foot, two-masted yawl (the *Agneta*) and spent a night on the fashionable Isle of Capri as guests of Italy's leading fashion designer, Princess Irene Galitzine (creator of high-end lounging pajamas favored by the newly dubbed "jet set"). They were serenaded by three singers at Galitzine's villa, then departed to Capri's most fashionable nightclub, where they danced till the early hours. Returning to Conca dei Marini at dawn, the boating party boisterously sang "Volare."

The *Agneta* turned out to be a refuge from their refuge, as it allowed them to escape what Jackie termed "the locusts"—the constant flashbulbs of photographers vying for pictures of the First Lady.

Cropped photographs showing Jackie striding alongside Gianni Agnelli gave rise to rumors of a liaison between them—just as there had been rumors of an affair between Lee and Gianni. But the constant presence of Gianni's wife, Marella, and Secret Service agent Clint Hill casts doubt on that rumor. Another photograph of Gianni about to apply suntan lotion to a black-bathing-suit-clad Jackie further fueled the rumors, but a countess who knew Gianni well felt that Gianni would not have wanted the complications of such an affair. And Jackie was writing ten-page letters to Jack describing her sun-swept days: "I miss you very much, which is nice though it is also a bit sad—because it is always best to leave someone when you are happy & this was such a lovely summer . . . but then I think of how *lucky* I am to miss you . . ." She waited up till 3 a.m. for his phone calls, including two incoming calls that were from an imposter.

They took a day trip down the coast to the ancient city of Paestum, originally named Poseidonia after Poseidon, the Greek god of the sea, and known for its well-preserved Greco-Roman temples. Without a port for the *Agneta*, the party was rowed ashore in a rather rough sea, then rowed back among a gaggle of photographers who had found them out.

After two glorious weeks, Jackie opted to stay on an additional week. These had been halcyon days for both sisters and their children, and Lee would devote pages to their Ravello adventure in her first book, *Happy Times*, describing their stay as

> carefree, with no set hours for lunch or dinner except that they were very late. Only a vague rhythm existed, of waking to hear fishermen below calling to one another, the hum of the motorboat in the distance, then the shutters opening over an endless stretch of sea.

Just before Jackie departed, she was made an honorary citizen of Ravello, and the Conca dei Marini beach where they swam every day was renamed the Jacqueline Kennedy Beach—an honor not extended to Lee.

*

FOUR MONTHS AFTER Jackie and Lee's excellent adventure, the agonizing thirteen days of the Cuban Missile Crisis gripped the Western world. The crisis began on October 16, 1962, when a photographic mission revealed that the Soviets had begun installing ballistic missiles in Cuba. It quickly escalated into a confrontation between the two nuclear nations, bringing the world to the brink of mutual annihilation. Jackie—and, soon after, Lee—would be among the first to know that something was terribly wrong.

In an interview with Arthur Schlesinger for the Kennedy archives, Jackie recalled that she was with her children at Glen Ora, sunbathing, when "this call came through from Jack and he said, 'I'm coming back to Washington this afternoon. Why don't you come back there?'" She remembered that "there was just something funny in his voice . . . it was so unlike him."

She quickly woke her children from their naps and returned to Washington, later saying, "When you're married to someone and they ask something—that's the whole point of being married—you just must sense trouble in their voice and mustn't ask why." For the next thirteen days, the world held its breath. "It seemed there was no waking or sleeping," Jackie remembered.

Kennedy responded by placing a naval blockade around Cuba and insisting that the missiles be removed. Many members of the cabinet, the Joint Chiefs of Staff, and White House personnel made arrangements for their wives and children to leave town, but Jackie pleaded with her husband, "Don't send me away to Camp David. Please don't send me anywhere. If anything happens, we're all going to stay right here with you . . . even if there's not room in the bomb shelter in the White House." She told Kennedy that she just wanted "to be on the lawn when it happens . . . I just want to be with you, and I want to die with you—and the children do too—[rather] than live without you."

Kennedy promised not to send them away.

Jackie also recalled one late night during the crisis when she tiptoed into Kennedy's bedroom, dressed in her nightgown. "I thought he was talking on the phone . . . and suddenly, I saw him waving me away—'Get out, get out!'" National Security Advisor McGeorge Bundy was in deep consultation with the president. Bundy "threw both hands over his eyes," Jackie recalled. "Poor Puritan Bundy, to see a woman running in her nightgown!"

She also recalled never feeling closer to Kennedy than during the days and nights of the Cuban Missile Crisis, with the sword of Damocles hanging over their heads:

> . . . that's the time I've been closest to him, and I never left the house or saw the children, and when he came home, if it was for sleep or for a nap, I would sleep with him. And I'd walk by his office all the time and sometimes he would take me out—it was funny—for a walk around the lawn. He didn't often do that. We just sort of walked quietly, then go back in. It was just this vigil.

Lee and Stas were staying with Jackie during what Lee later described as "the most memorable, extraordinary time of the White House years that I knew."

> There was one moment nearing the end when we—that's Jackie, the president, and myself—were in their private rooms upstairs, and the phone rang and it was McGeorge Bundy saying that there was extreme trouble ahead . . . the President put down the phone and said, "In three minutes we'll know if we're at all-out war or not." . . . You pictured missiles rising all over the world, submarines submerged . . .

She remembered that the phone rang after an agonizing few minutes. "The President had an extraordinarily tense expression on his face and hung up and said, 'The Russian ships turned back.'"

When it was finally over—when Nikita Khrushchev backed down and withdrew his missiles from Cuba—Bundy told Jackie that if the crisis had continued for even just a day or two longer, "Everybody would have cracked, because all those men had been awake night and day . . . everyone had worked to the peak of human endurance."

To commemorate those perilous days, Kennedy presented to Jackie and those who had weathered the crisis along with him a silver engraved Tiffany calendar for October 1962 with the fateful thirteen days highlighted in bold. It would remain on Jackie's desk in the family quarters of the White House for the rest of her husband's presidency.

*

THE CUBAN MISSILE Crisis brought Jackie and Jack Kennedy closer together. But what Jackie didn't know at the time was that Lee's marriage to Stas was unraveling. They remained a couple, but any pretense of monogamy was a casualty of Lee's sexual rejection of her once adored husband. Though Stas took up with other women, there was no doubt that he still loved Lee, even to the point of expressing a kind of admiring exasperation over how profligate with money Lee could be, especially when it came to her wardrobe. He once sighed to a friend, "You have no idea what that tiny little body cost me."

As she had in her marriage to Canfield, Lee looked elsewhere for romantic and sexual fulfillment. First it had been Nureyev, but the impossibility of that relationship soon became clear to her, though she would always count him as a close friend.

The press got wind of the couple's troubles. In September of 1962, *Time* magazine ran an unflattering article about Stas and Lee with the title "Unhitching Post." (Jack Kennedy was so incensed by the piece that he complained to Time Life founder Henry Luce, summoning him to the Oval Office for a personal rebuke.) Ironically, Lee's annulment of the Canfield marriage was finally granted on November 24, 1962, allowing Lee and Stas to have their Catholic wedding the following July, but by then it was too late to save their marriage.

What both sisters discovered over the course of their marriages was that they could abide infidelities—but not insolvency. Lee and

Jackie both knew that the style to which they were bred needed constant infusions of cash—and those infusions invariably came from the men in their lives. So when Lee met a swarthy, black-haired shipping magnate reputed to be one of the richest men in the world, she was utterly entranced. Lee would soon find a way to, if not trump Jackie, at least match her with a consort as worldly, influential, and charming to women as John Kennedy, but far, far richer: the Greek shipping tycoon Aristotle Onassis.

Onassis was born in Smyrna, in 1906, to a prosperous Anatolian Greek family. His father, Socrates Onassis, had been a successful tobacco merchant, but there were tragedies in Ari's early life. His mother died when he was six. As Greek Orthodox Christians living in Islamic Turkey, the family suffered extreme prejudice. The 1922 genocide of Greek and Armenian citizens at the hands of the Turkish state was intensely brutal: women were raped and murdered; men were rounded up into city squares and their throats were slit. As a boy, Ari witnessed terrible things: the hanging deaths of three uncles, the crucifixion of the priest who had married his parents. By the time he was a teenager, the Turkish government had burned down the family's warehouse, and the military had confiscated their villa. His father was dragged off to prison. Eventually, Ari escaped to Argentina on an ocean steamer and spent his youth in a hardscrabble existence, working as a dishwasher and peddling cigarettes. Throughout it all, he taught himself business and learned several languages, investing his money and immigrating to New York during the Second World War. Though born to wealth, he was clearly a self-made man, amassing millions in the shipping industry and marrying into a wealthy family when he wed Tina Livanos. By the time he met Lee Radziwill, his marriage had ended in divorce, caused by his affair with the great opera star Maria Callas.

. . .

Lee, like Jackie, had already fallen in love with Greece during her and her sister's brief hiatus there after her daughter's christening. And she found Onassis "magnetic. He walked like a potentate, noticing and wanting to be noticed . . . an habitual cigar in his hand. His hair was thick with brilliantine and his olive skin was smooth. His voice sounded like soft gravel—raspy, but low." His estimated worth was $300 million, equivalent to $2.1 billion today.

Onassis completely thrilled Lee, and not just because of his immense wealth and power. He was warm with an earthy charm and a strong sexual presence. (Lee later confided that she liked his "primitive vitality," and she described his "sexual prowess, his Oriental tastes in that area.") Onassis was twenty-seven years older than Lee; as had been the case with Stas, Lee was attracted to a man who reminded her of her father.

The "Golden Greek," as he was known, was still very much involved with Maria Callas when he met and wooed Lee, though Callas was married and their open affair created a scandal in Europe. Callas later said about her rival, "I never disliked Jackie, but I hate Lee. I hate her. I have a dream all the time. I dream about Onassis. I want to help him but I can't." With world-weary acceptance of his wife's affair, Stas was mollified by being made a director of Olympic Airlines, owned by Onassis.

Many speculated that Onassis's interest in Lee had indeed been enhanced by her connection to the White House. John and Bobby Kennedy actively disliked and mistrusted Onassis, considering him "a pirate . . . a crook." He had been indicted by the US government for illegally operating a fleet of ships he had bought from the US, and had ended up paying a $7 million fine. By the spring of 1963, the affair was being noticed: Drew Pearson wrote in the *Washington Post*, "Does the ambitious Greek tycoon hope to become the brother-in-law to the President?"

There has been speculation that it was Onassis himself who leaked his affair with Lee—or, possibly, Maria Callas's husband,

Giovanni Meneghini. Lee, still in an amicable marriage with Stas, was certainly discreet, even to the point of dissembling about her affair with Onassis. It was most likely the men who gave her away—either Onassis, who employed a press agent to keep his name in the news, or Meneghini, perhaps to force Callas's hand.

Onassis nursed a lifelong hatred of the Kennedys, especially Bobby. The fact that he now had the president's sister-in-law on his arm, spending nights with him on the *Christina*, moored off the Amalfi Coast in the shimmering Mediterranean, must have made the affair all the more satisfying for him. Onassis loved women, he loved money, he loved power—but he also loved revenge.

*

RUMORS OF LEE'S affair with Onassis continued to surface. Bobby Kennedy, who regarded the affair as "a betrayal of the whole family," hit upon the idea of luring Lee away from a cruise down the Amalfi Coast on Onassis's 325-foot yacht by asking her to accompany Jack on a state trip to Berlin and Ireland. Jackie was seven months pregnant at the time and, having already suffered one miscarriage, did not want to risk traveling.

The June 1963 trip featuring Lee in a leading role was another triumph, with adoring crowds and a prominent place at the Berlin Wall when Kennedy made the now historic remark "*Ich bin ein Berliner.*" "It was the most thrilling experience of my life," Lee recalled. It was followed by a deeply personal trip to Ireland, where Kennedy visited his sister Kathleen's grave; soon after becoming Lady Hartington, Kathleen had died in a plane crash.

If Jackie resented Lee taking her place on the triumphant trip to Berlin, adding to the growing rivalry between the two sisters, it remained unspoken. Afterward, Lee returned to London and to Greece, where she resumed her relationship with Onassis.

*

ON AUGUST 9, 1963, Jackie gave birth to Patrick, who died a few hours after being born. He was the second baby Jackie had lost—her first child, given the sweet name of Arabella, had been stillborn. Lee received the news while on board the *Christina* on an Aegean cruise with Onassis. She immediately flew to Boston to attend Patrick's funeral and to comfort her sister, who was plunged deeply into grief and postpartum depression. Terribly concerned about her sister, Lee urged Onassis to invite Jackie aboard the *Christina*. Kennedy didn't want her to go, but Jackie couldn't face returning to Washington so soon after the loss of their baby. Jack worried that Lee wanted Jackie along to act as her beard in her affair with Onassis, so he and Bobby turned to Franklin Roosevelt Jr., the son of FDR and a good friend of the Kennedys, and his wife, Suzanne, to accompany Jackie on the cruise to add an "air of respect" to the trip. Still concerned about bad publicity as the next presidential election loomed, Jack actually went down on one knee, his Washington friend Martha Bartlett recalled, to beg Jackie not to make the trip. But she was determined to go.

What many didn't know was that Jackie was allowed to go on the cruise to take the opportunity to persuade Lee *not* to marry Onassis, for the sake of the Kennedys.

So on October 2, 1963, Jackie flew to Athens. Two days later, the *Christina* departed from Piraeus on its way to Istanbul and the farthermost Greek island of Mytilene. Once aboard the sumptuous yacht, Ari left Lee and Jackie alone for much of the cruise, where once again they became the whispering sisters, exchanging confidences in the yacht's luxurious cabins (Jackie's state room was replete with solid-gold fixtures in the shape of dolphins). Onassis had even offered to stay away for the cruise, aware of the Kennedys' disapproval, but Jackie wasn't going to take advantage of his hospitality only to banish him. By many accounts, he stayed in his state room for the first three days of the cruise, making business calls and dining on lobster thermidor, while his guests sunbathed, read, and swam in the mosaic pool on the aft deck. Like in the classic fairy tale "The Beauty and the Beast," Onassis at first hid himself from the prized beauty until he suddenly appeared, offering Jackie all the hospitality his wealth and generosity afforded.

Debarking at Istanbul, they continued on a guided tour of Smyrna, in Turkey, where Onassis had been born. Photographs began appearing in the States of Onassis and Jackie threading their way through the winding streets of the ancient city— photographs that Maria Callas and President Kennedy both saw, and were alarmed by.

Back on board the *Christina*, it was difficult for Jackie to remain in close contact with Jack. Despite the modern conveniences of the yacht, the communication system was frustrating, and the time difference added another difficulty. She would place a call to the White House but would often have to wait three hours before it went through—and the local switchboard often lost the connection. She took to writing Jack long letters ("punctuated with dashes like everything she wrote," observed one presidential historian), describing how much she missed him and how she regretted that he could not be with her to share the calming pleasures of the Mediterranean.

However, once Jack saw newspaper photos of Jackie strolling with Onassis, her hand in his, he managed to get through to her on the *Christina* to ask that she cut her trip short. Jackie refused. She had always been deeply interested in Greek culture and myth, and to be given a tour of classical sites with Onassis as her guide was a true pleasure.

What neither Lee nor the Kennedys had counted on was the special attention paid to the First Lady once Onassis joined his guests, especially evidenced by the gifts he gave them at the end of the cruise. Suzanne Roosevelt was given a gold evening clutch (a minaudière), Lee received three diamond-studded bracelets, but he gifted Jackie with a dazzling diamond-and-ruby necklace, estimated at $50,000.

Lee was miffed, and she perhaps sensed that hers was a farewell gift. She wrote to her brother-in-law that she felt Jackie's rubies outshined her "dinky little bracelets that Caroline wouldn't wear to her own birthday party." But she had become used to that—gifts to ladies-in-waiting were always less magnificent than gifts given to queens.

Jackie left the cruise genuinely rested and restored to better spirits, but she wasn't prepared for the negative press her trip had inspired. Joe Alsop wrote in his column, "How terrible it was of Jackie Kennedy to go off on the Onassis yacht. Everyone knew that Lee Radziwill was having an affair with Onassis, and that Jackie was along as cover . . ." Schlesinger feared that "Jackie's rest" appeared to the American public as "La Dolce Vita in the Greek Isles." It was the second time Jackie received chiding press, a surprising reversal since the media had just praised her dignity and extended sympathy on the loss of her infant son. She worried that Jack now saw her as a political liability.

Chagrined by her husband's disapproval, Jackie agreed to help Jack campaign. She was a reluctant campaigner at best, but Kennedy knew she added glamour to the ticket. Jackie even considered accompanying him to the historic Army-Navy football game— though she loathed football.

"I'll campaign with you anywhere you want," she told him.

Kennedy asked whether that might include his upcoming trip to Fort Worth and Dallas with Lyndon Johnson. She took out her red leather appointment book and showed Kennedy the page where she'd scribbled "Texas" across the dates for November 21, 22, and 23.

*

NO LESS THAN the evangelical preacher Billy Graham had advised Jack Kennedy not to visit Dallas in his attempt to shore up Southern support for the Democratic Party in the upcoming 1964 presidential election. Right-wing conspiracy groups flourished there—the John Birch Society, the Minutemen, the Patrick Henry Society—and the ultraconservative oil billionaire H. L. Hunt exerted his anti-Democratic influence. As William Manchester, who would write the first and most detailed account of the assassination in his powerful book *Death of a President*, observed:

> In that third year of the Kennedy presidency, a kind of fever lay over Dallas country. Mad things happened. Huge billboards screamed, "Impeach Earl Warren." Jewish stores were smeared with crude swastikas . . . Radical right polemics were distributed in public schools; Kennedy's name was booed in classrooms; junior executives were required to attend radical seminars.

A "Wanted" poster was circulated in Dallas the day of Kennedy's visit, accusing him of "turning the sovereignty of the U.S. over to the Communist controlled United Nations" and "appointing Anti-Christians to federal office." Dallas was also a city awash in gun violence: 110 murders in 1963, three out of four by gunfire. "Texas led the United States in homicide, and Big D [Dallas] led Texas," Manchester wrote, in describing the city's "dark streak of violence." When Kennedy's assassination was announced to a fourth grade class in a wealthy Dallas suburb, the fourth graders burst into applause.

The night before the assassination, in their hotel room in Fort Worth, Jack asked Jackie what she was going to wear for the events planned in Dallas. "There are going to be all these rich, Republican women at that lunch, wearing mink coats and diamond bracelets," he said. "And you've got to look as marvelous as any of them. Be simple—show these Texans what good taste really is." Jackie held out several dresses in front of her——"beige and white dresses, blue and yellow suits, and, for Dallas, a pink suit with a navy blue collar and matching pink pillbox hat."

Jackie vividly remembered other details of that night and the following day: She recalled how Jack had asked her not to stay the night with him because he had to rise early the next morning to make a breakfast speech. She recalled how his aides had removed the hotel's mattress and replaced it with a special mattress he always traveled with to ease his chronic back pain. She recalled looking into the mirror and fussing over finding a new wrinkle. She recalled their long good-night embrace, not knowing it would be their last night together.

The next day, she remembered that Jack asked her to remove her oversized sunglasses so the crowd could see her face. "You're the one they've come to see," he told her. She did so.

She also remembered that after the first shot rang out, Kennedy slumped at her side. He'd been shot in the soft tissue of the shoulder, and the bullet exited through his trachea. Later, Dr. Kenneth Salyer, who treated Kennedy at Dallas's Parkland Hospital, speculated that had Kennedy not been wearing the back brace he usually wore to ameliorate his back pain, he might not have remained upright and thus a vulnerable target for Lee Harvey Oswald's second, fatal gunshot to the head. Part of his skull shattered in a pink mist.

She did not remember crawling to the rear of the open car in her blood-spattered pink Chanel suit, to seek aid from Agent Hill, who was following directly behind the black limousine. Hill gave Jackie his suit jacket, which she used to desperately wrap her husband's head wound.

She did remember struggling with Agent Hill to place Kennedy's body on a stretcher outside of Parkland Hospital. "I'm not going to let him go, Mr. Hill," she remembered saying. "You know he's dead. Let me alone."

She remembered that the back seat of the SS-100-X six-passenger Lincoln was soaked in her husband's blood.

She remembered asking Dr. Kemp Clark, one of the surgeons who tried desperately to save the president, if she could see her husband in his coffin before it was closed.

When he said no, she remembered saying, "Do you think seeing the coffin can upset me, Doctor? . . . His blood is all over me. How can I see anything worse than I've seen?"

She remembered trying to remove her left glove so she could place her wedding ring in the coffin alongside Kennedy's body, but fumbled with the glove. She remembered holding out her wrist to police sergeant Bob Dugger, who undid the glove and peeled it from her hand.

She remembered Vice President Lyndon Johnson—now suddenly made president—and Kennedy aides asking her to change out of her bloodied suit for the swearing-in of Johnson on board Air Force One, and that she refused.

"Let them see what they've done," she said.

A dress manufacturer named Abraham Zapruder caught the life-shattering event on 8 mm Kodachrome II safety film. He'd planned to head out of Dealey Plaza that day to join the throng of well-wishers along the path of the presidential motorcade, but he was going to leave his camera at home. It was an overcast day, but when the sun came out, his secretary said, "Mr. Z., you march right back there. How many times will you have a crack at color movies of the President?"

Zapruder protested, saying, "I'm too short. I probably wouldn't even get close." But he ran home and twenty minutes later returned to his office at the Dal-Tex Building on Elm Street, across from the Texas School Book Depository building with his new Bell & Howell Zoomatic home-movie camera. He wanted to record the glamorous young president and First Lady on their visit to Dallas for his children and grandchildren to treasure. Instead he found himself caught up in a horrific moment in American history.

It has become the most studied piece of film in history, and the most famous home movie, known as the Zapruder film: a 26.6-second strip of silent, grainy color film that just happened to capture the crime of the century.

After the first shot rang out, Zapruder continued to film, while others—some of them professional photographers—ran for safety or were so frozen with fear they were unable to capture the event. Zapruder immediately returned to his office and locked his camera in a safe. A reporter for the *Dallas Morning News* contacted the Secret Service to inform them that someone had possibly filmed the assassination, and before the terrible day was over, *Life* magazine contacted Zapruder and began their race with the Secret Service and the FBI to gain access to the film. By that evening, the footage was developed and three copies were made: two were handed over to the Secret Service. It was the first time in American history that a piece of film would become crucial evidence in a murder case.

While other news agencies and everyone from William Paley to Edward R. Murrow clamored for Zapruder's home movie, *Life*'s regional editor Richard Stolley craftily negotiated to pay $50,000 for the print rights and managed to slip out a back door with the original film. The Warren Commission then subpoenaed the film from *Life*. *Life* published thirty frames in black-and-white in the November 29, 1963, issue, and later in color, in a December 6, 1964, special JFK memorial issue.

In the first days after the assassination, the country was plunged into shock and grief. The slain president was flown to Washington, where his casket was laid in state in the Capitol Rotunda before the funeral Mass at St. Matthew's Cathedral and burial in Arlington National Cemetery. The line of grieving citizens filing by the catafalque reached five miles as it snaked through the streets of Washington, DC.

In the aftershock of her grief, Jackie's deep engagement with history helped her make decisions about the funeral. She modeled her husband's procession after Abraham Lincoln's, with a horse-drawn casket that wound its way through the chilled streets of the city, a riderless horse accompanying the casket. Jackie refused to ride in the government-issued black Cadillac. She chose to walk behind the casket, leading a delegation from ninety-two nations which included Charles de Gaulle. A White House aide, Larry O'Brien, commented, "We were supposed to be the tough ones, but this frail girl turned out to have more strength than any one of us." For America, the assassination of John Kennedy stood alone, but for Jackie, the assassination and the death of Patrick just a few months earlier became entwined as an inseparable tragedy.

In London, it was 6:21 p.m.—1:21 p.m. Eastern time—on November 22, 1963, when Lee received the call. She was at home at 4 Buckingham Place, and Stas was at the St. James's Club. Lee took the first available plane to Washington to be with her grieving sister. Stas, who had loved Jack Kennedy, followed the day after.

Lee was met at Dulles Airport in a driving rain by Janet and Hughdie. When she arrived at the White House, Lem Billings told her it was nice of her to come. Lee turned on him and shouted, "How can you say that? Do you think that I wouldn't?"

Before departing for Washington, however, Lee had called Onassis in Hamburg, Germany, where his newest tanker was being launched, and asked him to attend the funeral. She invited him to stay at the White House—one of only six invitations issued. Onassis reminded her that he had been warned to stay out of America until after the election, a year away.

"I don't think that matters very much now," Lee whispered.

Some have speculated that Lee extended the invitation out of gratitude for Onassis's role in helping restore Jackie to better spirits after the death of Patrick. A less charitable interpretation was that she'd hoped that by inviting Onassis to an intimate family setting at such a vulnerable moment, she might rekindle his interest in her. Truman Capote, who would enjoy an intense but short-lived friendship with Lee, told his Random House editor, Joe Fox:

> The invitation had actually been Jackie's idea. The First Lady knew that she could not invite "The Greek" herself . . . but by having Lee include him in her personal party, he automatically got one of the family's invitations to stay at the White House. Lee was deeply in love with the Golden Greek . . . but she played right into Jackie's hands.

Whatever the origins of his invitation, Onassis arrived at the White House and indeed proved himself a useful and diverting guest.

Not accustomed to an old-fashioned Irish wake, Onassis was surprised at the somewhat rollicking atmosphere when he arrived; it was all very different from how Greeks mourned their dead. The Kennedys, still in shock and in a forgiving mood, teased him about his yacht, and Bobby Kennedy wrote up a mock will for the shipping magnate to sign, pledging to give half his fortune to the poor of Latin America. Aristotle Socrates Onassis gallantly signed his full name to the document, in Greek. His presence introduced an element of levity in those somber days. Even Jackie was seen walking arm in arm with him down White House corridors.

Lee and Stas were supposed to sleep in the president's executive suite, but Stas was so devastated by Kennedy's death that he couldn't bring himself to sleep in the president's vacated bed in the most intimate room in the White House. The very sight of the four-poster bed, Kennedy's medicine bottles on the side table next to it, and the toy boats and bath toys that he used when bathing

John-John in the adjacent bathroom all filled him with sadness. A cot was ordered from the White House staff, to be set up at the foot of the bed.

"Poor Stas," Jackie said when she entered the room and saw the cot.

The next morning, Stas couldn't bring himself to shave and wash in the president's bathroom, so he was found wandering the halls, his toothbrush and razor in hand, looking lost.

*

"MY SISTER SHOWED so much courage, but it was the courage of a great actress," Lee recalled fifty years after the tragedy. "In private, alone with her children, it was unbearable. And there was no one really with whom she could share the true horror of it." Lee had been moved by her sister's public stance, "her self-composure in the face of all that pity," as she remembered. "It's interesting to see in many of the published diaries of the time, by people in so many different walks of life, what has been written about that day."

But even the noted writers of the day were often unable to fully grasp what had happened on November 22, 1963. Noël Coward wrote in his diary from Philadelphia during the tryouts for his musical *Sail Away*:

> The whole country is in a state of deep shock. Mrs. Kennedy . . . has behaved throughout with dignity, grace and magnificent self-control. I watched her today on television accompanying the President's body from the White House to the Capitol and was moved to tears . . . Hardly conducive to writing frivolous lyrics and music . . . I feel that I am living through too much history.

Joe Alsop expressed his grief and shock over Kennedy's assassination in his memoir:

I can only say that it was a shattering sensation to discover quite abruptly that one had lived the best years of one's life between the ages of forty-eight and fifty-three. I had never known I loved the President . . . until I felt the impact of his death . . . Why I should so irrationally mind the President's loss, and it much more than the loss of my own father, I cannot say. But, clearly, after that bright, blustery November day, nothing would be quite the same in my life again or . . . in the life of this country.

Schlesinger heard the news in New York while sipping cocktails with *Washington Post* publisher Katharine Graham, economist John Kenneth Galbraith, and several editors of *Newsweek*. He wrote in his journal: "A man entered in his shirtsleeves and said, a little tentatively, 'I think you should know that the President has been shot in the head in Texas.' It took a few seconds for this to register. Then we rushed for the radio . . ."

Schlesinger flew to Washington later that day. He recalled,

Everyone is stunned. Fortunately the practical details of the funeral engage everyone's attention and sidetrack us from the terrible reality. I still cannot believe this splendid man, this man of such intelligence and gaiety and strength, is dead. The wages of hate are fearful . . . It will be a long time before this nation is as nobly led as it has been in these last three years.

Before the funeral, Schlesinger wandered around the White House, and at 2 a.m. observed workmen draping black crepe over the windows and pillars of the grand portico. He watched as Kennedy's casket, wrapped in an American flag, was carried into the East Room and placed on a catafalque. "Jackie followed," he recorded in his journals:

. . . a boy appeared to light the tapers around the bier. The third taper took a painfully long time to light . . . A priest said a few words. Then Bobby whispered something to Jackie. She approached the bier, knelt in front of it and buried her head in the flag. Then she walked away. The rest of us followed.

Jackie retreated to her upstairs rooms, along with Bobby and Ethel Kennedy and Jean Kennedy Smith. A few minutes later, Bobby came down and went into the East Room with Robert McNamara. He came out, and asked Schlesinger and Nancy Tuckerman to help them decide if the casket should remain open.

"I went in," Schlesinger recorded,

with the candles fitfully burning, three priests on their knees praying in the background, and took a last look at my beloved President, my beloved friend. For a moment, I was shattered. But it was not a good job; probably it could not have been with half his head blasted away. It was too waxen, too made up. It did not really look like him.

Reminding Bobby that Franklin D. Roosevelt's casket had remained closed for his funeral, he and Tuckerman advised Bobby and Jackie to do the same.

Some Kennedy aides tried to talk Jackie out of leading the funeral parade of dignitaries, which included Charles de Gaulle, Prince Philip, and the new president, Lyndon Johnson, in the long procession up Connecticut Avenue toward St. Matthew's Cathedral. They were afraid that her athletic vigor would show up the older heads of state, but Lee encouraged her to walk in the procession.

Whether by choice or by coincidence, the symbolic riderless horse following the caisson bearing the president's body was named

Black Jack. If Jackie noticed, she did not remark on it; her somber dignity left an indelible impression on the American psyche, elevating her in the eyes of the world to not just America's First Lady, but America's First Widow, nothing less than a living saint.

Like the girls and women of their class, Jackie and Lee were taught from a young age that there was one way to be in public and another in private. The public face was the one that mattered. Jackie's stoicism and composure during those terrible days in November were real, but they masked the crushing grief and hopelessness she felt in the days and months that followed. Each woman could walk through a public storm with a book still perfectly balanced on her head.

Later, near the grave site, Air Force One soared over Arlington in a final salute to the president. Jackie missed it, but when Lee saw it pass overhead, her tears fell.

*

IT WAS LEE to whom her sister turned during the days and weeks following the assassination. Lee had been the first of the two sisters to discover Edith Hamilton's *The Greek Way*, and Jackie gave a copy of the book to Robert Kennedy soon after his brother's death. Written in 1934 by the Bryn Mawr classicist, it was a distillation of history and tragedy in fifth-century Greece and it resonated with Bobby Kennedy. Lee knew her history as well as anyone. Bobby, Jackie, and Lee would take to heart the cry of the herald in *Prometheus Bound*: "In agony learn wisdom."

Lee stayed on in the White House to comfort her sister, and for a time she provided the only respite for Jackie's grief. They were again the closest of sisters, brought together by tragedy. One night, Lee crept into Jackie's bedroom and left a note on her pillow, addressed "To Jacks, from Pekes." It read: "Good night my darling Jacks—the bravest and noblest of all. L."

Jackie made plans to leave the White House, a bitter move not only because of the terrible circumstances, but also because she felt a close bond to the home she had so lovingly and diligently restored to its historic glory. She bid good-bye to the White House staff, and then hand wrote the following text for a plaque to be placed in the Lincoln Bedroom:

> In this room lived John Fitzgerald Kennedy with his wife Jacqueline during the two years, ten months, and two days he was President of the United States.

It was placed just beneath the inscription, "In this room, Abraham Lincoln slept during his occupancy of the White House. March 4, 1861–April 13, 1865."

Eleven days later, Jackie, accompanied by Lee, moved into a Georgetown house at 3038 N Street Northwest, temporarily lent to her by former New York governor Averell Harriman. Once out of the public eye, as Lee had observed, Jackie gave in to her sense of loss and despair, holing up in her bedroom, weeping to her secretary, Mary Gallagher, and asking her, "Why did Jack have to die so young?"

She and her children managed to join Lee and Stas for a brief getaway at the Kennedy compound in Palm Beach before returning to Georgetown and buying a house at 3017 N Street, on the same block as the Harriman house.

She brought Lee with her while she unpacked cartons and worked with decorator Billy Baldwin, but her activity and Lee's presence did little to assuage her sorrow. She asked Gallagher to help her go through a file of clippings about Jack, admitting to her, "At night when I'm alone . . . I just drown my sorrows in vodka."

Throughout the winter, Lee stayed by her sister's side and became concerned at how unhinged and bitter Jackie had become.

Jackie lacerated herself that she had not done enough to save her husband's life. Lee confided in Cecil Beaton that she "had gone through hell" trying to help her sister. "She's really more than half round the bend! She can't sleep at night—she can't stop thinking about herself and never feeling anything but sorry for herself!"

At one point, after Lee had challenged her to get on with her life, Jackie slapped her across the face. Lee told Beaton that Jackie was "so jealous of me, but I don't know if it's because I have Stas and two children, and I've gone my own way to become independent. But she goads me to the extent that I yell back at her and say, 'Thank heavens, at last I've broken away from my parents and from you and everything of that former life.'"

Jackie spent the next several months trying to put her life back together, protecting her children and working to burnish the legend of her husband's brief presidency by summoning the image of Camelot, inspired by the Columbia Records soundtrack of the musical which she and Kennedy had listened to countless times in the White House.

What Lee didn't realize at the time was just how deep an impression Jackie's somber dignity left on the American psyche. If she had been merely famous before Kennedy's death, she was now an icon. For five years in a row, before and after the assassination, Jackie was named "the most admired woman in America" by a Gallup poll. During her brief time as First Lady, she had captured the world's imagination to an astonishing degree. As Carl Sferrazza Anthony, author of *As We Remember Her*, noted:

> Composer Rudolf Friml wrote an operetta in her honor . . . Her face was carved in a one-thousand-foot portrait in the snow of Mount Jaillet at Megève, France, by artist Rene Cazassus . . . Louis Foy in the *Paris Press* thought Congress should replace all images of George Washington with Jackie . . . Movie magazines offered scurrilous covers, with no story inside. One magazine

gave advice on "How to Be Your Town's Jackie Kennedy" . . .
There were Jackie dress-up dolls, cutout dolls, and Barbie dolls . . .

If Jackie did indeed envy Lee's marriage and intact family—
and her relative freedom and privacy—Lee knew there was no
way she could compete with an icon.

*

IN THE WEEKS following the assassination, Jackie was besieged
by journalists clamoring for interviews and information. Sphinx-
like, she kept her silence, until it became clear she would need to
cooperate with a writer to tell the whole story as she had lived
it. A Hearst newspaper columnist and writer of popular histo-
ries named Jim Bishop, she learned, was already researching a
book on the subject, without her cooperation. Bishop's 1955 book,
The Day Lincoln Was Shot, was a bestseller, and he was already
at work on a book titled *A Day in the Life of President Kennedy*,
which the president had cooperated with ten days before the assassination, and which Bishop would publish the following year,
with the inevitable title change.

Jackie hated the idea. She would have preferred that no book
be written, but as that was not likely, she decided to choose an author whom she knew and liked and felt she could work with. Her
first choice was Theodore H. White (*The Making of the President*), whom she trusted and to whom she gave her first interview,
a week after the cataclysmic events in Dallas. With Theodore
White, she began to describe the Kennedy years as a kind of now-
vanished Camelot, and she mused on what life might be like for
her and her children, with Jack gone. What she revealed was her
struggle with "a downward spiral of depression or isolation." She
felt sure that she would reject a public life now that she was on
her own.

I'm not going to be the Widow Kennedy—and make speeches like some people who talk about the family. When this is over I'm going to crawl into the deepest retirement . . . I'm going to live in the place I lived with Jack . . . That was the first thing I thought that night . . . Then I thought—how can I go back there to that bedroom?

Jackie also confided in Pierre Salinger, "There's only one thing I can do in life now—save my children. They've got to grow up without thinking back at their father's murder."

Theodore White ultimately turned down her request to write the official account of the assassination, as he was already deep into another work and he might also have been wary of the pitfalls of a family-commissioned book. Bobby Kennedy, working with Jackie in finding a suitable writer, assured her that they would have final approval over any manuscript written on the subject.

Salinger suggested William Manchester, a prolific writer of novels and biographies, a World War II veteran, an ex-marine, and a former foreign correspondent for the *Baltimore Sun*. He had already met with Kennedy and published *Portrait of a President*, and both men had enjoyed the encounters. Manchester later wrote about the experience:

I'd see Jack at the end of his last appointment for the day. We'd have a daiquiri and sit on the Truman Balcony. He'd smoke a cigar and I'd have a Heineken. He'd let loose—things he couldn't discuss with anyone else.

Jackie agreed with Bobby that a writer who already admired Kennedy, whose family was also from Massachusetts, and whose World War II experience was similar to Kennedy's (both had been awarded Purple Hearts, and Manchester had fought in Guadalcanal when Kennedy was commanding PT-109 a few miles away, near the island of Tulagi in the Pacific Theater) was the right choice. Here was someone the Kennedys felt they could trust. More important for Jackie, perhaps, was that she was impressed by Manchester's rich, lyrical writing style. She knew a superb writer when she saw one.

Bobby worked out a deal with Manchester and Harper & Row, the house that had published Kennedy's *Profiles in Courage* and was considered the official publisher of the Kennedy family. Jackie agreed to meet with the thirty-nine-year-old, angular ex-marine with the poetic prose style for an agreed-upon ten hours of interviews. Bobby had persuaded Jackie that she would only have to go over the ghastly events once with Manchester, not "again and again and again."

On April 7, 1964, roughly four and a half months after the assassination, Jackie greeted the writer at her town house in Georgetown for the first of two five-hour sessions. Jackie, then thirty-four years old, was dressed in yellow capri pants and a black jersey when they first met, and Manchester was fascinated by her "camellia beauty." He later wrote:

> My first impression—and it never changed—was that I was in the presence of a very great, tragic actress. I mean that in the finest sense of the word. There was a weekend in American history when we need to be united in our sadness. [Jacqueline Kennedy] provided us with an unforgettable performance as the nation's heroine.

The only way a still grieving Jackie could get through the lengthy interviews was with plentiful daiquiris. Manchester could hear the clinking of ice cubes when he played back his Wollensak tape recorder, as well as the sound of countless matches being struck, as both Jackie and Manchester smoked throughout the sessions. Manchester later wrote that "half the people I

interviewed displayed deep emotional distress while trying to answer my questions. None of the other sessions were as affecting
as those with Jackie." Because the assassination had occurred in
broad daylight, she couldn't bear to talk about it during daylight
hours, so they met as the sun was going down—what the French
call *"l'heure bleu."* Manchester was struck not only by her dark-
haired beauty but by how vividly and accurately she remembered
everything that had happened. "She had a great visual eye and
great recall," he wrote. "She remembers every god-damn thing
about that assassination . . . It was like expunging herself—the
wound was still pretty raw."

Five months after the assassination, with the country still in grief
and shock, Jackie was invited to spend Easter with her friend
Bunny Mellon at her home in Antigua. Lee and Stas were invited,
as were Bobby Kennedy and Chuck Spalding. In an attempt to
escape the gloom and pity that surrounded her, Jackie accepted
the invitation, and she and Lee were again closer than ever. The
sisters water-skied and swam and sunbathed. They planned picnics on nearby islands, and in the evenings in Bunny's splendid
villa, they played pop music at top volume to help drown out their
sorrows—popular hits of the day such as Steve Lawrence and
Eydie Gorme's "Blame It on the Bossa Nova," the Chiffons' "He's
So Fine," and Kennedy friend Andy Williams's "Can't Get Used
to Losing You." Bobby Kennedy would have none of that, so he
secluded himself in a corner of the villa, where he devoured *The
Greek Way.*

Manchester moved with his family to Washington, DC, from his
home in Middletown, Connecticut, where he had been working as
an editor at Wesleyan University Press, and immersed himself in
his research, working twenty hours a day on occasion. He became
obsessed with the book, spending time in Dallas retracing every

detail of the ill-fated day. Jim Bishop had decided to go ahead with his own unauthorized book about Kennedy's death, and Manchester realized the family wanted him to beat Bishop to market. He worked so intensely and relentlessly that he ended up hospitalized for exhaustion. And then Jackie and Bobby decided they didn't want the book published, once it was finished, because Jackie had found it too much a violation of her privacy.

When Jackie learned that *The Death of a President* would be serialized in *Look* magazine, she panicked, believing it would be "tasteless" to publicly expose her private memories of that terrible event. She had expected the book to be "bound in black and put away on dark library shelves," she would later say. Bobby went along with Jackie's wishes, reneging on his promise to Manchester to not interfere with publication. Their efforts to suppress *The Death of a President* brought Jackie truly negative publicity; for the first time, her popularity declined in national polls.

Manchester was devastated. He had put his heart and soul into the book and it had nearly wrecked his health. The fight over its publication was such a public scandal that Bayer Aspirin offered the writer $35,000 to endorse their headache remedy (he turned them down). Jackie filed an injunction to stop publication, finally settling out of court. Manchester agreed to cut 1600 words from the *Look* serialization and seven pages from the book's 654-page text. *The Death of a President* was serialized—and published—to great acclaim. Six hundred thousand copies were sold within two months and more than a million copies by the summer of 1967. Tom Wicker, reviewing the book for the *New York Times*, wrote, finally, that "it was worth the effort; it may even have been worth the pain."

But now, with John F. Kennedy gone and Jackie out of the White House, it was Lee's time to shine. She had always hated what had been written about her during the Kennedy years. "It seemed so empty, so jet set," she said about that era in her life. She had never liked living in a fishbowl, feeling that her attempts to soar were being tamped down by the Kennedys. "After the death of my brother-in-law," Lee admitted years later, "I was finally free."

7

SWAN DIVE

I'd love to act. Do you think it's too late?

—JACKIE

*Truman fell in love with me. He thought there was nothing
I couldn't do, and that I must go into the theater.*

—LEE

*I*n 1964, Lee convinced Stas that it was time to leave London and move back to the States to be nearer to Jackie in Georgetown and make it possible for Anthony and Tina to spend more time with Caroline and John Jr. Stas bought a duplex at 969 Park Avenue in New York. The return ushered in a happier time for both sisters. "Life was more gentle," Lee later wrote. "Everyone had more time to relax, appreciate looking at things, and visit museums. It was normal to lunch at people's apartments rather than in a restaurant."

Lee again turned to Renzo Mongiardino to transform the somewhat faded Park Avenue duplex into what many considered the most beautiful showplace in New York. She chose a dramatic cherry-red velvet for the living room. In the hall library she hung Francis Bacon's *Figure Turning*, which Stas had acquired when he'd covered the painter's gambling debts. The dining room walls were covered in a dark orange moire, surrounding one of her favorite works of art: a whimsical eighteenth-century "nursery" painting of a monkey shaking hands with a dog. Ferns and Anglo-Indian botanical watercolors transformed her bedroom into a greenhouse-like refuge. "When I woke up, I felt like I was in the country," was how she described it.

"A woman's home is her self-portrait," Lee believes, and though Jackie would receive world attention for redecorating the White House, Lee put her heart and soul into transforming her homes into places of exquisite color and design. She began spending more time in her duplex apartment, which overlooked Central Park and "the pale green leaded roof" of what is now the New York University Institute of Fine Arts, as she later wrote.

Jackie followed Lee's move to New York City to escape the fishbowl that Washington, DC, had become and the countless reminders of the thousand days she had lived in the White House with Jack. New York is known for its anonymity, though even there, Jackie would often be followed and stared at by the public, still fascinated by her mythic image.

It was Lee who had first suggested that Jackie go apartment hunting in Manhattan to break out of her shell of grief. Jackie, like Lee, had "always loved New York and everything about it— the museums, the parks, the people. She was always drawn back to New York," recalled Nancy Tuckerman. The two women went apartment hunting together, but to preserve her privacy (and no doubt keep the price reasonable), Tuckerman pretended to be the potential buyer and Jackie came disguised as the children's nanny. Nothing they saw, however, pleased her until Jayne Wrightsman told her about the five-bedroom, five-bath co-op suddenly available at 1040 Fifth Avenue.

The fifteenth-floor apartment was owned by Mrs. Lowell Weicker (her husband would serve as senator and governor of Connecticut and distinguish himself as a member of the Senate select committee on the Watergate investigation). It was not far from where the sisters had grown up, before Janet had married Hugh Auchincloss. Jackie could easily walk to favorite boutiques that she and Lee had once strolled through when Jackie was redecorating the White House—all pleasant memories of a happier time. It was seven blocks north of Lee's duplex apartment and walking distance to Caroline's school, the Convent of the Sacred Heart at 91st and Fifth Avenue (which had taught three generations of Bouviers, including the sisters' twin aunts, Maude Bouvier Davis and Michelle Bouvier Putnam).

"Ten Forty," as Jackie would come to call the building, was close to Lee's apartment, the Metropolitan Museum of Art, and the Carlyle Hotel, where the Kennedys had long maintained a duplex apartment on the top floor. Just as important to Jackie in her fragile state, her brother- and sister-in-law Peter and Pat Lawford lived nearby at 990 Fifth Avenue. Her in-laws Stephen and Jean Kennedy Smith resided at 950 Fifth Avenue, and her stepbrother Yusha Auchincloss was the outlier at 111 Park Avenue, still close enough for comfort. In many ways, she had come home.

Jackie bought the sprawling apartment for $250,000 ($1.75 million in today's dollars). She also maintained a separate four-room office at 400 Park Avenue, where she installed her two devoted secretaries, Tuckerman and Turnure.

From the Kennedy family suite at the Carlyle Hotel, Jackie and Lee supervised the transformation of the somewhat fusty Weicker apartment into a showplace reminiscent of the breezy Kennedy compound at Hyannis Port in Massachusetts and Lasata in the Hamptons, full of light and flowers. Typically, Jackie filled her apartment with books. With suggestions by the much-in-demand interior designer Mark Hampton, who wanted to reflect Jackie's classic style, Jackie kept the Louis XVI bureau on which John Kennedy had signed the nuclear test ban treaty in 1963. She displayed her collection of seventeenth-century animal drawings and miniature paintings from India, and the Empire desk that had belonged to her father and that Lee had generously given to her, knowing how much their father had doted on Jackie.

New York would give Jackie room to breathe, a place to be

herself. In New York, she could perhaps escape from her immense fame, just as Greta Garbo had moved to Manhattan at the end of her film career, saying, "I can live in New York or I can live in hell."

*

WITH JACKIE NOW the nation's widowed queen, no longer squarely in the limelight, Lee's life began to take center stage. She began writing articles on fashion and décor for *McCall's* and *Ladies' Home Journal.* The brilliant, diminutive writer Truman Capote completely flipped for Lee Radziwill, "the Principessa," and their friendship flourished.

Truman was one of Gore Vidal's rivals for the role of America's most famous living writer. His breakout novella, *Breakfast at Tiffany's,* was turned into a stylish film starring Audrey Hepburn and George Peppard. The serialization in the *New Yorker* and subsequent publication of *In Cold Blood,* his "nonfiction novel" about the murder of a Kansas farm family, catapulted Capote to stratospheric heights. A conflicted, transplanted Southerner making his way through New York's shark-infested society, Capote was known for his catty wit and brilliant portraiture of the women he admired and cultivated, known as his "swans." For a time, Lee was preeminent among them.

Capote admired Lee's "first-class intelligence," as well as her femininity: "I can't think of any woman *more* feminine than Lee Radziwill, not even Audrey Hepburn . . ." Lee began having regular lunches with the irrepressible Truman at fashionable restaurants like Quo Vadis and the Colony in New York, so much so that Capote's other swans—the society doyennes Babe Paley, Slim Keith, Pamela Harriman, and Gloria Guinness—were trumpeting their disapproval, their noses out of joint because their favorite writer, gossip, and escort-around-town was spending so much time at Lee's side. They missed his company, and they missed his flattery. One of them wrote to Capote, "I don't want to see another picture of you holding Lee Radziwill's hand. I want you to hold my hand." Suzy Knickerbocker groused in her society gossip column, "Somebody has got to tell Truman that Lee Radziwill can't have him ALL THE TIME. There's only one Truman and we saw him first."

Calling her "Princess Dear," Truman wrote in a *Vogue* appreciation of Lee, "I love everything about her. I love the way she looks, the way she moves, the way she thinks . . . Ah, the Princess! Well, she's easily described. She's a beauty. Inside. Outside." This is where he described her eyes as "gold-brown, like a glass of brandy resting on a table in front of firelight." As Truman's biographer Gerald Clarke observed, Truman imagined Lee as a character in a novel—a modern-day Becky Sharp from William Thackeray's *Vanity Fair*, making her way through society yet aware that she was playing an impossible role. Whereas Jackie seemed to have been born into a fairy tale, wife of a dashing young president, the most admired woman in the world, Lee had married a prince with a dubious title, had money but not a fortune, and seemed to be eclipsed by her sister in everything she did. It just wasn't fair. Truman seemed poised to balance the equation, hoping to mold her into someone who could outshine Jackie.

"She doesn't just want to be somebody's sister," he later explained. "She wants to have a life and an identity of her own. She's a very, very extraordinary girl. She has a really good first-class mind. It just has to get released."

The admiration was, at first, mutual. Lee told Gerald Clarke:

He's my closest friend. More than with anyone else, I can discuss the most serious things about life . . . I miss him *terribly* when I am away from him. I trust him implicitly. He's the most loyal friend I ever had, and the best company I've ever known. We've always been so close that it's like an echo. We never have to finish sentences. We just know what the other one means or wants to say. I feel as if he's my brother, except that brothers and sisters are rarely as close as we are.

Some were baffled by Truman's idolatry of Lee. Though lovely, slender, and stylish, she wasn't as charismatic as Babe Paley, as impossibly chic as Gloria Guinness, nor did she possess Pamela Harriman's persuasive charm and political influence. In fact, Lee seemed rather lost and uncertain compared to the confidence exuded by his other swans. Perhaps Lee and Truman recognized in each other their own gilded outsider status—they seemed to have everything (fame, popularity, taste), but somehow, it was never enough. Truman saw in Lee the desperation to make a name for herself. Truman knew that feeling, and he knew how she could do it.

He also saw how insecure Lee could be, sensing the way she felt about her sister. He wrote to Cecil Beaton from Switzerland as early as 1962, "Had lunch one day with a new friend, Princess Lee (My God, how jealous she is of Jackie: I never knew); I understand her marriage is all but *finito*."

Truman had actually met Jackie first, most likely at a party in New York in the summer of 1960 when Jackie was just the Georgetown wife of a relatively unknown senator from Massachusetts. The young couple kept an apartment in Manhattan, which Truman characterized as "this awful old apartment on Park Avenue." Truman would visit Jackie in the New York apartment, or they would go out to dinner or the theater when Jack was not in town.

After the election of 1960, Truman had sent a congratulatory telegram to the Kennedys, receiving a reply from Jackie, explaining that at first they thought the cable was from Harry Truman, until they realized "a) Harry wasn't in Switzerland, and b) wouldn't have signed it 'love and hugs.' Hah!" Truman found Jackie "sweet, eager, intelligent, not quite sure of herself, and hurt—hurt because she knew [Jack] was banging all these broads. She never said that, but I know about it, rather vaguely."

Truman was actually dismissive of Jack Kennedy's appeal as a ladies' man. His own taste in men tended toward the rumpled and the middle-aged, possibly as a way to recapture the love of the father who abandoned him in childhood. "What I don't understand," he told Clarke, "is why everybody said the Kennedys were so sexy."

But Jackie and Truman remained friendly for several years. Jackie always admired writers, and she was especially touched by the seven-line letter of condolence Truman had sent to her after Patrick's death. Jackie wrote to Truman her appreciation of his kind words:

> I keep thinking what power a great writer has. All the things you write move people. It is a selfish thought—but if all you have written all your life was just training to write those seven lines which were only seen by me—and Jack—I am glad you became a writer.

Their friendship would last only a few more years, however. Unable to keep the details of his closeness to the First Lady to himself, he bragged that she had once invited him into her bedroom in the White House as she dressed for the evening. When that got back to Jackie, she dropped Truman. (That was something else that Jackie and Lee had in common—their ability to simply drop a friendship when they felt betrayed, and to speak no more about it.) So perhaps Truman's great attentions to Lee—despite his genuine admiration of the Principessa—derived from an intention to get back at Jackie for having dropped him years earlier.

*

IN THE SUMMER of 1965, Jackie began to throw off her widow's weeds, going on skiing trips with Bobby Kennedy, who had turned to the beautiful widow to assuage his own grief at the loss of his beloved brother. The more time they spent together, the more rumors flew about a possible affair.

Three years after Kennedy's death, Jackie had traded in her tasteful A-line dresses and demure necklines for miniskirts. Manchester observed that once she finally emerged from mourning,

> she was photographed dancing, skiing, riding in a New Jersey hunt, cruising along the Dalmatian coast, greeting European nobility, and visiting Acapulco, the West Indies, and Spain . . .

The *National Enquirer* touted, "From Mourner to Swinger." *Women's Wear Daily* called her "the most elegant New Yorker and the most outstanding woman in the world" and gushed that she was now "one of the REAL GIRLS—honest, natural, open, de-contrived, de-kooked, delicious, subtle, feminine, young, modern, in love with life, knows how to have fun."

Once again, Jackie was in ascendancy. So when the brilliant, sought-after Truman Capote preferred Lee to Jackie, it meant something. Lee was equally besotted with Truman, telling her friends that she felt closer to Truman than anyone else in her life, even her sister. To this day, she remembers Truman as "her echo," describing him as "a great raconteur" and "the best company I've ever known. He could also be very generous, and sensitive to other people's needs."

Their friendship reached its apotheosis at Capote's famous Black and White Ball.

After the spectacular success of *In Cold Blood*, Capote "had the golden touch," wrote Gerald Clarke, "and was already looking forward to his next triumph, a party that would end the year as it had begun—with all eyes focused on him . . ." Held in the Grand

Ballroom of the Plaza Hotel on November 28, 1966, Truman's Black and White Ball was inspired by the Ascot scene in *My Fair Lady*, with costumes designed in black and white by his friend Cecil Beaton. The invitation read "Diamonds Only" to ensure no emeralds or rubies would ruin his visual scheme. It was a masked ball thrown in honor of the recently widowed Katharine Graham, publisher of the *Washington Post*, but it was really thrown to show New York society who was at the hot white center of that world: Truman Capote. As Slim Keith said, "He wanted to give the biggest and best goddamned party that anybody had ever heard of. He wanted to see every notable in the world, people of importance from every walk of life, absolutely dying to attend a party given by a funny-looking, strange little man—himself."

It was a huge success, attended by spectacular personalities who bridged show business, politics, society, and literature, including Frank Sinatra and Mia Farrow (Frank wore a cat-whisker mask), Candice Bergen in rabbit ears, the glamorous Marella Agnelli, the Maharaja and Maharani of Jaipur, Lynda Bird Johnson trailed by a phalanx of Secret Service agents, and Tallulah Bankhead (after begging for an invitation as the two former friends were on the outs). But no one was more invited than Lee Radziwill.

"People talked about the ball for months in advance—what kind of mask would they wear; whom would they order their black or white dress from; whose dinner they would attend; who was or wasn't invited," Lee later wrote. "My spiral silver sequin dress was made by Mila Schon, who came from Milan to London several times for fittings, as well as to oversee the mask."

After first dining with Bill and Babe Paley, Lee and Stas arrived at the Plaza's ballroom. It took her breath away:

> The elegance of the room was incomparable. The orchestra was impossible not to dance to, and everyone was at his best, full of expectation and ready to have a wonderful time. Lauren Bacall

danced with Jerome Robbins and cleared the floor. Stas and I left with Truman and Henry Ford at 5:00 a.m. We were so elated, and wished it wasn't all over.

After the gala, they went to have breakfast—not at Tiffany's, but at the Brasserie on Park Avenue.

The one person who didn't attend the party was Jackie Kennedy.

Jackie was of course invited and had selected an elaborate mask designed by Halston, who nearly had a nervous breakdown fulfilling orders for $600 masks for Truman's guests—but Bobby Kennedy, now a senator from New York already nursing presidential ambitions, had asked her not to attend. He feared it would create bad press for him if Jackie were to be seen at such an extravagant event while men were dying in Vietnam. In fact, the journalist and sportswriter Pete Hamill weighed in with a damning piece in the *New York Post*, contrasting the frivolity of the Black and White Ball with gruesome scenes from Vietnam.

So Jackie stayed home, but Lee—resplendent on Truman's arm in a fabulous mask—shined like the princess she knew herself to be, Stas trailing behind them.

During the filming of *In Cold Blood*, in Kansas, Truman's thoughts turned to how to help Lee find her rightful place in the world. What trumps politics, he thought, but movie stars! He and Lee had both loved going alone to the movies in the middle of the day, watching the big screen in a nearly empty theater, a habit Lee still enjoys five decades later. On paper, Truman's scheme seemed inevitable. Lee was beautiful. She looked good in clothes. Since her days at Miss Porter's, she'd always wanted to take center stage. More important, Truman had the connections, both in theater and in Hollywood, to launch his beautiful swan. He got Laurence Olivier's and John Gielgud's agent, Milton Goldman, to represent her.

"Truman fell in love with me," Radziwill reminisced in 2014, elegantly smoking one of her thin cigarettes in her Manhattan apartment, a rueful smile playing across her lips. "He thought there was nothing I couldn't do, and that I must go into the theater and I would be the perfect Tracy Lord," the madcap heroine of Philip Barry's comedy of manners about Main Line society, *The Philadelphia Story*, a role made famous on-screen by Katharine Hepburn. "He would arrange it with such taste. He was convinced that I could do this." When she hesitated to follow in the footsteps of Katharine Hepburn, Truman had said, " 'You'll act rings around Kate!' Truman could be a magnificent liar," she added with a laugh, "but nonetheless he did give me the courage to go on [the stage]."

Despite Lee's affairs with Nureyev and Onassis and the cooling of their marriage, Stas was still very much in the picture, as Lee continued to divide her time between New York, London, and Turville Grange. Unfortunately, Stas was "violently against" her going on the stage, Lee recalled: "He said, 'You have everything in life, a perfect life. Why do you want to go out and get criticized? Why?' I said, 'Because I've always wanted to do this.' There were so many things I couldn't do when my brother-in-law was president. Can I do this, can I do that? One had to be . . . well, why can't I do this now?"

Truman became obsessed with showcasing his favorite swan, arranging almost every aspect of the production. Remembered Lee, "Truman pushed and pushed, in spite of my husband being so against it. Truman could be so 'Honey, you have to have George Masters. He's the greatest makeup man in history! Jennifer Jones spends eight hours with him a day.' I said, 'Forget it. I'm not spending more than an hour, maximum, with him.' "

At Truman's insistence, Masters flew to New York from Los Angeles to meet with Lee. "So," Lee continued, "George Masters arrives from LA. The first thing he does is throw all the shoes in my closet out the window and says, 'You can't look like a typical little society girl, so I'm throwing all this stuff out.' That was pretty devastating when I came back to my room and found most of my things thrown on the floor." He then decided that she needed to lighten her hair. "You've got to be a blonde; your hair is much too dark," he told the princess.

"I began to get terrified," Lee recalled.

Lee had appeared in plays at Miss Porter's as a teenager—most memorably, Kaufman and Hart's *You Can't Take It with You*—and she had studied singing in Paris, so this plan did not come out of nowhere. She began taking lessons in breathing, moving, and extending her whispery voice to prepare for the role. The insouciant, privileged, spoiled socialite Tracy Lord seemed tailor-made for Lee, but only on the surface: Lee didn't identify with her at all. "She has none of the feelings I understand, of sadness, despair, or of knowing loss," Lee later said.

Lee was of course a novice, so Truman thought it best to open in a small theater-in-the-round in Chicago. The play was set to open at the Ivanhoe on June 20, 1967, for a four-week run.

*

THEY CHECKED INTO penthouse suite 1705 of the Ambassador East hotel in Chicago for the hurried rehearsals, with George Masters complaining about Yves Saint Laurent being brought in to design all of Lee's costumes. New York society hairdresser Kenneth was flown in from New York to do Lee's hair, and of course Truman was on hand to orchestrate the three-ring circus, coaching Lee and calming her nerves, while dancing backstage to his favorite records on a portable phonograph.

Dr. Max Jacobson came by to give the exhausted cast and crew vitamin B12 injections. Someone calling herself Cabala Woman read the cast's fortunes over the telephone, telling Lee that the signs were "very promising for theater work." The forbearing Stas, who valiantly accompanied Lee throughout the whole undertaking, smoked and drank throughout the ordeal, while George Masters kept calling him "Princie."

"So, all that didn't help my nerves at all for opening night," Lee reminisced. "George Masters was so excited that Rudolf Nureyev was coming that he almost lost his mind. He did dye my hair blonde, and he made me a nervous wreck by the time it opened. Then he spent the day on opening night, dressing [to impress] Nureyev, in an absolutely snow-white suit. I sat in my dressing room waiting for him, until Rudolf came backstage and just held me in his arms. I was weeping. Rudolf ignored Masters completely."

Lee wore Yves Saint Laurent's costumes so well that with each new entrance, in each new ensemble, Lee and her wardrobe were met by approving oohs and aahs from the audience. The costumes were indeed stunning: "I will always remember the very heavy white crepe dressing gown he designed for Tracy when she was carried to her room, somewhat the worse for wear," Lee reminisced.

Even though Lee had insisted on using "Lee Bouvier" in the credits instead of "Princess Lee Radziwill," the four-week run was sold out, and the first-night audience was brimming with bold-faced names. But when the play finally opened, Lee found herself alone on the stage, frozen with fear.

"I remember so well," Lee continued. "It was a theater-in-the-round, so no curtain, and the first scene opened with Tracy trying to write a letter. I could not move [my hand] to the end of the page. I was totally paralyzed."

There was some resentment on the part of the cast because Lee had been elevated to a starring role with so little training. And they had a point. Though she looked beautiful, she failed to command the stage. She later explained, "It's hard for someone raised in my world to learn to express emotion. We're taught early to hide our feelings." The reviews were mixed—ranging from "Miss Bouvier's Bravado Shines" to "Lee Lays Golden Egg"—yet the audience loved it. They knew exactly what to expect—glamour and eye candy and proximity to stars—and they got what they came for.

"I got terrible reviews," Lee recalled decades later, "but I really believe they were written before the play opened. I don't know why the press blew it up so . . . I couldn't understand it. You know Dina Merrill? She was a great heiress. Her mother was Marjorie Merriweather Post. She didn't have any of that [criticism], and she was always in films and movies. I couldn't understand why I was getting this barrage."

Another disappointment accompanied Lee's theatrical debut. Despite the celebrity audience, there was one empty seat, in the third row, and it was reserved for Jacqueline Bouvier Kennedy.

Jackie, who disapproved of Lee's new venture, was in Ireland and had decided not to cut short her visit. She had taken Caroline and John Jr. to Dunganstown, the ancestral village of the Kennedys, which Jack had visited with Lee in his final summer. She toured the Waterford glass factory, where she ordered chandeliers for the Kennedy Center, now under construction in Washington, DC.

Her choosing to remain in Ireland could be interpreted as not wanting to steal Lee's thunder or as a sign of her disapproval. Or could she have been envious? She had once told Gore Vidal, "I'd love to act. Do you think it's too late?" She had even thought of doing a screen test for Paramount, but as usual, the Kennedys wouldn't allow it. But Jackie, sainted by her widowhood, had become a kind of movie star in her own right, as Vidal later observed: "a silent star of unmade films, her face on every magazine cover almost to the end." William Manchester, too, had described Jackie as appearing like a "great, tragic actress" when he first met her soon after Kennedy's assassination.

Whatever her true feelings, Jackie sent a "pretty little mauve box" to Lee on opening night with her wishes for "extravagant luck," but she missed Lee's entire four-week run.

As for Lee, it hadn't been a total disaster. *Life* magazine put the radiantly smiling thirty-four-year-old Lee on the July 14, 1967, cover, for an article titled "The Princess Goes on Stage" (where the pull quote appeared, "Girls who have everything are not supposed to do anything"). Though the critics mostly panned her, the fashion editors continued to love her. Diana Vreeland arranged a ten-page fashion layout featuring Lee for the fall fashion issue of *Vogue*, bringing in the celebrated Bert Stern to do the shoot.

"Lee was like Marilyn Monroe to work with," the photographer recalled about that photo shoot. "Very sexy. Very sweet. I was surprised at how beautiful she was when I photographed her." Compared to photographs of Lee during her trip to India and Pakistan with Jackie several years earlier—in which Lee seemed too coifed, too careful, too repressed—Lee now glowed with confidence and a sense of freedom.

Lee presented an unsinkable spirit in both *Life* and *Vogue*, undaunted by the negative reviews, and in fact she made plans to appear in another high-profile production, again arranged by Truman. She would take on the title role of *Laura*, in a two-hour movie of the week filmed in London for ABC, to air on January 24, 1968. (Gene Tierney had played the haunting film noir heroine in the 20th Century–Fox film; at the height of her career, the actress had had a brief affair with the young John Kennedy.) Truman Capote himself wrote the adaptation, with David Susskind producing; Farley Granger costarred in the role of the smitten detective (played by Dana Andrews in the 1944 film); and wry, waspish George Sanders played the wry, waspish columnist Waldo Lydecker (Clifton Webb's role in the movie).

Despite the sometimes nasty reviews for *The Philadelphia Story*, Lee was excited about this new venture. "I wish we could begin tomorrow—it's going to be marvelous," she wrote to Truman from London. Susskind had arranged for *Laura* to be filmed in London to accommodate Lee, who had returned to 4 Buckingham Place. Stas grumbled the whole time, prompting another letter from Lee to Truman: "I was *so* happy to get your letter," she wrote, "except that it made me weep because I miss you so much & need you to make life worthwhile." Out of gratitude for her friend who saw great potential in her, Lee had a Schlumberger cigarette box sent to Truman, with the engraved inscription, "To My Answered Prayer, with love, Lee. July 1967."

But this substantial production foundered on Lee's delicate shoulders; she just wasn't ready to carry an entire film on live television, unable to step out of herself to entirely inhabit the character. The reviews, again, were not kind. She moved like a specter through the two-hour production, again wearing her wardrobe beautifully but expressing little emotion. "Reduced to a stunning clothes horse," is how the television critic of the *New York Times* reviewed it. *Time* magazine described her as being "only slightly less animated than the portrait of herself that hung over the mantel." As another writer expressed it, *Laura* was "widely watched, ferociously criticized." John Davis noted, "Few people, however, made allowances for the fact that, although it was an advantage in some respects, it was a disadvantage in others to be the sister of someone as famous as Jacqueline Kennedy."

One wonders in retrospect, however, if Truman's urging Lee to jump unprepared into two iconic starring roles was evidence of conflicted feelings he felt toward the Principessa. Lee's good friend Ralph Rucci believed that the flamboyantly gay writer "was in love with her, totally in love with her. And because he couldn't psychologically handle that he had to hurt her, which is so twisted and unfortunate." In trying to elevate her, Truman instead held Lee up to public ridicule.

Nonetheless, Lee was offered other roles, including a small part in *Rosemary's Baby.* "I did turn down, afterwards, a film with Sean Connery, and before that, a chance to go to the playhouse in Arizona with Maureen Stapleton. She was a brilliant actress, so I thought I could really learn something," Lee reminisced. But Stas had had enough. "He said, 'I'll never let you see the children,' so I couldn't do that. What a shame having gone through all that and now not being able to continue. A terrible shame."

Though her theatrical ambitions, finally, did not pan out, Lee had achieved something that had eluded her for decades—she had kicked off her mother's shoes and had succeeded in running away from home. Just six years earlier, atop a camel in Pakistan, Lee had resembled Janet. Now, on the cover of *Life*, her radiant smile announced a buoyant and joyful spirit. Her light brown hair tousled around her face, her sense of exuberance—at last Lee seemed to have come into her own.

When asked if she had pursued acting to become more famous than her sister, she answered, "Look, I am doing this to be myself, my own person, in a way, I feel I've never been allowed to be. . . . If one wants fame, I can think of easier ways of getting it." If she had taken this perilous course to become herself, she had succeeded. But it's also possible that on some deeper level, Lee never quite forgave Truman for holding her up to public criticism, and she would play out her wounded feelings several years later, when Truman's star spectacularly crashed.

8

THE GOLDEN GREEK

Ari was magnetic. He walked like a potentate,
noticing and wanting to be noticed.

—LEE

If they're killing Kennedys, then my children are
targets. I want to get out of this country.

—JACKIE

The two men in my life I found the most attractive were Ari and Rudolf—and they couldn't have been more different," Lee reminisced one afternoon in the sun-filled aerie of her Upper East Side apartment. (She prefers to spend her winters in New York instead of Paris because, as her longtime friend Reinaldo Herrera observed, "New York in winter has sunny days, whereas Paris, in winter, rarely does.") Of course she was referring to Aristotle Onassis and Rudolf Nureyev, two men she had loved and inevitably lost—the first to the Kennedys and then, famously, to her sister, and the second to Nureyev's sexual orientation, perhaps, or simply to fate, which continued to play a hand in the lives of both sisters. (Lee once wrote that Ari always wore dark sunglasses because "he had Mediterranean eyes—you could see the whole story of his life in them." But what she couldn't see was Ari's intention to marry her sister.) The two men, in their fashion, had courted her, and both had offered her—at least for a brief time—a life at the center of the universe.

. . .

Many felt that Jackie was betraying her legacy as America's widowed queen by marrying one of the richest men in the world, considered by many to be a crass vulgarian. But others observed that Ari—known as the Golden Greek—was in fact immensely charming, keenly intelligent, with a deep knowledge of Greek myth and of human nature. Both sisters had been captivated by his Homeric storytelling and command of five languages. Nicholas Gage wrote in his magisterial biography of Onassis and Callas:

> Onassis was a brilliant raconteur, in all of the five languages he spoke fluently. He suffered from insomnia, and it was his practice to pass the long nights regaling anyone willing to listen—guests on his yacht or local fishermen in a Greek harborside tavern—with his stories. Randolph Churchill, the journalist who was Sir Winston's son, once described in *The London Evening Standard* Onassis' Homeric gift for oral narration: "he is a born orator with a poetic sense and can build up a list of adjectives in an ascending order of emphasis and weight which are as perfect as a phrase of music."

When people asked incredulously what Jackie saw in Onassis, Gore Vidal rather waspishly wrote, "Ari was more charming and witty than she, and in the glittering European circus, where, to her credit, she did not particularly want to shine, the word was, 'what on earth does he see in her?' "

But for Onassis, Jackie was the ultimate trophy—world-famous beyond Lee and even Maria Callas, in need of his protection, and made even more beautiful by her tragic history. With her wide-spaced eyes and elegant lines, she closely resembled the fin de siècle artist Aubrey Beardsley's rendering of Helen of Troy. But perhaps more than that, this was the ultimate revenge against the Kennedys—Jack and Bobby—who had both loved her, and who had tried but failed to keep Onassis as far away as possible from both sisters.

On June 5, 1968, Bobby Kennedy was assassinated by Sirhan Sirhan, a disturbed young Palestinian, in the kitchen of the Ambassador Hotel in Los Angeles, just after winning the California primary in his bid for the presidency. Although Jackie did not campaign for Bobby in terms of giving speeches or hosting events (indeed, she never campaigned for anyone in that way), she had been supportive of her brother-in-law, saying, "Whatever Senator Kennedy will do I know it will be right. I will always be with him with all my heart. I shall always back him up."

Just as she had accompanied her husband's body on Air Force One from Dallas to Washington, DC, still in her blood-spattered suit, so Jackie accompanied Bobby's casket from Los Angeles to New York. Kennedy family friend and NBC correspondent Sander Vanocur saw how disturbed she was, especially as she mistakenly thought it the same Boeing 707 that had carried her husband's body home. It was not, but she couldn't help but feel that she was reliving the same cataclysmic event. "There are friends of the Kennedys," one journalist wrote, "who think that when Senator Robert Kennedy was shot . . . much died in this country, including something of them, and something of [Jackie]."

Jackie was still haunted by the horror of Jack Kennedy's death five years earlier. When Cecil Beaton visited her in New York to photograph her and escort her to the Balanchine ballet *Don Quixote*, he wrote in his journal on February 19, 1968:

Jackie shows signs of the awful experiences of the last four years. Her white skin has shadows and creases, as if underneath the surface something had broken . . . happily, none of this shows in photographs, and she is still the most photogenic person in the world . . .

That night at the ballet, when a few revolver shots rang out onstage, "Jackie nearly jumped out of her chair and over the rail in the dress circle," Beaton recalled. "I felt sorry for her, in such a state of nerves."

Many believed that it was Bobby's murder that propelled Jackie into the arms of Onassis, when in actuality, she had considered marrying him several weeks earlier. They had taken an intimate cruise on the *Christina* around the Virgin Islands, and at least one of her friends, Dorothy Schiff, publisher of the *New York Post* in its earlier, more liberal days, believed that Jackie was keener on marrying Onassis than the other way around. In any case, she had discussed her plans to marry Onassis with Bobby, whom she completely trusted.

Given his disapproval of Lee's earlier involvement with Onassis, Bobby denounced Onassis as a "rogue" and asked Jackie to at least wait until the presidential election was over before making any public announcements. Ironically, his sudden death at the hands of an assassin freed her of any agreement to wait, and it also compelled her to seek the protection offered by Onassis.

Skorpios, Onassis's private four-hundred-acre island in the Ionian Sea, which he had bought for $110,000 in 1963, now seemed the kind of sanctuary Jackie needed. Manhattan, where she had thought she could live unmolested by gawkers, no longer felt safe. The photographer Ron Galella stalked her relentlessly, snapping her photo whenever she stepped onto the Manhattan pavement. He seemed to be everywhere, disguised in various wigs and false mustaches, even dating Jackie's maid to get inside information. His stalking went beyond Manhattan. Galella hung out on Capri to take photographs of Jackie and Ari dining together, and hunkered down in a skiff just off Skorpios. Like any stalker, he was obsessed with her, and his presence began to feel threatening. She finally went to court in 1970, taking out a restraining order against him. Galella reacted by suing Jackie for $1.3 million for "interfering with the pursuit of his lawful occupation" and—after Jackie had him arrested—for "malicious prosecution, false imprisonment, and harassment." Jackie countersued for $6 million, on the basis that Galella harassed her and violated her right to privacy. It took three years to resolve in the courts, culminating in a restraining order that required him to stay at least twenty-five feet away from her and thirty feet away from her children.

Even though she had moved to Manhattan in part to preserve her privacy, Jackie was still inundated by fans and curiosity seekers. One evening, Jackie went to the theater with Joan Thring, who recalled:

> When the interval came up, I said, "let's go and have a drink," and she said, "I can't, I can't do that." And suddenly, somebody said, "there's Jackie Kennedy," and there was this thunderous thing of feet running down either aisle . . . they just filed in rows in front of us, just staring. It was terrifying.

Thring asked if this happened often, and Jackie replied, "All the time. Just pretend it's not happening."

After the assassination of Bobby Kennedy, Jackie said, "If they're killing Kennedys, then my children are targets. I want to get out of this country." Not only that, it seemed everywhere she looked there was a new reminder of the life that was so suddenly and so cruelly taken from her: The National Cultural Center in Washington, DC, became the John F. Kennedy Center for the Performing Arts; Idlewild Airport in Queens, New York, was renamed John F. Kennedy International Airport; even Dealey Plaza in Dallas, Texas—where the unimaginable crime had occurred—was renamed John F. Kennedy Memorial Plaza. Cape Canaveral became Cape Kennedy (this one at Jackie's request, to recognize her husband's devotion to the space program with the goal of being the first nation to reach the moon). If she wanted to forget, it would be far more difficult to forget her former life, and her slain husband, in America. The country itself was becoming a kind of monument to her husband's martyrdom.

After Bobby Kennedy's assassination, Jackie felt that her life was "now shadowed by death," as she confided in her aunt Maude, one of her twin Bouvier aunts:

> I can't escape it. Whether I'm helping with the Kennedy Memorial at Harvard, or taking a plane from Kennedy airport, or seeing a Kennedy in-law, I always think of Jack and what they did to him.

*

HAVING MADE UP her mind to wed Onassis, whom she affectionately called "Telis," Jackie sought approval from Janet and her mother-in-law, Rose Kennedy, whom she called "Belle-Mère." One afternoon in June, she brought Onassis to meet her mother at Hammersmith Farm in Newport, Rhode Island. With him were his gracious and stylish sister, Artemis—known for her warmth and wit—and Onassis's daughter, Christina. Ari was there on a charm offensive, to help win Janet's blessing.

But Janet had already met Onassis, and she most definitely did not approve. There were all the usual reasons—including social snobbery aimed at the self-made, Turkish-born shipping magnate—but more important, four years earlier Janet had angrily confronted him in his Claridge's hotel suite in London in search of Lee. Unruffled, Onassis had informed Janet that Lee had just left his rooms.

Rose Kennedy, whom Jackie visited in Hyannis, was more amenable toward the Golden Greek. Their paths had casually crossed during Rose's trips to Europe. She and Joe Kennedy would sometimes run across him in restaurants, and she described their relationship as a "friendly acquaintance." Rose admired self-made men of immigrant origins—she married one—and she appreciated Onassis's commanding masculine presence. (Joe Kennedy, severely incapacitated by a stroke in 1961, was not able to offer an opinion. Did he even know that Onassis had had a fling with the actress Gloria Swanson, a longtime mistress of the Kennedy patriarch?)

Rose Kennedy, who preferred to stay in the dark about such matters, later recalled Onassis's visit in her memoir, *Times to Remember,* describing him as "quietly companionable, easy to talk with, intelligent, with a sense of humor and a fund of good anecdotes to tell. I liked him. He was pleasant, interesting, and to use a word of Greek origin, charismatic."

Jackie must have found that heartening, and even surprising. "She of all people was the one who encouraged me, who said, 'he's a good man,' and 'don't worry, dear,'" Jackie later recalled. "She's been extraordinarily generous. I was married to her son and I have his children, but she was the one who was saying, 'if this is what you think is best, go ahead.'"

By some accounts, it was Onassis who wasn't sure about the marriage, not Jackie, although he showered Caroline and John Jr. with gifts and attention. But he continued his affair with Maria Callas and gave little sign of ending that relationship. Maria believed that she and "Aristo" were still a couple.

*

WITH BOBBY GONE, younger brother Edward "Ted" Kennedy became the acting head of the Kennedy clan, and he stepped in to negotiate a prenuptial agreement with the Greek tycoon. They met on Skorpios and over two days began to sketch out an agreement, while Jackie discreetly stayed away. Ted Kennedy pointed out how much the Kennedy family, and America itself, were shocked by the impending union, and he asked for an up-front settlement of $20 million for Jackie. He pointed out that she would be giving up her $175,000 per year from the Kennedy trust, as well as her presidential widow's pension of $10,000 per year from the government, by remarrying.

Ted and Jackie had turned to André Meyer, chairman of Lazard Frères investment banking firm in New York and Jackie's financial adviser, to work out the details of the agreement. Meyer was very much opposed to the marriage, and, perhaps in a last-ditch attempt to scuttle it, he had devised the idea of a generous up-front settlement.

Furious over the demand, Onassis flew to New York on September 25, 1968, and met with Meyer at the investment banker's sumptuous apartment in the Carlyle Hotel. Onassis insisted that he wasn't *buying* a wife, but Meyer was adamant, and like two heads of state, they thrashed out an agreement.

In exchange for Jackie waiving her right under Greek law to inherit 12.5 percent of his estate upon his death, Onassis guaranteed $3 million for her and $1 million for each of her children. He also agreed to pay all of her expenses while their marriage lasted, and that after his death, she would receive $150,000 per year.

It wasn't an overly generous settlement for someone of Onassis's wealth, and in fact it was Ari, not Jackie, who was beginning to wonder what he'd gotten himself into. Was he spooked by the complications of working out the prenuptial agreement? Perhaps, as some have speculated, he was still in love with his first wife, Tina Livanos, mother of his two children, Alexander and Christina, and now married to his archrival, Stavros Niarchos. And he was still in thrall to his mistress Maria Callas, the affair that had ended his marriage to Tina.

According to Nicholas Gage's interview with Callas's butler, Ferruccio Mezzadri, Onassis called Maria two days before his wedding to Jackie, asking her to come to Athens to save him.

"How, Aristo?" she answered.

"If you come to Athens, Mrs. Kennedy will get angry and go back to America."

"You got yourself into this," Callas said imperiously. "You get yourself out of it." And she slammed down the phone.

Or, as Lee's friend Reinaldo Herrera wondered, did Onassis suddenly realize that "he would have been far happier with Lee"?

In any case, Onassis realized it was too late—there was no way he could get out of the marriage, especially after the *Boston Herald Traveler* reported on October 17, 1968, that the wedding "will take place before Christmas." (A close friend of Maria Callas, a Dallas socialite named Mary Reed Carter, believed that Ted Kennedy leaked the news to the *Boston Herald Traveler* in order to force Onassis to go through with the nuptials.) Ari confided to the chairman of Olympic Airlines, Ioannis Georgakis, "If I try to get out of the marriage now, it will cause a terrible scandal. I can't do that to Jackie. She's a mother with two young children."

Some believe that Jackie had not told Lee about her impending marriage. "Can you imagine not even getting a phone call, having to hear about it, reading about it in the newspapers?" Lee's friend Ralph Rucci marveled years later. But Truman Capote described Lee calling him and weeping bitterly over the telephone before the news was publicly announced. "I can't tell you what she said," Truman told friends, "but it's going to be in the news. It's the biggest piece of gossip there is, and she's crying her eyes out because of it. She's crying and weeping and sobbing. I can't tell you what she said."

The screenwriter Eleanor Perry, who was collaborating with Truman on adapting some of his short stories for television, was visiting him at his 870 United Nations Plaza apartment when Lee called. Truman had excused himself, taking the call in another room, but Perry claimed that she could hear Lee over the phone, hysterically saying, "How could she do this to me? How could this happen?"

Truman had an answer to that. His biographer noted:

> Truman looked upon those special few—the stylish rich—the way the Greeks looked upon their gods, with mingled awe and envy. He believed that money not only enlarged their lives; it also excused them from the ordinary rules of behavior—or, indeed, any rules at all.

Whether or not she knew about the upcoming wedding before the rest of the world, Lee was devastated. She put a brave face on it, however, saying publicly, "I am very happy to have been at the origin of this marriage, which will, I am certain, bring my sister the happiness she deserves." But it was a staggering blow. For Lee, a marriage to Onassis could have been equivalent to Jackie's marriage to President Kennedy—and Lee had been genuinely smitten with the Golden Greek. This was a blow from which their relationship would never completely recover, and what made it more painful was that it was Lee, of course, who had brought Jackie and Ari together.

After the news broke in the *Boston Herald Traveler,* the world seemed to go crazy. Nancy Tuckerman hastily made a public announcement of the forthcoming wedding, fending off journalists who clamored for more information. "I didn't even know until a half hour ago," she pleaded. In fact, when Nancy learned of Jackie's plans, she was taken aback. But Jackie had clearly made up her mind, and she told her friend, "Tucky, you don't know how lonely I have been."

Nor could she relieve her loneliness by haunting the streets of New York. She was hounded by gawkers wherever she went, whether to Schrafft's (around the corner from her apartment) or Bonwit Teller. She was becoming a prisoner of her Fifth Avenue apartment. If Lee had felt liberated by the end of the Kennedy reign, Jackie felt hemmed in by her sanctified widowhood and her indelible fame.

*

ONASSIS HAD BEEN there for her during three of the most devastating losses she'd endured: the death of Patrick and the staggering losses of Jack and Bobby. And Jackie did not want Caroline and John Jr. to grow up without a father figure in their lives, so it mattered that Onassis was affectionate with both children. Caroline was gifted with a twenty-foot sailboat bearing the name *Caroline*; eight-year-old John Jr. was given a red speedboat, also bearing his name. Onassis also brought in Shetland ponies for their entertainment, and flew in Coney Island hot dogs to please them. He even flew John Jr.'s pet rabbit from New York to Greece on an Olympic Airlines flight.

Onassis often took John Jr. on his knee aboard the *Christina* and regaled him with tales of Greek heroes. With Telis, Jackie would be starting her life anew, on beautiful, secluded Skorpios, which bore no remembrance of the Kennedys and her former life.

Nancy Tuckerman issued a wedding announcement that sounded like an engraved invitation: "Mrs. Hugh D. Auchincloss has asked me to tell you that her daughter, Mrs. John F. Kennedy, is planning to marry Aristotle Onassis sometime next week. No place or date has been set for the moment."

In Athens, Onassis was besieged by reporters in the lounge of the Hotel Grande Bretagne, where he was having a drink with friends. "Yes, it's true. I'm marrying her tomorrow—or in three days," he said, and he quickly left by a back entrance.

Everyone in café society had an opinion. The celebrated Welsh actor Richard Burton, whose own marriage to Elizabeth Taylor four years earlier had been an international *scandale*, wrote in his journal on Tuesday, October 22, 1968:

The Onassis Kennedy thing still fills the papers. It's odd that you have to search for the news of the three Yanks in orbit in the Apollo. The Vatican says that Mrs. Onassis has sinned against her Church, as expected as ever. We sent Onassis a telegram of congratulations yesterday.

Many in America did, indeed, feel betrayed. Edmund Wilson, writing in his journal of the 1960s, described several meetings with Arthur Schlesinger for lunch at the Princeton Club grill. On one such occasion, he wrote:

> Lunch with Arthur Schlesinger. When I talk to him about the Kennedy-Onassis marriage, he said that he was at first incredulous, then horrified. I said that she had evidently always had a café society side. He said that somebody . . . had told him that before she married Jack, she had cared about nothing but international society, and that Jack had got her away from this. But until she married Onassis, Arthur had never realized how important this element in her nature was . . . This event had profoundly shaken his faith in his ability to judge character.

Wilson further wrote that he, too, "enjoyed swinging" and that he had once encountered Onassis at El Morocco, the fashionable New York nightclub, where the Greek tycoon was surrounded by a "retinue of yes men," and had "held forth to Arthur with his fascist views." Arthur had suddenly said to himself, "What am I doing in El Morocco listening to this fascist?"

On October 17, 1968, the Olympic Airlines evening flight from New York to Athens was scratched, stranding ninety-three passengers, so that the flight could leave earlier with just eleven passengers on board: Jackie Kennedy, Caroline and John Jr., Janet and Hugh Auchincloss, Jackie's sisters-in-law Jean Kennedy Smith and Pat Lawford, the children's nanny, and three Secret Service agents. Lee was not on board.

When she arrived in Athens, Jackie was warmly greeted by Artemis, Ari's sister, who had already forged a friendly bond with the former First Lady. Artemis had first met Jackie in October of 1963 aboard the *Christina*, after the death of Patrick. Devoted to her brother, she had "a more patient and nuanced understanding of human nature than [Ari] did. She was extraordinarily humorous and hospitable," according to a friend of the Onassis family. Artemis was glad when Ari decided to marry Jackie, never having approved of his alliance with Maria Callas, and she urged her recalcitrant niece, Christina Onassis, to be more welcoming to her new stepmother. Jackie never forgot her kindness.

On Sunday, October 20, 1968, Jackie and Ari were married in a Greek Orthodox wedding on Skorpios, among the cypresses, bougainvillea, and trailing jasmine surrounding the tiny, private Chapel of Panayitsa (Chapel of the Little Virgin). It rained all day, considered good luck in Greece, though Onassis's son and daughter, Alexander and Christina, glowered throughout the ceremony, and Janet Auchincloss reportedly whispered into Jackie's ear even as she walked down the aisle with her stepfather, "You don't have to go through with this." But Jackie seemed radiantly happy, in a short beige lace dress by Valentino, with streaming ribbons in her hair. (The dress became Valentino's most popular couture in its history.)

The Greek Orthodox ceremony was officiated over by a tall, bearded metropolitan, and Artemis served as the *"koumbara,"* whose function was to ceremoniously change the crown of white flowers three times on the bride and groom. Among the twenty-one guests were John Jr. and Caroline—looking a little shell-shocked at the seemingly sudden turn of events—who followed

Jackie with long tapered candles. Alexander, who disliked Jackie from the moment he guessed she would be taking his mother's place, said bitterly, "It's a perfect match. My father loves names, and Jackie loves money."

Although the couple had issued a request for privacy during their wedding, thirty journalists descended on the island, only to be turned back by Onassis's staff and members of the Greek navy.

After the ceremony, the wedding reception was held aboard the *Christina*, with pink champagne and dancing. Janet, realizing that any further objection would be futile, finally toasted the marriage: "I know my daughter is going to find peace and happiness with you," she said to Onassis.

*

THE WORLD WAS not happy with Jackie and Onassis's marriage. Headlines such as "Jackie, How Could You?" and "America Has Lost a Saint"—even the cruel "Jack Kennedy Dies Today a Second Time"—lamented her marriage. Jackie did receive good wishes from friends and admirers, however, such as a telegram that arrived from Paris that read:

> *All the happiness in the world, magnificent Jacqueline. STOP. Wish my name were Aristotle Onassis instead of Maurice Chevalier.*

She received a warm note from Lady Bird Johnson, and Boston's Richard Cardinal Cushing, who had been the Kennedys' spiritual adviser, said publicly, "My advice to people is to stop criticizing the poor woman. She has had an enormous amount of sadness in her life and deserves what happiness she can find . . ."—a sentiment Jackie treasured. Jackie and Lee's eccentric cousin "Little Edie" Beale wrote from her home in East Hampton, telling Jackie that they should ignore people's disapproval of their marriage.

...

Theirs was not a typical honeymoon. Jackie remained behind on Skorpios, having sent Caroline and John Jr. back to New York, while Onassis returned to Athens to meet with Colonel George Papadopoulos, head of the military junta that had recently taken over the Greek government in a shocking coup. Onassis was trying to launch an ambitious $400 million deal to create an oil refinery, power station, air terminal, and shipyard that would allow him to keep his fleet of oil tankers afloat year-round, dominating the oil industry in the Mediterranean. While he was courting Jackie, he was spending as much time, if not more, wooing the colonels of the junta in order to launch his dream, which he called "Project Omega." As Nicholas Gage noted:

> Many observers, journalists, and Greek patriots would criticize Onassis for getting into bed with the despised colonels at the same time he was getting into bed with America's sainted first lady.

Indeed, some thought that was part of his motivation for the marriage: to use Jackie's glamour to appeal to the colonels. He had her entertaining Colonel Papadopoulos over a luxurious dinner at Glyfada, his lavish family compound in a suburb of Athens, and the sight of Jackie in a diamond necklace and black dress did indeed dazzle the colonel. "It was obvious that he saw that marriage as a good career move," remarked one American steel executive.

For Jackie's part, she said that she was pleased to help her husband, but one wonders how the widow of the leader of Western democracy could so cozily dine with the leader of a hostile military takeover.

As for Lee, she arrived in time to be part of the wedding party, and she kept her counsel about her hurt feelings and her sense of betrayal, especially after the Kennedy brothers had warned

Lee against becoming involved with the Greek tycoon. But Lee managed, once again, to make peace with it, publicly defending her sister's marriage in the face of America's disillusionment. She wrote in *Cosmopolitan* in September of that year:

> If my sister's new husband had been blond, young, rich, and Anglo-Saxon, most Americans would have been much happier . . . He's an outstanding man . . . active, great vitality, very brilliant . . . a fascinating way with women. He surrounds them with attention. He makes sure that they feel admired and desired . . . My sister needs a man . . . who can protect her from the curiosity of the world. She's tired of having to exercise such enormous control over herself, not to be able to move without all her gestures being judged and all her steps being traced . . . Onassis is rich enough to offer her a good life and powerful enough to protect her privacy.

Years later, when questioned about their suitability, Lee's eloquent answer was, "The map of love is uncharted. You don't need an intellectual passion to sustain a relationship, to be happy. There are many kinds of love." But in the weeks and months after Jackie's marriage to Onassis, Lee became convinced that Ari had only pursued her as a way to get to her sister. He had given Lee a promontory in Athens as a kind of farewell gift, another prize that seemed petty and insignificant compared to the riches Jackie was heir to. Yet Lee visited Skorpios, spending part of the summer with her sister and Ari, and acting as graciously as possible.

A few weeks following the wedding, Jackie and Ari visited Lee and Stas at Turville Grange, spending a weekend there with Lee's other guests, Nureyev and Margot Fonteyn. But the strain of putting on an approving public face occasionally showed itself, as when another guest criticized Jackie over some social trifle, and Lee commented, "It is about time somebody spoke to Jackie like that . . ."

Lee returned to her amicable but sexless marriage to Stas, but four months after the wedding, in February of 1969, Lee entered a clinic in Lausanne, Switzerland, suffering from insomnia and possibly anorexia. (She had often disliked being described as "fashionably thin" because even when she had wanted to gain weight, she couldn't.) Now she was nearly gaunt, but mostly she needed a place to rest—and perhaps to hide.

*

IN THE EARLY weeks and months of her marriage, Jackie seemed supremely happy, despite frequent trips to Manhattan with her children, as they were still attending school in the States. In photographs, she and Onassis appear intimate and playful. Onassis sometimes snatched Jackie's cigarettes out of her hand to discourage her from smoking too much. On her fortieth birthday, celebrated on Skorpios, Onassis gifted her with a pair of jewel-encrusted, twenty-two-karat gold earrings he'd designed himself, in honor of the July 20, 1969, Apollo 11 moon landing, which took place eight days before her birthday. The earrings were ostentatious—not her style—and she only wore them once, but she was touched by the gesture, especially because it had been President Kennedy, after all, who had pledged to put a man on the moon. "Next year," Ari had promised her, "if you're good, I'll give you the moon itself."

Onassis lavished gifts on Jackie, and she thanked him by putting together an album of photographs she took of Ari on Skorpios, posing as Odysseus alongside English translations of Homer's *Odyssey*. She doted on her husband, buying him colorful neckties to brighten up his dark suits, and getting Pierre Cardin to design new uniforms for Olympic Airlines stewardesses. (She later advised them to ditch the new sleeveless uniforms, having belatedly realized that Greek women didn't shave under their arms.)

When a visiting friend asked her why she had married Ari, she answered, "For the privacy." But it was far more than that. As one journalist close to Jackie wrote:

> She has always been drawn to men of power, of strength, who took the deepest risks and expected to win . . . He has built the buffer zone, cushioning her from a curious world unable to ever stop watching that famous widow. Perhaps, too, he makes her laugh . . . and he has stories to tell she has not ever heard. Perhaps he is a man she can lean on when she feels like it, but who lets her breathe and be alone when she needs that.

And then, of course, Jackie and Lee had been in love with Greece and its ancient culture since their idyllic vacation there in 1961. Jackie was a student of Greek tragedy, once disagreeing with Arthur Schlesinger's description of Jack Kennedy as a classical Roman, suggesting instead that her husband had been more like the ancient Greeks, in that the Greeks fought with their gods, and with fate. "Greeks have esteem and respect for the gods," she once wrote, "yet the Greek was the first to write and proclaim that Man was the measure of all things. This conflict with the gods is the essence of the Greek tragedy . . ." Even earlier, when Jack Kennedy first confided his intention to run for the presidency, Jackie's response was to write him a poem comparing him to the Greek hero Jason, writing: ". . . he would find love / he would never find peace / for he must go seeking / the Golden Fleece."

Jackie had in common with the Greek people a belief in the crucial role that fate plays in human lives. She had already had her own reckoning with fate, but she didn't know when she married Onassis that she would continue to live in what increasingly felt like a Greek tragedy. But now, she bloomed in the hot climate of the islands. She especially loved being on Skorpios, an island shaped like a scorpion and ablaze with flowers and light.

The main house on the island was a neoclassical stucco building known as the Pink Villa; it was beautiful and comfortable, tended to by a cheerful staff. With their help, Jackie served great casual meals ("lush—nonstop Dom Perignon and O.J.," as one guest described it). She put together fabulous picnics. There were guest cottages as well, and Onassis had spent a fortune turning the rocky island into paradise. He put in orchards and planted bougainvillea, jasmine, and oleander. As a tribute to the memory of his grandmother, he planted the trees of the Old Testament, which flourished in Greece—olive, fig, almond, cypress, pine. He built a harbor where he could dock the *Christina* and installed a livestock enclosure, reminiscent of Hammersmith Farm, where he housed the Shetland ponies (he had classical music piped in, to keep the livestock calm). With her children, Jackie swam, sunbathed, and water-skied, and whenever she had time for it, she painted watercolors and made beautiful, outsize scrapbooks. In the evenings, she practiced yoga and meditated on the beach, while the small island owls—sacred to Athena—swooped in gold crepuscular light.

Jackie learned Greek and embraced Greek culture, learning to dance the traditional *surtaki* and, on one occasion, dressing in the native dress of Corfu. She learned how to make dolmades; she made arrangements from the orchids, tulips, and roses that grew on the island. In Athens, she scoured antique shops for books on Greek art and antiquities. She attended classical performances at the fourth-century-BC amphitheater Epidavros, accompanied by Alexis Miotis, the director of the Greek National Theater. She attended Mass at the Church of St. Francis on Corfu.

And all around her was the sea. Her friend the archaeologist and curator Karl Katz described Skorpios and its surrounding waters as

an absolutely fantastic place. The warm water was a color that is often mentioned in Greek mythology as wine colored, a deep

purple that wasn't blue, the clearest, most beautiful water . . .
The sun was everywhere, the setting sun, the rising sun, shining
on the other islands in the distance . . .

Surrounded by sea and bathed in sunlight, this was the closest Jackie would come to re-creating the ambience of Lasata. She
once described the Greeks as mystics, writing, "This mysticism
can be traced to the influence of the sea—the boundlessness and
mystery of the sea respond to the yearning of the Greeks for a su-
pernatural rapport with divinity."

There's a sweet story told about Jackie visiting a flea market
at the foot of the Acropolis on Athens's Pandrossou Street. There,
she met a sandal maker named Stavros Melissinos, who was also a
poet. His sandals were fashioned after those depicted on the gods
and goddesses of ancient statuary. Admiring his wares, she engaged him in a conversation about Pandrossou Street, which was
marked for destruction to make room for an archaeological dig.
The Greek government had already posted notices that the street
and market would soon be torn down.

"It would be a pity," the sandal maker told her, "if this street,
which has its own character, were destroyed." Two days later, the
Ministry of Public Works called Melissinos to say that plans had
changed to tear down the street and market. Jackie had inter-
vened, just as she would years later in Manhattan, spearheading
the preservationist movement to protect the city's great land-
marks, such as Grand Central Terminal and Columbus Circle.

The Greek people seemed to love her, asking her to pose with
them for photographs, greeting her with smiles and good wishes.
In countless photographs, she looks radiant: behind oversized sunglasses, seated next to Onassis aboard the *Christina*; beaming at
the camera in a Greek skirt and jewel-green shawl at an outdoor
tavern as her new husband reads a newspaper; dazzling in sandals

and a short cotton dress festooned with stars and quarter-moons—
her hair in pigtails!—smiling at a somberly dressed Onassis.

Rose Kennedy continued to be supportive of Jackie's marriage,
and she visited her in Greece three times, whereas the Auchinclosses only visited once. "It seems to be a good marriage," she
later commented. Even Christina, Onassis's unhappy, somewhat
spoiled and overly cosseted daughter, at first warmed to Jackie, as
Jackie sought to bolster the young woman's self-confidence. "Maria Callas never liked me very much," Christina confessed, "but
Jackie is my stepmother and great friend." Alexander, however,
never accepted his stepmother and continued to look upon her as
an interloper and a gold digger.

In 1972, to celebrate their fourth wedding anniversary, Jackie
threw a party in the Champagne Room of Manhattan's famous El
Morocco. One of their sixty-two guests was the highly respected
journalist Gloria Emerson, one of the few women who had covered the war in Vietnam (she would win a National Book Award
in 1978 for *Winners and Losers*, her book about the war's casual-
ties). Emerson was born into the same debutante class as Jackie
and Lee. Through her acquaintance with Jack Kennedy, she and
Jackie had become friends, and the journalist wrote about the former First Lady for *McCall's* in 1974.

By then Emerson had traded in her society-page reportage for
wartime journalism, but she covered the anniversary party, noting that Jackie "wore a black top, a long white skirt and a heavy
gold belt that looked Moroccan. I thought she had the tiniest rib
cage of any grown-up woman I had ever seen." The eight round
tables were draped in a pale pink linen, with centerpieces of
pink-and-white carnations and tiny pink rosebuds. The Pol Roger
1964 champagne was "very cold and good," served along with a
1967 Saint-Émilion wine. She also noted that Lee Radziwill was
present, wearing orange and being amused by the director and

man-about-town Mike Nichols. And she noticed that when a toast was made to the bride and groom, Lee—ever so slightly—grimaced.

Emerson was delighted to see her old friend looking so well. "She was still herself," she wrote,

> after all the years that had passed . . . she still wants fresh flowers and the pink tables. Not many women I have known have driven back upon themselves as she had. It is a long and hard journey none of us need envy. She is a survivor, someone who has shown that the world couldn't finish her off . . .

*

LEE AND STAS and their children continued to visit Jackie on Skorpios. As far as Lee was concerned, things changed for the better when Jackie invited a new friend to visit: the dashing photographer, diarist, adventurer, and wildlife advocate Peter Beard, who was Kennedyesque in his boyish good looks and his vast appeal to women. The Yale-educated man-about-town was described by one wag as "half-Tarzan and half-Byron," and Jackie and Lee both delighted in his company. It's quite possible that Jackie had invited Peter to Skorpios to spend time with Lee, as a kind of consolation prize now that Jackie had married Lee's former lover.

As a youth, Beard had been inspired by Isak Dinesen's *Out of Africa*. After graduating from Yale, he'd moved to Kenya and worked at the Tsavo National Park, where he documented and photographed endangered wildlife, including the African elephant, and published his work in several books, beginning with *The End of the Game* in 1965. He bought a property in East Africa called Hog Ranch, seventeen miles from Nairobi and not far from Baroness Karen Blixen's (Dinesen's) coffee farm. He divided his time between his camp in Africa and New York City, supporting himself as a freelance fashion photographer (he was later briefly married to one of the models he photographed, 1980s "California Girl" Cheryl Tiegs). An earlier marriage to Minnie Cushing, one of the famous, socially prominent Cushing sisters, lasted only a year. Though born to a prominent family—his great-grandfather James Jerome Hill was a founder of the Great Northern Railway—all that came to him from a once glorious railroad fortune were a few small trust funds that he had to supplement with photography, documentary filmmaking, and book publishing. Thus he was not rich enough for Lee, but she was drawn to his vibrancy and creativity—and to his sun-kissed male beauty. Years later she would write in her second coffee-table book, "Peter Beard changed my whole life. He opened so many windows for me, because he taught me to be insatiably curious."

Jackie had invited Peter to visit her in Skorpios in part to entertain and photograph Caroline and John Jr. A talented artist and collagist, he involved Jackie's children in his creativity, when they weren't swimming and water-skiing. Besides working on a book titled *Longing for Darkness*, which retold the tales from Dinesen's *Out of Africa* as related by Dinesen's cook, Kamante Gatura, Peter was always working on his extensive journals. He carried a volume with him wherever he went, and continually added to it, collage-like, pasting in photographs, newspaper clippings, drawings, notes to himself, various musings. It was botanical (including insects and dried flora) and personal and a record of his travels. It also contained "pages and pages of Jackie, Caroline, John-John, and Bobby . . . Hanging out with the Kennedy women was almost a fixation with him," writes Diana DuBois, who published an unauthorized biography of Lee in 1995.

If Lee continued to nurse any hurt feelings about Jackie's marriage to Onassis, by the end of that summer on Skorpios, the sisters seemed to have made a cold peace, made easier when Peter and Lee became lovers.

Peter was five years younger than Lee, so she had broken the pattern of falling for men who were versions of her father. For the first time Lee had not been drawn to a mate who could provide her with financial security or high social status; this was fascination, lust, discovery—even love. They began a secret affair on Skorpios, which they had to hide because Lee was still married to Stas. She would sneak into Peter's bedroom at night, in the Pink Villa, leaving her husband and children asleep in nearby rooms. What made it more difficult for Lee was that Stas and Peter became friends; a few months later Stas would go on safaris in Kenya led by Beard. But at least on Skorpios, Stas seems to have suspected nothing.

At summer's end, Peter went back to Kenya, and Lee accompanied Stas and their children to Warsaw to attend the funeral for Edmund, Stas's brother, who had died that August.

Lee was sorry to see the summer end.

*

THE EARLY MONTHS of Jackie's marriage seemed blissful, but there was trouble in paradise. Onassis began to resent the amount of time Jackie spent in Manhattan, as she was virtually commuting from Skorpios. It was easy enough when your husband owned an airline, but the truth was that she felt an obligation to the memory of her late husband to raise their children as Americans, and she wanted to keep them in their Manhattan schools. "To my sister," Lee said once, "America was New York."

He endured her long and frequent absences and, when they were together, her preference for staying in and reading instead of going to nightclubs. Leo Lerman, the legendary Condé Nast editor and a close friend of Maria Callas, noted in his diary for January 6, 1969:

[She] will not sit in El Morocco with him and his three or four cigar-smoking Greek chums with their lavish, blondine females while the Greek men talk business. Mrs. K likes "intellectuals"— Galbraith, Schlesinger—but this is not why he married her. He wants to display her; she won't be displayed. Onassis is bored with Mrs. K. They never planned a single day past their wedding day on Skorpios.

There was another irritant, as far as Onassis was concerned. Almost from the beginning, he found fault with Jackie's extravagant spending, just as Jack Kennedy had. On frequent visits to Manhattan, she reportedly spent $1.25 million on couture in the first year of their marriage. ("Jackie O continues to fill her bottomless closets," tattled *Women's Wear Daily.* "She's making Daddy O's bills bigger than ever with her latest shopping spree. She's buying in carload lots.") At one point, when Onassis received a bill from Valentino for a dress costing $9,000, he exclaimed, "What does she do with all the clothes? I never see her in anything but blue jeans." What Onassis didn't know was that Jackie embellished her $30,000-a-month allowance from him by buying couture and then, after one or two wearings, selling to consignment shops, usually Encore at 1132 Madison Avenue, three blocks from her New York apartment. (This is a time-tested method for people who are being supported by others to scare up some extra cash.) She would also auction personal possessions, such as picture frames and nursery furniture, at the William Doyle Galleries or Sotheby-Parke Bernet in Manhattan. Profits would be channeled through Nancy Tuckerman—who was placed on Onassis's payroll as Jackie's secretary—and would make their way to Jackie's bank account.

Jackie spent lavishly on redecorating the Pink Villa, flying in one of her favorite interior decorators, Billy Baldwin, to fill the villa with flowered chintz, which Onassis disliked and had removed. When Onassis discovered that Jackie had lost $300,000 of her prenuptial funds in bad investments made against his advice, he had her allowance reduced to $20,000 a month.

But an even bigger problem loomed. Soon after their marriage,

Onassis saw his luck begin to desert him. Rival ship owners had once looked upon him as the Golden Greek for his success and the fact that he'd lost only one ship in three decades. A year after marrying Jackie, four of his vessels were damaged and he suffered big losses. The good luck that had rained down upon him during their wedding on Skorpios seemed to disappear. His long-cultivated Project Omega, forged with the colonels who had taken over the Greek government, collapsed, in part due to the interference of his rival, Stavros Niarchos. He was threatened with financial ruin, and his once Midas touch was beginning to desert him. Even the military junta felt he was becoming bad luck.

On July 22, 1970, one of his Olympic Airline flights was hijacked by four Palestinians. Onassis boldly marched onto the blazing-hot tarmac to offer himself as a hostage in place of the eighty passengers and crew, but the hijackers turned him down. He had to persuade the Greek government to meet the hijackers' demands.

If Jackie was feeling happy, safe, and cosseted in her marriage to Onassis, a spooked and superstitious Onassis was calling Maria Callas.

Onassis flew to Paris and showed up at 36 Avenue Georges Mandel, home of his spurned lover, by some accounts as early as one week after the wedding. (Lerman once described Callas's apartment as luxurious, but full of "the emptiness of waiting.")

One of the opera star's servants, Ferruccio Mezzadri, recalled:

A week after the marriage, he was outside the door . . . shouting, whistling for Madame to let him in. He called from the corner and I spoke to him myself . . .

In a corroborating account by one of Callas's American friends, Mary Reed Carter, Onassis came to the apartment and started whistling a sailor's whistle to call her out, but she refused to see him. Then he called from a nearby bistro and begged to be allowed in. She still refused to see him in her apartment, but after Ari's multiple entreaties on multiple trips to Paris, she agreed to have dinner with him at Maxim's.

After that, as Mezzadri recalled,

> ... he was in Paris all the time, every four or five days. He would tell her how miserable he was, everything he was doing. He shared everything with her. Even when Mrs. Kennedy [sic] was in Paris, he would go to dinner with his wife, but would come first to Madame, to have a drink and talk.

Over dinner at Maxim's, Onassis reportedly confessed that he missed her terribly and that she was the only woman he'd ever loved. Callas laughed at that, and though she relished his confession, she still refused to sleep with him or to believe that he would ever divorce Jackie.

But Onassis would not be easily deterred. A month after his wedding, according to Lerman, Onassis slipped into her bedroom and undressed, but the diva ran to the window, flinging it open to shriek into the empty Parisian streets, "Shame on you! And on the anniversary of your second wife's first husband's death!" It was November 22, 1968, five years after Kennedy's assassination.

Callas was still angry at what she saw as Ari's betrayal, but their bond was deep and passionate. As Mezzadri observed, she "filled his life like no one else ... Madame adored him, that's for sure, and he too was strongly bound to her."

Onassis continued to woo Callas behind Jackie's back. On four successive nights, Ari dined with her at Maxim's, followed by intimate hours spent at Callas's apartment. She refused to sleep with him as long as he was married to Jackie, but she could no longer deny him her emotional support.

When Jackie got wind of Onassis's renewed courtship of Callas, she was, understandably, incensed. She considered divorcing him. Jackie had put up with Jack Kennedy's countless flings, and she was used to the idea that men of wealth and power could—and would—have mistresses on the side, but this time she did not want that kind of marriage. She flew to Paris, where she and Ari were photographed in an intimate dinner—at Maxim's.

When Maria Callas saw photographs in *Le Monde* of Ari dining with Jackie at "their" table, in "their" restaurant, she became despondent. If Onassis had promised that he would divorce Jackie, here was proof that the marriage was still intact, and that Ari had lied to her yet again. Four days later, Callas was rushed to the hospital, and Radio Luxembourg announced that she had attempted suicide by overdosing on barbiturates. (Callas denied the report, claiming that she had only taken sleeping pills to calm her mind, and in fact she successfully sued Radio Luxembourg and a tabloid that picked up the story, winning 20,000 francs in damages.)

Against her better judgment, Callas still hoped that Ari would divorce his famous wife and return to her. Ironically, as Lerman would note in a February 1971 diary entry, the Greek public looked upon Jackie as "the other woman" and considered Callas "a wronged woman, splendid in her dignity . . . All of which is an indication of the morality of these times: The mistress is the wronged one, and the loyal wife the villainess."

9

THIS SIDE OF PARADISE:
RETURN TO NEW YORK

I felt this terrible claustrophobia . . . these trees
closing in on me. I longed for the sea.

—LEE

If you are a good mother it does not matter
much what else you have done.

—JACKIE

Back in London with Stas, Lee missed Peter Beard terribly and wrote him passionate letters. They would meet again in February of 1972, when Lee decided to accompany Stas on a safari in Kenya, something she normally would not have done. She arrived a week ahead of Stas, traveling with a friend, Alan Jay Lerner's fifth wife, Karen Lerner, who acted as a beard, giving Lee an opportunity to spend time with her lover.

Despite its humble name, Hog Farm attracted many aristocrats and luminaries. Stas arrived with Baron Ashcombe, with whom he had been on many shoots, and they embarked on the safari with Lee trailing behind. Lee, however, managed to sneak back to camp for an assignation with Peter. She resolved to end her marriage to Stas, yet the deception continued for several more weeks. After the Kenyan safari, Peter stayed with the Radziwills at their London house for several days, and then joined them at a villa in Barbados, lent to them by Baron Ashcombe. Soon Jackie and her two children arrived. If Stas knew that Lee and Peter were in love, he did not let on, nor did he make a scene. Instead, he flew to London after their Barbados idyll, while Lee and her children accompanied Jackie and her children to New York, on a private plane owned by Onassis.

And that was how Lee's thirteen-year marriage ended.

Lee had had enough, not just of her passionless marriage to Stas—whom she still admired and loved in her way—but of her life in London and at Turville Grange. She was lonely. She was homesick. She no longer wanted to live as an expat. She wanted to spend more time with her sister in Manhattan, and in the Hamptons by the ocean that had always nourished her spirit. And she wanted to be with Peter Beard. She was thirty-nine years old, she had recently undergone a hysterectomy, and she felt strongly that it was time for a major change in her life.

Perhaps Stas was not surprised when Lee left, but it broke his heart.

*

BACK IN MANHATTAN, Lee continued her love affair with Peter Beard. One night, he invited Lee and Jackie to dine with him in Chinatown, where he introduced the sisters to Andy Warhol, notorious for his entourage of drag queens and dwellers in Manhattan's drug-infused demimonde. While Peter took endless Polaroid shots throughout the dinner, Lee no doubt relished being in the company of the avant-garde artist, whose unconventional appearance and lifestyle belied his serious gifts as an artist, and the profound, game-changing effect his art and ideas would have on contemporary arts and culture. Lee was usually more open to new ideas, especially in realms of art and design, than Jackie, who was at heart a traditionalist. Lee had a more adventurous spirit.

In early spring of 1972, Lee and Peter joined Warhol and his friend the avant-garde filmmaker Paul Morrissey on a drive out to the fishing village of Montauk at the farthest tip of Long Island's south shore. Warhol and Morrissey had bought a sprawling compound with stunning views of the ocean, comprising a rustic central lodge surrounded by four whitewashed cottages. Originally a fishing camp built by an Idaho family for summer vacations, it was bought mostly as an investment property, but its seclusion on twenty acres made it especially attractive to the celebrities Warhol had planned to rent to during the summer months. ("Andy just bought it and never spent a night there," Lee later recalled.) It was a bohemian version of the Kennedy compound in Hyannis, and Lee immediately rented the lodge house, inviting Peter to move in with her. He did.

It ushered in a glorious summer for Lee, and for her sister as well. When she was in New York, Jackie would drive out for long visits with Caroline and John Jr., who delighted in the company of their cousins. Warhol seldom came out to the compound because he was at heart a city boy who hated the sun and the sea ("It seemed to us he was allergic to air," Lee later wrote). However, from boyhood he had been a fan of movie stars and celebrities, and he appreciated the value of having the famous sisters as his tenants and guests. He joked about putting up gold plaques that would read, "Lee slept here," and "Jackie slept here," and even framing the toilet seats used by the most famous sisters in the world.

Lee later described staying at Andy's Montauk lodge as "really roughing it, but it was by the sea, and I adored that." Indeed, Lee seemed younger, freer, and more alive than she had been in a long time. She loved the lodge house, redolent of pine and cedar and fresh sea air, with its two fireplaces and stone floor. Anthony and Tina loved it, too, and spent long summer days swimming, burying each other in the sand, or taking trips in a Mercedes-Benz convertible, often to the landmark lighthouse on Montauk Point at the tip of the island.

. . .

Peter was the catalyst that brought the two sisters back together after Jackie's divisive marriage to Onassis. He was a wonderful friend and mentor to all four children, involving them in art projects and botanical expeditions, windsurfing and swimming with them, and both Jackie and Lee appreciated their offspring's delight in his company. If Peter had been something of a peace offering from Jackie to Lee, it was now Lee who could offer Jackie and her children resplendent vacations from the city, and from the darkening clouds gathering over her life on Skorpios.

If Peter had been more malleable, he would have been something of an exciting boy toy, but in fact Peter was then and has remained a truly independent spirit, challenging Lee to open her mind to new adventures and to move further away from the proper society girl she was raised to be. That meant giving Peter the space to take off for Africa when the spirit moved him, and it also meant maintaining a rather open relationship. Peter continued to see other women while he was with Lee, and Lee tolerated it, as long as it didn't show up in the gossip columns.

They made for an interesting pair: the immaculately dressed Lee Radziwill and the disheveled Ivy League adventurer dressed in moccasins and old clothes, sometimes sleeping in his station wagon bedecked with rattlesnake skins and animal bones. One of Peter's oldest friends, Porter Bibb, commented:

> Peter always looked like he had just been sleeping in his car, but he was so damned good-looking and appealing and visceral that he was irresistible anyway. He loved the ability to drop out of the sky into Lee's life and then go back into his own life, and in that sense I saw him as being in control. Peter was desperate to be in control of every aspect of his life.

Another friend of Peter's was the Yale-educated James "Jay" Mellon, heir to the Andrew Mellon fortune and an enthusiast of African safaris. (He was also the author of a number of books, including the oral history *Bullwhip Days*, about the depredations of American slavery, and *The Face of Lincoln*, a compilation of daguerreotypes of Abraham Lincoln that Jackie would later have a hand in publishing.) He often joined Lee and Peter in Manhattan for drinks at Lee's apartment, followed by dinner on the town. Mellon felt that "Peter and Lee were obviously in love," but he noted the social dissonance between the two: "She was always pecking away at him for his slovenly behavior, and he didn't give a damn. They quarreled a bit here and there."

Lee and Jay Mellon started a flirtatious friendship that lasted over a year, but Jay came to be disillusioned with what he saw as Lee's superficiality and fascination with money and status. He felt that was true of both sisters, but with Lee,

> I had a feeling quite often that there was another person inside of her who was really quite a nice person, actually. And Peter would often say to me that if you get Lee out to the country and put some blue jeans on her, she becomes a completely different and a much nicer person. The problem with her starts after a few days when she gets the itch to go back to the city . . . [because] she isn't being seen in the right places and going to the right parties. Then this uptight quality of hers asserts itself . . . the publicity-conscious part that wants to build up her image in various ways.

Another of Jay Mellon's friends, journalist Steven M. L. Aronson, agreed that Lee was "a marvelous and genuine person if you can get her away from the strobe lights." That's what Peter offered her: a chance to step away from the pecking order of London and Manhattan society, to live a freer and more sensual life.

Truman Capote was a third wheel in Lee's relationship with Peter, and his adoring friendship was one of the currents that pulled Lee back to Manhattan, back to the fierce Darwinian struggle for recognition and triumph in the eyes of the world. Just as he had tried to launch Lee as an actress, he encouraged her in a new venture: writing a memoir. Lee wrote an article about her halcyon childhood in East Hampton for *Ladies' Home Journal*, based on the memoir she was intermittently writing, and the redoubtable woman's magazine gave her a cocktail party at the Four Seasons to celebrate the article and hopefully attract publishing interest. It was just before Christmas, and the champagne flowed, and the centerpiece of the party was a cake in the shape of a book. Norman Mailer was present, as well as Jackie's friend John Kenneth Galbraith and, of course, Lee's biggest champion, Truman Capote, who made it known that Lee "wrote it herself," referring to the thousand-word *Journal* article, adding, "I see the book going to forty thousand words. The title, 'Opening Chapters,' is good."

Soon after, Lee and her children flew to Sun Valley, Idaho, for a skiing holiday.

*

"REMIND ME TO tell you about being on tour with the Rolling Stones," Lee said one winter afternoon. In June of 1972, Lee, Peter Beard, and Truman Capote joined the Rolling Stones on their 1972 North American concert tour. Capote was to cover the tour for *Rolling Stone* magazine, with Peter supplying the photographs.

It was originally Lee's idea. She thought it would help Truman with a case of the "blahs"—a word both Lee and her sister used for a sense of dissatisfaction with life, as in "he's just going through a bad case of the blahs." By the early 1970s, Truman was very much adrift, struggling with his roman à clef, *Answered Prayers*, the book that he claimed would be his Proustian masterpiece, according to Gerald Clarke. But Truman, Clarke wrote, "seemed eager to do nearly anything rather than lock himself away and confront the problems inherent in any long and complicated novel." Unable to write, he was restless, recovering from yet another misguided love affair, though drinking less than he had been in the preceding two years.

Lee had a brainstorm. With Peter Beard and Jann Wenner, editor of *Rolling Stone* magazine, she persuaded Truman to cover the 1972 Rolling Stones tour of North America. Lee suggested that Peter accompany Truman and photograph the Stones on the road as they toured the country. It would be marvelous, Lee told Truman, and she encouraged him by suggesting that the article could eventually be expanded into a book, a variant of an earlier piece in the *New Yorker* that became the celebrated *The Muses Are Heard*, Truman's account of traveling with the Everyman Opera Company when they toured the Soviet Union performing George Gershwin's *Porgy and Bess*. Lee knew Truman's work well, and knew she could flatter him with it. It worked.

Lee did not blame Truman for the debacle of her acting career—though some thought that he had set her up for public embarrassment out of his conflicted romantic feelings toward the Principessa. She also knew that Truman vowed to tell the secrets of his "swans" in his new book, deep-dish gossip he'd heard as the world's most celebrated houseguest and intimate of society luminaries Babe Paley, Slim Keith, Gloria Vanderbilt, and Carol Matthau. Lee knew there wasn't anyone Truman wouldn't betray for a good story—even her—so perhaps she wanted to distract him with a new project, or just keep her status as his favorite swan.

Truman invited Lee to join him on the tour. "He had taken me to see several Stone concerts at Madison Square Garden," Lee recalled decades later, "so he said, 'Honey, you gotta come.' And so I said I would adore to. And so that's how it started." So she, Truman, and Peter Beard joined the Stones in late June, midway through their two-month tour of thirty-one cities.

Ironically, given the city's historical significance to the Kennedys, they joined the tour in Dallas. Lee had never been there before. Just nine years after the assassination, the Texas School Book Depository on Dealey Plaza had been turned into a museum. Truman was eager to spend time there, given his fascination with crime stories (*In Cold Blood* had cemented his reputation as one of America's greatest living writers). But Lee found herself "horrified to see that what was on display . . . were the newspapers where Dallas was conspicuously mentioned, as if it were a source of pride," writes biographer Diana DuBois.

After touring the museum, Lee spoke witheringly of former governor John Connally, who had been struck by one of Oswald's bullets but had survived, saying that the Texas governor "just screamed his head off when he was shot and never contacted the family afterward." For Lee, Dallas raked up images of the assassination and of Jackie's perilous grief.

They continued with the tour, Lee and Truman sleeping in bunk beds on the tour bus. The highlight for Lee was being backstage before each concert, which "was always wonderful, as they were tuning up and exercising and screaming and—you felt such an air of excitement." She immediately saw that Mick Jagger was "absolutely the leader, always in command, the one that stayed so straight so he could keep everybody else under his control. I can see how people found him sexy, but I found him a little repulsive," she admitted.

Clarke claimed that the Rolling Stones liked Truman and he liked the Stones, but Keith Richards recalled in his 2010 memoir, *Life*, that they often teased and terrorized the brilliant writer with the high-pitched, querulous voice. "We had some sport with Truman Capote, author of *In Cold Blood*, one of the group of Mick's society friends," he wrote, "who had attached themselves to the tour and who included Princess Lee Radziwill, Princess Radish to us, as Truman was just Truby. He was on assignment from some high-paying magazine, so he was ostensibly working."

Actually, he *was* working, but mostly working on just surviving the tour. He found the concerts deafening and was reduced to wearing earplugs to maintain his sanity. "Truman found the amplified instruments and the roar of the crowd almost unbearable," Lee recalled. That was one of the things that bothered Keith Richards, who wrote, "Truby said something bitchy and whiny backstage—he was being an old fart, actually complaining about the noise." He decided he was going to teach "this motherfucker" a lesson:

> I mean this snooty New York attitude . . . it got a little raucous. I remember back at the hotel, kicking Truman's door. I'd splattered it with ketchup I'd picked up off a trolley. "Come out you old queen. What are you doing around here? You want cold blood! You're on the road now, Truby! Come and say it out here in the corridor."

After the difficult experience in Dallas, putting up with Truman's complaints about the noise and the Stones' rabble-rousing, Lee had had enough. She was eager to return home and she expected Peter to return to New York with her. She ought to have known by now that Peter would do whatever Peter wanted to do. When he informed Lee that he wanted to continue the tour, in part to keep an eye on Truman, she was furious. At the height of their argument, Lee told Peter that she had long suspected that Truman was envious of their heterosexual relationship. After all, Peter had been the first serious romance in Lee's life since she and Truman had first met. She insisted that Truman had asked him to remain on the tour just as a way to break them up.

It was Lee and Peter's first serious argument, and she went back to New York alone.

However, on July 27, Lee did attend the tour's final, three-hour performance, held at Madison Square Garden, followed by a gala birthday party thrown for Mick Jagger by Atlantic Records founder Ahmet Ertegun on the rooftop ballroom of the St. Regis hotel. Lee reunited with Peter and Truman, who were joined by Andy Warhol and Bob Dylan. For Lee, that party was the beauty part of the whole shebang—the only time in the entire tour that she felt she was at the white-hot center of American culture. She knew it was through Peter that she was able to enter this exciting world that Jackie had only glimpsed from afar. "The demimonde was too much for my sister," Lee said.

With Truman comfortably returned to his country house in Sagaponack to begin writing the piece for *Rolling Stone*, Lee was there to act as midwife. He began by reading bits and pieces aloud to her and Peter. He took its working title, "It Will Soon Be Here," from a nineteenth-century painting of farmers in the Midwest trying to save their harvest from a threatening storm—very likely suggested by Lee, with her deep interest in nineteenth-century painting.

Despite Lee's best efforts to keep Truman focused, the deadline passed, and then another, and the article was never finished. "It may have been that he did not have the energy or power of concentration to devote himself to any significant piece of prose," as Clarke proposed, or else, as Truman told Lee and Peter, there was simply nothing really to write about. All that hysteria and energy was simply a well-oiled machine whose excitement was as exaggerated as the elongated tongue that appeared onstage as the Stones' logo. "I can't be bothered," Truman explained. "Maybe if I had been younger."

Lee had tried. Truman's alcoholism and occasional cocaine use was already alienating Lee, as was his parade of, in her words, "inappropriate boyfriends." Soon Truman would need real rescuing and would be bitterly surprised when Lee failed to help him.

*

JUST TWO YEARS after the wedding, rumors of divorce loomed over Jackie's second marriage, as bad luck continued to dog Onassis. His daughter, Christina, hastily married a man twenty-eight years her senior whom she'd met poolside at a hotel in Monte Carlo. They divorced after eight months when Onassis cut off her trust fund. Tina Onassis, Ari's ex-wife and mother of his children, secretly married Stavros Niarchos, who had been formerly married to Tina's sister, Eugenia. That marriage had ended with Eugenia's suicide (she had taken twenty-five Seconals), and Onassis believed that Niarchos had physically abused her, contributing to her death. He was incensed when his archrival had married Tina, whom he still cared deeply about.

On January 4, 1973, Onassis dined out with his son, Alexander, and discussed his plans to divorce Jackie. He planned to start proceedings using the ruthless New York lawyer Roy Cohn. Alexander was delighted to hear of his father's intentions. He had always held out hope that his parents would reunite, and he'd been just as devastated when Tina married Niarchos following his aunt Eugenia's suicide. Alexander, like his father, felt that Niarchos had had something to do with Eugenia's death, and now the young man actually feared for his mother's life. It was easy for him to blame Jackie for preventing a reunion between his parents.

Alexander, just twenty-four, had come a long way from his youthful years as a wealthy brat. He was still a shy, somewhat inarticulate young man, more comfortable working on engines or piloting planes than hobnobbing with society, but he was well liked among his father's Olympic Airlines employees, where he had been put in charge of a charter service that flew to the smaller Greek islands. His stewardship had been a success, and Alexander had further endeared himself by piloting small planes under emergency situations, rescuing people ill or stranded in remote areas. Despite the poor eyesight that prevented him from getting a commercial pilot's license, he would often fly where more experienced pilots would not go. In one instance, Alexander rescued a fisherman's son whose hands had been blown off by dynamite, and flew him to safety. When the boy's father pressed a hundred-drachma tip into Alexander's hands—worth about 30 cents—he accepted the gift, so as not to injure the fisherman's pride.

Onassis and his son had reached a rapprochement in their once contentious relationship. He was proud of his son and heir, often referring to him as his "alpha and omega." Alexander left the dinner elated that his father planned to divorce Jackie, and pleased that he'd agreed to replace an antiquated company plane, the Piaggio, that he felt was unsafe.

But on January 22, 1973, less than three weeks after that dinner in Paris and three months after Onassis's fourth wedding anniversary, Alexander was piloting the Piaggio in a test run with two other pilots on board. The plane crashed seconds after takeoff. Alexander's right temporal lobe was crushed in the accident. Covered in blood, he was rushed to a hospital in Athens.

Onassis and Jackie were in New York when they received the horrible news. They immediately flew back to Athens, and Ari sent a plane to fly Christina in from Brazil. She had heard about her brother's crash over the radio. Onassis also flew in a leading neurosurgeon, London's Dr. Alan Richardson, in a desperate effort to save his grievously injured son. Heartbroken, Onassis told Dr. Richardson, "If I give you my entire fortune, can you save my boy's life?" As Gage reports, "All the money, the business deals, the yachts and villas and ships—his kingdom had been accumulated for this boy."

But after examining Alexander, Dr. Richardson concurred

with two other surgeons that Alexander was beyond help, having suffered irreversible brain damage.

Onassis made one more attempt to turn the balance in his son's favor: he flew in an icon of the Virgin Mary sacred to the Greek island of Tinos, a place where the sick and dying make pilgrimages. He called Archbishop Ieronymos of Athens to beg him to bring the sacred icon from Tinos to his son's bedside. He did so, but to no avail. Ari was beside himself with grief.

Jackie, who had already lived through the death of two infants and the horrific murder of her husband, remained somewhat stoic in the face of Ari's grief. She had learned to cling to the mundane facts of life in the grip of terrible events, like the poet Robert Desnos reading palms and telling fortunes while a prisoner at Theresienstadt. But at least two accounts of her behavior at Alexander's bedside do not flatter her: knowing that Ari was considering divorcing her, Jackie reportedly approached Alexander's lover, Baroness Fiona von Thyssen-Bornemisza, to ask if Alexander had mentioned a settlement amount to bestow upon Jackie if they divorced.

Alexander had fallen in love with Fiona when he was nineteen and she was thirty-five, struck by seeing her step out of a sports car during a snowstorm in St. Moritz. He described her as "tormentingly lovely," and he carried a torch for the baroness, though his father disapproved. Jackie probably gravitated to her because both were still considered outsiders in the close-knit Onassis family.

Fiona had no answer for Jackie but to ask Ari himself.

After Christina arrived from Brazil and saw her brother, Onassis made the decision to remove Alexander from life support, telling Christina, "Let us torture him no more."

Still unable to accept the death of his only son, Onassis considered having him cryonically frozen by the Life Extension Society in Washington, DC, with the hope that one day science could repair his injured brain. However, his close friend Ioannis Georgakis convinced Onassis that such a move would interfere with the migration of Alexander's soul. Greek Orthodox Christians believe that it takes forty days for a soul to leave earth and reach paradise.

Alexander lay in a gold-plated casket for three days, while thousands filed by to pay their respects. For Jackie, it must have felt as if she were reliving John Kennedy's funeral: present were royalty and heads of state, including the prime minister of Greece and head of the military junta that ruled the country, George Papadopoulos. Leaders from around the world sent their condolences: President Nixon, President Pompidou, Queen Elizabeth, and even Constantine, the exiled king of Greece.

Onassis finally left the church on the third day, hand in hand with his daughter, Christina. The family was beginning to close its ranks against outsiders, and Jackie seemed to be increasingly shut out. Ari appeared to have aged overnight. When he threaded his way through the crowd outside the church and suddenly stumbled, an ancient seaman called out, "Courage! Stand up, old man." Onassis did so, and walked on.

Alexander's body was buried on Skorpios.

In the weeks after his son's burial, Onassis was inconsolable. He wandered the island in the company of a stray dog and spent long nights at his son's grave. He would sit for hours in the grass, talking to Alexander and drinking ouzo, pouring a glass for his lost son. Jackie was worried; she had been through that kind of suffering, and she tried to console him and to repair their relationship. She tried to distract him by inviting guests like the Pierre Salingers aboard the *Christina* on a trip to the Antilles. She tried to ingratiate herself with members of his family, and she took him on trips to Mexico, Spain, the Caribbean, and Egypt. On a visit to New York, she asked Yusha Auchincloss to bring along pretty girls of his acquaintance to distract Ari—something she had done while planning state dinners for Jack Kennedy. Nothing seemed to rouse Ari from his grief.

The only person who could really console him was Maria Callas, because they understood each other, and because early on in their affair, they had lost an infant son. When he first arrived at her Paris apartment after losing Alexander, he fell into her arms.

"My boy is gone," he wept. "There's nothing left for me."

*

THOUGH SHE WOULD later deny it, Lee's affair with Peter Beard essentially ended her marriage to Stas. Lerman noted in his diaries that as early as February 20, 1971, Truman Capote called Stas over the "blower" (in a bit of British slang) to say that Lee was "hysterical over Peter Beard . . . She's gone to England to arrange a divorce. He's bad news, isn't he? Maybe she won't marry him, but she thinks she will . . ."

Jackie, always fond of Stas, was not pleased. Seeing the impending loss of his family, Stas asked Jackie to intervene by persuading Lee to stay in the marriage, just as the Kennedys had once asked Jackie to convince Lee to end her affair with Onassis. Jackie was critical of how Lee's behavior and a divorce would affect Anthony and Tina, feeling that her sister already spent too much time away from her children. Lee resented Jackie's interference and her lack of support. "You don't have to live with his moods," Lee told her sister, even going so far as to say that Jackie's marriage to Kennedy would not have lasted if he had lived. It was a low point in their relationship, stoking the embers of Lee's sense of betrayal over Jackie's marriage to Onassis. According to one source, "Their youthful closeness was gone."

Stas finally sued for divorce, hurt by Lee's affair with Peter, whom Stas had counted as a friend. Their divorce was announced on March 3, 1973, Lee's fortieth birthday, and was finalized the following year. His fortunes had dwindled considerably by then, and he had become a rather haunted figure, reminiscent of Jack Bouvier near the end of his life. Despite Stas's own occasional affairs, Lee was still the love of his life, and after the marriage ended, he fell into a depression and was often heard to lament, in his Polish-accented English, "Why did Princess leave? I can't understand why Princess left."

Bordering on bankruptcy after the 1971 death of his friend and business partner Felix Fenston and the crash of the real estate market, Stas had to sell Turville Grange. It was heartbreaking for both him and Lee—they had spent many blissful summers there, and Lee especially had derived great pleasure in turning the country house into a splendid retreat. Fourteen-year-old Tina went with Lee to Manhattan while fifteen-year-old Anthony remained with his father so he could continue to attend Millfield School in Somerset. Anthony and Tina were desperately unhappy at being separated, and it could not have been a preferable solution for Lee, whose relationship with Tina had always been strained, while she openly adored her only son.

Stas gave Lee a generous settlement, in part to move his remaining funds to America to avoid the high taxes levied in England and thus safeguard his children's future. He allowed her to keep Francis Bacon's *Figure Turning,* which Lee hung in her Manhattan duplex apartment. In a rare public statement about her divorce, Lee later told *People* magazine in her characteristic whisper, "It was stale for a long time. It just took a long time to work out the details." She also explained in a 1974 interview with the *New York Times*:

I was a foreigner married to another foreigner, living in a foreign country. That's fairly difficult in a way. We both missed our own countries a lot. Divorce is a 50-50 thing, and it can be a number of petty things that finally drive you out of your mind.

*

JACKIE'S MARRIAGE WAS also approaching its end. Besides being a personal tragedy for Onassis, the loss of his son was the death knell for their marriage, and he began to take out his grief on Jackie. Peter Beard, on his several visits to Skorpios, recalled:

> I can't tell you how many meals I sat through when Onassis would scream at her. He used to make insulting comparisons, right to her face between Jackie and Callas. He said Jackie was superficial and Callas was a "real artist." Jackie just sat around and took it.

Beard also noticed that Onassis was nicer to Jackie when they were in London, visiting Lee, or in Manhattan, but on Greek soil, "all the macho in him came out. When he exploded, everybody ran for cover." He returned to his favorite subjects, berating Jackie for her extravagant spending, and for deserting him for Manhattan on too many occasions. During one such tirade, Peter and John Jr. ran for cover, hiding in the shower.

Jackie called her eccentric cousin Edie Beale, confiding in her that everything seemed to go wrong after Alexander's death and that Ari's personality had undergone a sea change. "Mr. Onassis really lost his mind when his son died in that airplane crash," she recalled years later. "Onassis was no longer interested in life. He became a perfect horror to live with."

In Acapulco during the first winter after Alexander's death, Jackie and Ari visited Loel and Gloria Guinness. Another of their guests, the fashion doyenne Eleanor Lambert, recalled:

> When it was midnight and the fireworks began, Ari started to sob. Jackie put her arms around him, just like the Pieta, and held him. She let him cling to her for what seemed like ten minutes.

It was so touching because he was not kind to her. But she stuck by him in this awful time when he was mourning so terribly.

There's a Greek saying that if you turn your back on love, your luck will turn against you. That seems to be what happened to Onassis, if indeed Maria Callas was the woman he most loved. In his superstitious Greek soul, Onassis began to blame his bad luck on what he perceived to be Jackie's "*malocchio*"—her evil eye—as so many around her had died early and tragic deaths. Even Christina, who had at first been warm toward Jackie, now believed she had brought the gods' wrath down upon their family. According to Gage, Christina

> always felt that the union with Jackie had brought a curse on the family; now she was certain of it and openly said so to her father. Even Artemis, who bowed to no one in either her superstitions or her defense of her sister-in-law, felt it necessary to assure a guest at her dinner table, "It is just bad kismet. Jackie's not responsible for it."

"Greeks are very fate-oriented, and he felt that it was a curse that Alexander had died," Letitia Baldrige later remarked. "He unfairly blamed her . . . so it became inevitable for that marriage not to work." Peter Evans, one of Onassis's biographers, wrote that the woman he had once praised as "cool and sharp at the edges, fiery and hot beneath the surface," now seemed "cold-hearted and shallow," no longer "my class A lady" (inspired by the slogan on her L&M's "20 class A" cigarettes). Onassis once believed that some marriages are made in heaven, but the best ones are made on Skorpios. As he turned against Jackie, that was no longer true for him.

Maria Callas, who had never stopped loving her Aristo, took little satisfaction in the "Jackie jinx" and its effect on Onassis and his family, although the idea had taken root among Onassis's employees and even the Greek people. Even the tabloids blamed Onassis's unprecedented run of bad luck on "the Kennedy curse." His regret over the marriage gradually became an obsession, and he sought to rid himself of an alliance that seemed to have turned fate against him.

*

IN THE SPRING of 1972, Lee set out to make a documentary about her childhood in the Hamptons with the legendary avant-garde filmmaker Jonas Mekas, a friend and sometime collaborator of Peter Beard's. What Lee had in mind was a lyrical tribute to her happy memories of growing up with Jackie in East Hampton, coupled with images of Caroline, Anthony, Tina, and John Jr. enjoying the same summer pleasures. The Lithuanian-born Mekas, then in his late forties, came out to Montauk to film.

Mekas strove for a diaristic effect in his films ("like little sketches of people, friends, locations, even the weather"). His distinctive style, seen in his documentaries of groundbreaking artists such as John Lennon, Yoko Ono, Harry Smith, Allen Ginsberg, video artist Nam June Paik, and Andy Warhol, has been described as "a marriage between avant-garde poetics and 'home movie' amateurism," achieved through handheld camerawork and natural or overexposed lighting.

Given Mekas's experimental style, television producers passed on the project, and the few dollars she and Peter Beard raised barely covered expenses. However, Jackie saved the day by hiring Mekas to teach her children the fundamentals of photography and filmmaking. The documentary, *This Side of Paradise*, was shot over several summers in Montauk, with occasional forays into Lee's and Jackie's Manhattan apartments.

Each segment is connected by intertitles. "Home scenes" looks very much like a home movie of Tina Radziwill's birthday party, an intentional device of Mekas's to convey the intimacy and spontaneity of private events. In "Oh, yes, the summers of Montauk," we see John Jr. and Anthony boisterously wrestling and spraying each other with shaving cream. Later, Tina and Caroline swim in the Atlantic while Anthony, John Jr., and Peter Beard cavort in the sand. Scenes at the beach are shot in overexposed film that renders the sunlight blinding, like a home movie true to the heady pleasures of heat, sea, and sand.

Besides being a record of languid summers on Montauk, *Paradise* also shows the close bonds between the two sets of cousins. Keeping in mind that Caroline and John Jr. had endured the sudden, unthinkable murder of their father, the bothersome predations of paparazzi, and the adjustments of moving to Greece as the stepchildren of a Greek tycoon who already had grown children of his own, the two seem like normal, happy teenagers. Gloria Emerson recalled Jackie once saying that "if you are a good mother it does not matter much what else you have done." Jackie was nothing if not a good mother, attending their baseball games and school plays, taking them to their favorite movies, and making sure they were well educated—Caroline at Concord Academy, a boarding school in Massachusetts, and John Jr. at the private Collegiate School in Manhattan.

Anthony and Tina had also suffered hardships. They'd recently seen the separation of their parents, which meant a kind of banishment of their beloved father and the loss of their childhood home, Turville Grange. Yet in *Paradise*, they, too, are blissfully unaware of the fates that would catch up with them, in the present moment swimming, roughhousing, tasting all that summer has to offer. They appear, as film critic Aaron Scott describes, "unselfconscious and carefree, deeply engaged with one another and their surroundings."

Unable to raise the funding to complete the project, Mekas drifted out of their lives, but he'd loved working with Lee and found her to be "very talented and smart." In the end, *This Side of Paradise: Fragments of an Unfinished Biography* would not be edited or released to the public for another twenty-seven years, except for footage Mekas used in his 1990 film short, "Scenes from the Life of Andy Warhol" (which he dedicated to Lee). But it did lead to another film that would become a camp classic and inspire a Tony Award–winning musical and an Emmy Award–winning film for HBO.

When Mekas departed the scene, Peter Beard's friend Porter Bibb suggested that the documentarians Albert and David Maysles might agree to complete the film with the possibility of Lee's friend Truman Capote narrating. Bibb had worked with the Maysles brothers as a producer on *Gimme Shelter*, a groundbreaking documentary about a 1969 rock concert featuring the Rolling Stones in Altamont, California. (The concert had gone terribly wrong when a Hells Angels gang member, hired for security, knifed an audience member to death, unwittingly captured on camera.) Once the Maysles brothers signed on, Lee introduced them to her aunt and cousin living in a dilapidated house on Georgica Road in East Hampton, thinking it might be a good idea to film them as part of *Paradise*, to show the Hamptons before it was spoiled by overdevelopment and tourism. But once again, a project conceived by Lee ended up not only being about two *other* Bouviers, but leaving Lee out of the final cut altogether. Once the Maysles brothers met the oddball Beales in their gothic setting, they had found their subject.

During her summers in Montauk, Lee had renewed her friendship with her Bouvier aunt and cousin, "Big Edie" and "Little Edie" Beale, major presences during Lee and Jackie's summers in Lasata. Reduced by penury and hobbled by their own eccentricity, which included the OCD illness of hoarding, mother and daughter were living in their once beautiful but now decaying twenty-eight-room mansion in East Hampton, known as Grey Gardens.

"It was my idea," Lee recalled decades later, "when Stas and I lived in England at Turville, to go back to East Hampton, which I had so much nostalgia about as a child, and have my extremely eccentric aunt be the narrator for my memories." Lee recalled her aunt Edie's "wonderful singing voice" as well as her eccentricity. "She'd say anything. Her imagination was quite extraordinary, and her daughter, Edie, 'Little Edie' we always called her, was almost as eccentric."

Little Edie, however, didn't start out as pixilated as her mother. She'd graduated from Harvard, had wanted to work in the theater as a costume designer and an actress, had come out as a debutante celebrated for her beauty, and had flirted with Joseph Kennedy Jr. She was creative and imaginative. She had tried to set herself up in New York City to pursue her dreams. "It was when her mother locked her up as her companion at Grey Gardens," Lee observed, "and she never left East Hampton for twenty-five years," that Little Edie became as eccentric—and lost—as her mother. Lee knew that it would take days—weeks—just to get them to open their door. It wasn't enough to knock. "Oh, no, no, no, no," Lee recalled. "You bang and you scream."

Appalled by the squalid condition of their once splendid home and gardens—over thirty cats roamed the filthy corridors, and raccoons nested in the walls—Lee galvanized Jackie to help them save their home from demolition by the local board of health. It was Peter's idea to get the Maysles brothers to come in with their 16 mm cameras. He thought that "the Maysleses will be charmed by them," and he was right. As Lee recalled:

The Beales were terribly attracted by the Maysleses because they adored to have their picture taken and they adored to scream at one another constantly. And they said, listen, we don't want this to be an Edie narrating for you, for your nostalgia. We can really make something extraordinary out of this.

The writer Bob Colacello, editor of Andy Warhol's *Interview* magazine from 1970 to 1983, accompanied Lee and Jackie to Grey Gardens once the restoration was under way. As he later wrote:

> Lee was doing a good job, given the incredible decay into which the house had fallen—and the incredible state of mind into which her cousins had fallen . . . Big Edie was propped up in her bed and her bedroom, which had not yet gotten that Radziwill touch. A tree branch extended into the room through an open window to the middle of Big Edie's bed, and squirrels and raccoons climbed in to eat potato chips and pretzels. The bedcover was a trash heap of cracker boxes and candy wrappers, half-eaten tins of tuna fish and cat food, spilled milk, assorted other droppings, and piles of old *Confidentials* and new *Enquirers*, all with Jackie covers.

What got left out of the now-legendary documentary, titled *Grey Gardens*, is the degree to which Lee spearheaded the rescue mission. The documentary filmmaker Matt Tyrnauer, a friend of Lee's, described outtakes from the Maysles brothers' documentary as

> incredible footage. She's actually cleaning the house. But who got the credit for cleaning up Grey Gardens? Jackie. But it's Lee actually moving the refrigerator out of the kitchen. Then the Department of Health comes. Lee deals with [them] and she's amazing. She comes off so well. She's so nice to Big and Little Edie, so sweet. And Big Edie's so excited to have her there. There's this great part where she's screaming to someone, "Lee! Lee's here! My niece, Lee's here from Montauk!" And Lee looks

so beautiful. It's really like she's in Technicolor in the black-and-white scenes from *The Wizard of Oz*, in this perfect A-frame sundress, with the hair, and the kids are with her.

Although Jackie is much spoken of, Lee and Jackie do not appear in the documentary, and *Grey Gardens* is not at all a film about Lee's memories. Instead, it is the Maysles brothers' darkly humorous investigation of privilege, penury, and ruined dreams.

For the two sisters, other fates awaited.

*

JACKIE'S MINISTRATIONS FAILED to assuage Ari's grief and rescue their marriage. Onassis's health was failing; he developed the painful condition of myasthenia gravis, which caused one of his eyelids to droop so severely that he needed to tape it open. He began divorce proceedings, but before they could be finalized, he was rushed to the American Hospital of Paris in Neuilly-sur-Seine, suffering from respiratory failure. He managed to take one item with him to the hospital—a red blanket that had been given to him by Maria Callas.

On March 15, 1975, at the age of sixty-nine, Aristotle Onassis—whom many had considered a force of nature—died in Paris.

Jackie, who had found it increasingly difficult to be with Onassis, was in New York at the time of his death. Onassis's doctors had informed Jackie that he could indeed die at any time, and many criticized her for not staying with him in Paris. John Jr. was visiting with a friend in New York City when his mother called with news of his stepfather's death. Biographer Christopher Andersen notes that John "registered some small sadness at the news," but his stepfather's harsh treatment of his mother after the death of Alexander tempered any sorrow he might have felt.

Jackie flew to Paris. When she arrived at Orly Airport, she issued a public statement about her controversial and troubled marriage: "Aristotle Onassis rescued me at a moment when my life was engulfed with shadows. He meant a lot to me. He brought me into a world where one could find both happiness and love." It was a gracious comment, and it was true.

John Jr. and Caroline arrived in Athens from New York, accompanied by Ted Kennedy, Janet Auchincloss, and Jackie's half brother, Jamie Auchincloss. They were descended upon by photographers, though John Jr. tried to hide behind a comic book. Giving up, he stuck out his tongue at the Furies that surrounded them. Onassis's sister, Artemis, still maintained her friendship with Jackie and greeted her warmly.

Christina, Onassis's only daughter, was shattered by her father's death coming so soon after Alexander's tragic accident. Emotionally vulnerable and unable to cope with so much loss, Christina attempted suicide. (She was photographed leaving her father's hospital room with a bandaged wrist.) For Christina, all this misery and misfortune would be laid at her stepmother's door. She called her the Black Widow. "I don't dislike her, you know," Christina had once told a friend. But after her father's death, Christina's cold peace with Jackie melted away overnight. "I hate her" was her passionate response of blaming Jackie for her father's death, although the two women embraced when Jackie arrived in Athens from Paris for the funeral, clinging to each other for emotional support and protection against the swarm of reporters and paparazzi.

It rained on the day of Onassis's funeral, as it had on the day of his wedding to Jackie. He was carried aloft in a coffin made from the walnut trees on Skorpios, to be buried next to Alexander.

In a reverse image of President Kennedy's funeral, Jackie was elbowed to the back of the line of mourners, far behind Onassis's grieving family, even though she was the official widow. It was so unusual that the presiding Greek archdeacon was moved to say,

"In all my years in the church I don't recall another funeral where the widow was pushed into the background this way." There she stood, in black sunglasses and black trench coat, holding on to John Jr. and looking like a tragic Helen of Troy, while Onassis was laid to rest next to the grave of his son.

"Jackie was humiliated and hurt, and John certainly knew it," wrote Arthur Schlesinger, who had remained close to Jackie after Kennedy's assassination. "Just look at the photos taken at the time. The look of dismay in both their faces, especially John's, is extraordinary." John Jr. had always been protective of his mother.

Lee did not join her sister at the back of the funeral procession. There was speculation that Lee had wanted to attend her former lover's funeral but that Jackie had forbidden it, claiming that her presence would cause too much of a disturbance. But it's possible that Jackie, as DuBois notes, "could be just as jealous of Lee as Lee was of her. Jackie sensed with envy that the men in their circle were attracted to Lee for herself rather than for her position. Not only was Lee the more sensuous, some of them considered Jackie to be asexual altogether." Her fame had made her insecure, understandably, about her suitors' motives, so if there was something she envied Lee for, it was Lee's ability to live a more private life, and to trust the affection and love offered by the men around her. If Jackie had power, Lee had passion, and Lee wasn't as constrained about expressing her emotions.

For the year and a half following Onassis's death, Jackie and Christina battled over Onassis's will and Jackie's prenuptial agreement. When the two women agreed to meet to work out the financial arrangement, Christina refused to be in the same room with her stepmother, leaving it to their lawyers to work out a settlement while they sat in separate rooms. Christina actually wanted to adhere to the prenuptial agreement, which specified that instead of the 12.5 percent of his entire estate that Jackie was entitled to

John "Black Jack" V. Bouvier III. Jackie and Lee's father lost his fortune and his wife, but his two daughters loved him till the end. "Style is a habit of mind . . . it's what makes you a Bouvier," he once said, which both daughters took to heart. 1930.
Photo credit: Getty Images

The Auchinclosses. Janet with her new husband, Hugh D. Auchincloss. Jackie [l., back row] and Lee [r., middle row] were plunged into a new life and a new family with three Auchincloss stepsiblings: Hugh (Yusha), Nina, and Thomas. Janet holds her newborn, also named Janet, and they would have a son, James.
Photo credit: John F. Kennedy Presidential Library

Jackie with her father, "Black Jack" Bouvier, who was at this point living in somewhat reduced circumstances and missing his daughters. East Hampton, July 23, 1947. *Photo credit: Getty Images*

Jackie and Lee in ball gowns, photographed by Cecil Beaton for *Vogue*. Both sisters were named "Debutante of the Year"—Jackie in 1948 and Lee in 1951—by society columnist Cholly Knickerbocker (Igor Cassini). 1951.

Photo credit: Cecil Beaton/Getty Images

Michael Canfield, Lee's first husband, rumored to be the illegitimate son of the Duke of Kent. She dated the adopted publishing scion from the age of fifteen. At twenty, Lee was the first to marry, but the union only lasted six years. Pictured here with Jackie. *Photo credit: John F. Kennedy Presidential Library*

Photo booth snapshot of Jackie and her husband, Senator John F. Kennedy, possibly taken during their honeymoon in Acapulco and Beverly Hills in 1953. *Photo credit: John F. Kennedy Presidential Library*

Lee with her second husband, Prince Stanislaw (Stas) Radziwill, whom she married in 1959. Her mother said, "Why, he is nothing but a European version of your father," which delighted Lee. He was twenty years her senior, and they would have two children, Anthony and Anna Christina (Tina). *Photo credit: Getty Images*

Jackie's brief three and a half years as First Lady brought her closer to Lee. The Kennedys and the Radziwills spent holidays together, and Lee and Stas Radziwill were frequent guests of honor at the White House. Jackie with German shepherd Clipper, Lee, and the Radziwills' daughter, Tina. January 1963. *Photo credit: John F. Kennedy Presidential Library*

Turville Grange, Lee and Stas Radziwill's eighteenth-century country estate in Oxfordshire, which Lee transformed into a magnificent retreat. Nureyev described Lee's homes as "two of the prettiest houses in England." *Photo credit: Alamy*

Jackie appeared on the cover of *LIFE* more than thirty times. In 1961, she embarked on an ambitious restoration of "The People's House," with superb and historically accurate results. Her uncluttered, elegant style influenced a generation of women, bringing them out of the kitschy 1950s.
Cover photo: © Mark Shaw/mptvimages.com
Photo credit: Getty Images

President Kennedy asked Jackie to make a diplomatic trip to India and Pakistan, and Jackie brought Lee along as her closest companion. The trip was a spectacular success, with thousands turning out to cheer "America's Queen" and her "lady in waiting." Karachi, Sindh, Pakistan, March 1962. *Photo credit: John F. Kennedy Presidential Library*

Lee with her daughter, Tina, in the sumptuous drawing room at her London house at 4 Buckingham Place. She worked closely with the designer Renzo Mongiardino to achieve a richly layered, nineteenth-century décor. She would later be drawn to an airier, more minimalist style. *Photo credit: Cecil Beaton Studio Archive/Sotheby's Picture Library*

With Jackie's help, Lee
sought an annulment of
her marriage to Michael
Canfield, so her civil
marriage with Radziwill
could be sanctified in the
Roman Catholic Church.
Jackie looks serene and
unknowable, as always.
Lee looks distraught.
At the Basilica of Saint
Petrus, Rome, 1961.
Photo credit: Alamy

While living in London,
Lee began her lifelong,
passionate friendship
with Russian dancer
Rudolf Nureyev, pictured
here in snake-skin jacket
and boots. Both shared a
love of living grandly in
baroque style. Lee and
Jackie had what Truman
Capote described as "the
sense of the right to
luxury."
Photo credit: Alamy

Lee invited Jackie to join her on a summer vacation in Ravello, Italy, the "jewel of the Amalfi coast." She and Stas rented a beautiful cliff-side villa that overlooked the Gulf of Naples. Jackie's Secret Service detail and flocks of paparazzi were the only things that marred their idyllic seclusion. 1962.
Photo credit: Benno Graziani/Photo12

Lee with shipping tycoon Aristotle Onassis, at the beginning of their affair. "Ari was charismatic," she said, but the Kennedys asked her to end the relationship, worried about John F. Kennedy's upcoming re-election. 1961.
Photo credit: Getty Images

Jackie and Robert F. Kennedy, mourning the death of President Kennedy. Jackie planned the obsequies along the lines of Abraham Lincoln's state funeral. Jackie's regal, veiled dignity elevated her to the iconic status of America's First Widow. November 25, 1963. *Photo credit: Keystone-France/ Gamma-Keystone via Getty Images*

A luminous Lee on the cover of *LIFE* on the occasion of her debut performance as Tracy Lord in *The Philadelphia Story*, as orchestrated by Truman Capote. "Principessa, you must go on the stage!" he insisted. July 1967. *Photo credit: Pierre Boulat, Getty Images.*

Lee with Truman Capote at the Black and White Ball. It was a genuine friendship until his drinking, prescription drug abuse, and a feud with Gore Vidal put an end to it. *Photo credit: Getty Images*

Onassis with his longtime mistress, the opera diva Maria Callas. An American-born Greek, Callas was married to Giovanni Meneghini, but her affair with "Aristo" was an open secret, and the two shared an intense emotional bond. She hated Lee and was devastated when Onassis married Jackie. *Photo credit: Getty Images*

Jackie at work in her office at Viking Press in 1975, as a consulting editor. She moved to Doubleday two years later.
Photo credit: Getty Images

Lee with her son, Anthony Radziwill.
Photo credit: Jodie Burstein/ Globe Photos LLC Presidential Library

Lee with the A-list film director Herbert Ross, whom she married in 1988. He brought her the glamour of Hollywood; she delighted in his wit and style. Their thirteen-year marriage didn't survive the devastating loss of her son, Anthony, who died of cancer at the age of forty. *Photo credit: Getty Images*

DAILY⊙NEWS

40¢   NEW YORK'S HOMETOWN NEWSPAPER   Friday, May 20, 1994

JACQUELINE KENNEDY ONASSIS
1929-1994

COMPLETE COVERAGE BEGINS ON PAGE 2

Jackie passed away in 1994 at the age of sixty-four, from non-Hodgkin lymphoma. The world noted her passing, and throngs kept vigil outside of her Fifth Avenue apartment. Jackie's will left generous bequeaths to all of her family members except Lee. *Photo credit: Getty Images*

On July 16, 1999, John F. Kennedy Jr.'s small plane plunged into the Atlantic, killing him and his new bride, Carolyn Bessette, and her sister, Lauren. Jackie was spared this cruel tragedy, reminiscent of the death of Onassis's son, Alexander. *Photo credit: Getty Images*

under Greek law, she was to receive instead $150,000 annually for the rest of her life. Fearing that Jackie might sue for the 12.5 percent of the estate, Christina offered her stepmother a $20 million settlement, plus an additional $6 million to cover taxes, which Jackie had insisted upon. It was a generous settlement—roughly $130 million in today's dollars—but many of Onassis's associates were surprised because Jackie would have received far more had she taken her case to the Greek courts.

"There was not a lot of love lost between them," recalled Ari's spokesman Nigel Neilson. Christina would never forgive the Black Widow for blighting her family's life, leaving her adrift without her father and brother. She was suddenly the world's richest woman, but it was cold comfort. Many Greeks, including Christina, believed that when the gods turn against you, it is useless to fight back.

Alone, without her father to protect her, Christina was vulnerable to fortune hunters, something Onassis had always warned her about. She embarked on a series of doomed marriages. Christina quickly abandoned her fiancé, the shipping heir Peter Goulandris, who had had her father's approval, to take up with the scion of a Greek banking family, Alexander Andreadis, marrying him just four weeks after their first meeting. That marriage lasted fifteen months. Christina then became infatuated with Sergei Kauzov, a Russian bureaucrat rumored to be a KGB agent, and they were married in Moscow. But Christina missed Skorpios and she divorced Kauzov and returned to Greece, giving him an oil tanker as a divorce settlement. In March of 1983, Christina would marry Thierry Roussel, heir to a French pharmaceutical fortune. The wedding took place at the Paris town hall, followed by a celebration dinner at Maxim's for 125 guests. Roussel became the father of Christina's only child, Athina, but Christina would soon learn that her husband had also impregnated his mistress, a Swedish model who gave birth to Roussel's second child shortly after Athina was born. She divorced Roussel in May of 1987. "It was her tragedy to be passionate without being lovable," one of her suitors cruelly said about Christina.

In an attempt to stay slim and attractive as the paparazzi buzzed around the richest woman in the world, Christina made use of amphetamines, and her extreme weight fluctuations no doubt contributed to her ill health. In November 1988, the year following her divorce from Roussel, Christina would die in Buenos Aires from an acute pulmonary edema of the lung, which had produced a heart attack. She was just thirty-seven years old. After Christina's death, her three-year-old daughter, Athina, became the richest girl in the world, sole heir to the Onassis fortune.

*

IN 1974, AFTER a few summers of renting Warhol's Montauk lodge, Lee soon fulfilled a lifelong dream and found a beach house to rent on Gin Lane in Southampton. Settled on three wooded acres at the end of Main Street, it had a pool and two hundred feet of beach access. Though the house was rather modest, it was nestled among some of the most expensive properties in the country; her neighbors included Gloria Vanderbilt, financier Felix Rohatyn, socialite Anne Ford (Henry Ford's great-granddaughter), and *New York Times* publisher Arthur "Punch" Sulzberger.

As before, Lee took great pleasure in decorating the small A-frame house, transforming it into a year-round showplace. She designed sleek dining chairs and a coffee table and, using wicker and sailcloth upholstery, created an airy, sea-inspired retreat. "I wanted the house . . . for any time of year," she explained, "a house that focused on the natural environment, an unencumbered place that would constantly renew the spirit."

Lee swam every summer day, continued to develop her interests and talents, and worked intermittently on her memoir, which many years later would be published as *Happy Times*, a book of photographs and reminiscences, by the publisher Assouline. It was a place not only for her to thrive, but for her children as well: "Although they were only a year apart in age," she later wrote, "Anthony and Tina were completely different. Anthony loved sports and animals; Tina was passionate about ballet and the arts." But like their mother and aunt, they both loved their summers by the sea.

Jackie, now an extremely wealthy woman, returned to Manhattan to live full-time. The sisters would enjoy a period of closeness, brought together in part by their friendship with Peter Beard and through the camaraderie among their four now-teenage children. When not spending time in Manhattan or on Long Island with Lee, Jackie vacationed in a country house she owned in the hunt country of Peapack, New Jersey, an hour from the city. There she was able to indulge her lifelong love of horseback riding, a pastime that Caroline also shared. ("Keep her riding," Jack Bouvier had once advised a young John Kennedy, "and she'll always be in a good mood.")

But there would be one more lonely death in the Onassis family romance.

In 1975, while Aristo's health was deteriorating, Callas had begun a world tour. The celebrated diva had not sung publicly for eight years, and she was enthusiastically welcomed back by her ardent fans. In Hamburg, Germany, Callas was given a five-minute standing ovation as soon as she appeared onstage. Four years earlier, Lerman had noted that when Callas simply appeared in the audience of an opera at the Met, she was greeted with "applause and shouts of 'Brava, Callas!' Cascades of adulation."

Now, however, the critics were not kind, noting that her voice was no longer the fabulous instrument it had once been (one critic compared it to "a monochrome reproduction of an oil painting").

When Aristo was hospitalized in Paris, Callas had visited him, making sure to arrive when Christina was not present, and assuming—correctly—that Jackie would not be making an appearance at her husband's bedside. Knowing he was near death, she reportedly bent down to kiss her former lover good-bye, at which point Aristo roused himself to tell Maria that he loved her.

After his death, Maria Callas began to decline. She thought about moving permanently to Palm Beach, Florida, but instead returned to her home in Paris, where she became something of a recluse, canceling dates with friends and continuing to mourn the loss of Aristo. She could often be seen peering through her curtained French windows—a haunted, shadowy figure—but mostly she sat alone inside her apartment, watching Westerns on television day and night.

Lerman noted in his diary that on the morning of September 16, 1977, her maid, Bruna,

> served her breakfast in bed, then [Maria] got up and took a few steps toward the bathroom. She crumpled to the floor, falling against a bureau . . . [Although] Bruna tried to revive her with three spoonfuls of coffee, by the time the doctor arrived, she was dead. [A] Turkish fortune teller had accurately predicted that she would die young, but without suffering. She was 53 years old.

On the occasion of her death, the *New York Times* music critic Harold C. Schonberg wrote:

> Her career was short and toward the end she was displaying only the shreds of a voice . . . But for some 15 years after 1947 she was a symbol fired into the very psyche of the opera goer . . . She drove her audiences wild; she had a kind of electrical transmission that very few musicians have ever approached . . . Callas, dead at 53, blazed through the skies and was burned out very early. But what years those were!

To their credit, both Lee and Jackie had admired Callas's artistry, Lee going so far as to describe her as "a force of nature, a gifted child, impossible to please. It took an outsize personality like [Onassis] to tame the hurricane that was Maria."

*

"FOR THE FIRST time, I really feel true to myself," Lee told Judy Klemesrud of the *New York Times* in a September 1974 interview. Since leaving her marriage to Stas, Lee was experiencing a burst of creative activity. Besides the Rolling Stones tour, her involvement in Jonas Mekas's and the Maysles brothers' documentaries, and trying to write her memoir, Lee had embarked on a television career. If Jackie was finally found, Lee refused to be lost.

Described by Klemesrud as a "society blueblood, ex-princess" and "little sister to one of the world's most famous women," Lee swept "into her bright red living room on Fifth Avenue . . . to talk about her latest endeavor: working." Throughout the 1970s, this was how she was often portrayed—a storm looking for a port. Pencil thin, dressed in a white silk shirt and navy pants, Lee chain-smoked throughout the interview. When Klemesrud asked why someone of her background wanted to "become a working woman"—that old question—Lee answered in the parlance of the times:

> I'm obviously all for women's lib, but . . . this is no classic case of women's lib. The most important thing, I've found, is to be self-reliant. I just felt I was being true to myself by returning to New York and starting a life of my own. In London, I found I was no longer able to contribute to anyone else's life except my children's, and they're at an age now where they no longer need me very much.

Her friend William Paley, founder and chairman of CBS and husband of Babe Paley, had agreed to create a pilot of six "Conversations with Lee Radziwill" to be made available to five

CBS-owned news programs, with the goal of her own syndicated program. It was Lee's "dream job"—a half-hour interview show of her own, with one guest at a time. Lee conducted six interviews, mostly with celebrated friends of hers: John Kenneth Galbraith, Gloria Steinem, Rudolf Nureyev, Halston, *Jaws* author Peter Benchley, and the Harvard psychiatrist and writer Robert Coles. Nureyev rarely appeared on television, but he could not refuse Lee, nor could the fashion designer Halston.

Lee was often motivated as much by the things she disliked as by the things she admired. She clearly disliked the talk show hosts of the mid-'70s, describing them as "literally offensive. They're so glib, and have done little homework on their guests' backgrounds. Their questions have no substance or value . . . The one exception is Barbara Walters, who is absolutely great."

Lee had indeed done her homework, impressing Nureyev with her knowledge of ballet, and especially coming to life in her interview with Halston, given her deep appreciation of couture. At one point Lee asked Halston what a woman could buy with twenty-five dollars. "Nothing," he said.

Galbraith characterized his interview with Lee as "thoroughly rehearsed spontaneity." (Lee later described him as "the only man I ever met wearing a nightgown. It was madras with long sleeves, a Moghul idea he got when he was in India.") When Lee asked Nureyev if he ever planned to get married, the great dancer blushed at the teasing question, but gave back as good as he got: "One doesn't expect close friends to ask silly questions."

The most winning of all the conversations was the one Lee herself was most nervous about because she knew him the least: Peter Benchley. Lee charmed and flirted with the bestselling writer, who later admitted that his time with Lee was "one of the most delightful afternoons I ever spent," describing her as "one of the most charming, solicitous, sweetest women I ever met in my life . . . she framed interesting questions and was well prepared."

But Benchley, who was himself acquainted with the medium, nonetheless felt that Lee was, if anything, too polite, too eager to avoid controversy. Considering it nothing but "soft news," most of the local stations turned their backs on Lee's hard work. The time lag between when the interviews were conducted and when they finally went on the air made them seem out of date, especially in an era when television news was confronting the upheavals of the '70s counterculture.

Lee blamed the show's failure to ignite on Sam Zelman, the CBS news chief at the time, feeling that he had truncated each interview. "They were quite good and people were quite candid," she said, "but it was traduced to nothing. They had a feast and they turned it into canapes."

However, Ray Beindorf, CBS programming executive at the time, observed:

> Talk television had not surfaced yet. It was still in its early stages, so we didn't know how to present it properly. I thought Lee was coachable, and certainly we all liked her personally. The consensus was that she had a quality that was attractive. She wasn't Barbara Walters, but she held her own. The problem wasn't her performance. The problem was that the form had not established itself . . .

Or, as Lee's friend Taki Theodoracopulos wrote about Lee in *Esquire*, when comparing her to other talk show hosts of the day, "Lee came on like a genius."

But Lee found another way to shine. That same year—1974— saw the publication of *One Special Summer* by Delacorte Press, with an initial print run of 100,000 copies (and it was also an alternate selection for the Book-of-the-Month Club). On a visit to Merrywood to see Janet and their stepfather, Jackie and Lee had come together to sort through old diaries, letters, and artifacts stored in the attic. Lee was hoping to use what she found in her ongoing memoir. That's when the two sisters discovered "A Special Summer," the sweet, funny, girlish record they had made of their first trip to Europe together in 1952 as a present to their mother. It had survived as an artifact, and a testament to how close they had once been. After some persuading, Lee convinced Jackie—still shy about publicly revealing any aspect of herself— that they should publish it, just as it was.

The following year, Lee had hoped to finish her memoir, tentatively titled "Opening Chapters," but instead she appeared on the February 2, 1975, cover of Warhol's *Interview* magazine. In the accompanying interview, she confessed to Warhol that her "deep regret" was that she "wasn't brought up to have a métier. I'm mainly interested in the arts, but because of my kind of education, my interests were never channeled in any particular field . . . I should have been in the decorative arts as I'm a very visual person."

Warhol and his cohort Bob Colacello had a firsthand glimpse of Lee's visual eye and knowledge of art history. They arrived one rainy day at Lee's Fifth Avenue apartment to accompany her and Jackie to the Brooklyn Museum. The sisters were waiting in the lobby, dressed in identical trench coats with scarves on their heads, both looking like sane versions of Edie Beale.

"After the usual greetings," Colacello described, "Mrs. Onassis's first words were 'So tell me, Andy, what was Liz Taylor like?' I couldn't believe it. Here was the only person in the world who was more famous than Elizabeth Taylor and she wanted to know what Elizabeth Taylor was like . . . And what's more, it was asked in the voice of Marilyn Monroe! If Marilyn had gone to Foxcroft and Vassar, that is. The same girlishly sexy breathiness."

At the museum, Colacello noticed that

Lee seemed to know everything there was to know about the exhibition. "Oh, look, Jackie," she would say, "that bowl is just like the one we saw in the Cairo Museum." She could list the Pharoahs and the dates they ruled. She seemed to have the mind of a curator, and the taste of an aesthete. Jackie looked at her the way a pupil looks at a teacher, intently, taking it all in. Lee talked, Jackie listened. Lee led, Jackie followed. And there was no sign of their reputed competitiveness.

Secure in her own territory—the visual arts—Lee did not have to compete with her sister.

*

LEE'S PASSIONATE LOVE affair with Peter Beard was tested by his lack of interest in exclusivity and marriage and the differences in the ways they liked to live. Peter purchased a small cabin on sixteen acres in Montauk to refurbish, with an old windmill as his main abode. In the meantime, Lee found staying at the cabin cramped and uncomfortable. When she moved to Southampton, she began to see less of Peter, but what really ended their affair was Peter's involvement with a sultry model named Barbara Allen, who moved in with him. Lee showed up and made a huge fuss, insisting that Peter was *hers*. Although he found it rather amusing, their love affair was over, though Lee and Peter have remained good friends. Actually, of all of her lovers, Peter is the one who has remained most loyal to Lee in the ensuing years.

10

WORKING GIRLS

I have always lived through men. Now I realize I can't do that anymore.

—JACKIE

There's no necessity of doing anything when nothing is demanded of you . . . maybe fate will come to get me.

—LEE

fter the death of Onassis in March of 1975, Jackie returned to the Kennedy compound in Hyannis Port for a brief visit. She felt overwhelmed by memories of her life there with Jack: "This was the only house where we really lived, where we had our children, where every little pickle jar I had found in some little country lane on the Cape was placed, and nothing's changed since we were in it, and all the memories came before my eyes," she remembered.

That evening, Rose Kennedy invited her to take a walk on the beach, not wanting to leave her alone. "I can't remember Jack's voice exactly anymore," she confided, "but I still can't stand to look at pictures of him." (Photographs of Jack remained in her children's rooms but nowhere else in her Manhattan apartment.) When she was left alone, she dipped into the works of two of her favorite poets, C. P. Cavafy and George Seferis. Even before her Greek sojourn, she'd loved these poets, and now the melancholy tone of Seferis's "The Last Day" spoke to her mood:

*"This wind reminds me of spring," said my friend
as she walked beside me gazing into the distance, "the spring
that came suddenly in the winter by the closed-in sea.
So unexpected. So many years have gone . . ."*

When she returned to Manhattan in September, Tish Baldrige noticed how listless Jackie seemed. John Jr., 14, was still attending the Collegiate School on the Upper West Side of Manhattan, and Caroline, 17, was planning to study art at Sotheby's in London. (Gloria Emerson noted that "it is Caroline who now writes the verses and sketches. Her mother does not write or paint, which is too bad, for genuine gifts were once there.") They did not need her as much, and Jackie found herself at loose ends. She sought help from a psychiatrist and from an acupuncturist, Lillian Biko, who told *Cosmopolitan* that Jackie "had problems because she's so secretive. Which is why she sees me." Tish suggested that Jackie consider going to work.

"What—me work?" Jackie had joked, but she immediately warmed to the idea. Tish, no longer Jackie's private secretary but still her friend, and now the head of a Manhattan public relations firm, later told the *New York Times*:

> I really felt she needed something to get out in the world and meet people doing interesting things, use that energy and that good brain of hers. I suggested publishing. Viking was my publisher, and I said to her, "Look, you know Tommy Guinzburg—why don't you talk to him?"

Jackie arranged a lunch at Le Perigord on East 52nd near Sutton Place with Tom Guinzburg, Viking's publisher, whom she had met years earlier through George Plimpton (they had been young men in Paris together) and through her stepbrother Yusha, who had been a hall mate of Guinzburg's at Yale. It was not lost on the publisher that Jackie, now forty-six, would be of inestimable value to any publishing house, given her high profile, her vast range of friends and acquaintances, and the cachet that her name would bring. "What author could not be lured to Viking by the promise of having Jacqueline Bouvier Kennedy Onassis as his or her editor?" commented Christopher Andersen, one of Jackie's many chroniclers. Guinzburg also felt that if Jackie ever decided to write a memoir, he would be there to catch the bouquet.

The publisher immediately offered her a part-time job four days a week as a consulting editor at a yearly salary of $10,000. She would acquire books but would not necessarily have the daily labor of editing them. Obviously not needing the money after her $26 million settlement from the Onassis estate, she accepted.

By the second week of September 1975, Jackie showed up at Viking's office at 625 Madison Avenue to begin work, the first paying job she'd undertaken in over twenty-two years, since being the Inquiring Cameragirl for the *Washington Times-Herald* for twenty-five dollars a week. Despite the hordes of fans crowding the lobby of Viking's offices trying to get a glimpse of her, Jackie quickly made it apparent to her coworkers that she did not expect—or want—any special treatment. She settled into her small office and was seen making pots of coffee for her colleagues and staff. She also did her own typing and filing and phone calling. "I expect to be learning the ropes at first," she told reporters. "You sit in at editorial conferences, you discuss general things, maybe you're assigned to a special project of your own. Really, I expect to be doing what my employer tells me to do . . ." She also realized that "like everybody else, I have to work my way up to an office with a window." As much as she tried to fit into the editorial corps at Viking as a fledgling editor, there was still no escaping her off-the-charts fame and mystique. No sooner had she begun working than renowned *Life* photographer Alfred Eisenstaedt was sent by the magazine to photograph Jackie in her new job.

. . .

Among the first of several books she worked on at Viking was Barbara Chase-Riboud's *Sally Hemings: A Novel*, a then controversial work about Thomas Jefferson's enslaved mistress, and a novel she was especially drawn to by Nancy Zaroulis, titled *Call the Darkness Light*, about a nineteenth-century mill worker in Lowell, Massachusetts. "I realized that the story would illuminate a period of American history and lives of a whole group of women," she commented, lives far from the protected privilege that the Bouvier girls had been born into.

Jackie also took partial credit for Jay Mellon's *The Face of Lincoln*, a collection of Lincoln daguerreotypes, though the editors of note, Barbara Burn and Elisabeth Sifton, had no recollection of her involvement. But as Jay Mellon was a friend of Peter Beard's, it's possible that she had a hand in acquiring the book for Viking. The book certainly reflected her keen interest in American history and in particular the American presidency.

Two of the books she edited for Viking reflected her long interest in tsarist Russia: *In the Russian Style* in 1976 and Boris Zvorykin's *The Firebird and Other Russian Fairy Tales* in 1978. The first came out of Jackie's friendship with Diana Vreeland, who'd asked her to accompany the Metropolitan Museum of Art director Tom Hoving to Russia. Vreeland was curating a show at the Met's Costume Institute and needed help in persuading the Hermitage Museum to lend the Met clothing once worn by Alexandra, the last tsarina of Russia. Jackie commissioned Audrey Kennett, a former editor of British *Vogue* who had traveled to the USSR during the Cold War era, to write the copy, while Jackie selected the photographs and provided the captions. The Costume Institute exhibition was extremely popular, and *In the Russian Style* was well received, except for a caviling review by Russian composer Nicolas Nabokov in the *New York Review of Books* in which he complained that the book was "the work of a dilettante." Jackie was embarrassed by the review, but she continued her association with Vreeland, writing a catalogue for another of the fashion doyenne's exhibitions, *Vanity Fair*, meant to be a refutation of the seventeenth-century writer John Bunyan's attack on the human foible of vanity. (This struck close to home: Bunyan's *Pilgrim's Progress* was one of Jack Kennedy's favorite books.) Jackie's catalogue essay was in the form of an interview with Vreeland, titled "A Visit to the High Priestess of Vanity Fair." In it she and Vreeland extol the superb craftsmanship of couture ("the sewing, the cutting, the intricate beadwork"), noting that cultivating fashion helps to keep these ancient skills alive.

Through her friendship with Andreas Brown, owner of the Gotham Book Mart, Jackie was introduced to the work of the Russian artist and illustrator Boris Zvorykin. As an editor at Viking, she was able to bring out a new edition of his illustrated *The Firebird and Other Russian Fairy Tales*.

Three years later, Jackie would have another occasion to express her admiration of Russian artists. In December of 1981, the Polish poet and Nobel laureate Czeslaw Milosz was invited to be the guest of honor at a dinner held for prominent patrons of Poets & Writers, the nonprofit organization devoted to writers and the literary arts. It was an annual event meant to thank major donors for their support, but when Milosz bowed out because his wife was ill and in the hospital, the program director at the time, Eva Burch, suggested replacing him with the émigré Russian poet Joseph Brodsky.

As this was six years before Brodsky himself was awarded the Nobel Prize in Literature, the organization's executive director, Galen Williams, worried that he would not be well-known enough to the assembled guests. Eva suggested that Mikhail Baryshnikov—who was a close friend of Brodsky's—accompany him as cohost of the evening. So it was arranged and held at the home of investment banker and arts patron Terry Kistler, who lived at 1040 Fifth Avenue—Jackie's building. Guests included

Susan Sontag, Michael and Alice Arlen, David Rose, Timothy Seldes, the Arthur Schlesingers, and Jackie Onassis.

Everyone arrived before the guest of honor, and everyone was dressed to the nines (except for Susan Sontag, who wasn't, and Brodsky and Baryshnikov, who arrived together in corduroys and jeans). Jackie appeared resplendent in a black-sashed red tunic and black wide-legged silk pants, looking for all the world like a Russian Cossack.

As soon as Brodsky walked through the door, she stood up and said as loudly as her whispery voice would allow, "I can't believe I'm meeting you at last! Is it going to be as it is in my dreams?"

Abashed, Brodsky turned red and mumbled, "I hope we have a chance to talk later," before spinning off to the bar for a glass of Jameson Irish whiskey, his favorite libation.

When it came time to be seated for dinner, the name places apparently had been switched by one of the guests, so Jackie found herself seated across from Brodsky, instead of at his side, at a table so wide that it made conversation difficult. Things got more awkward when the guest who had seated herself next to the Russian poet told him he had the profile of Napoleon. Already worn out from having to make small talk with people he didn't know, Brodsky suddenly jumped up and left the table. Baryshnikov and Sontag followed him out of the room, and out of the party.

After he left, Jackie stayed for a while longer, smoothing things over by telling Terry Kistler, "Russians are so emotional. You should see how Nureyev behaved."

But she had relished the evening. In Brodsky, two realms Jackie admired merged completely: poetry and Russian culture. Ironically, a decade earlier the American poet Robert Lowell had become obsessed with Jackie during one of his manic phases, writing to her constantly. Perhaps if he had been Russian, she might have written him back.

(Lowell wasn't the only writer obsessed with Jackie and, by extension, with Lee. In the early '70s, Gore Vidal wrote a novel titled *Two Sisters* about two women who are clearly modeled on Jackie and Lee, a novel much discussed among literary and social circles but not a critical nor a commercial success. When the novelist and relative-by-marriage Louis Auchincloss read it, he commented that he "fervently hoped Gore had finally gotten them out of his system." He had not.)

*

THOUGH SHE HAD always been a traditionalist in her views of women's place in society, since starting her job at Viking, Jackie's perspective had undergone a sea change. She now believed that "what has been said for many women of my generation is that they weren't supposed to work if they had families"—a lament that Lee had been making for decades. Sixteen years after Betty Friedan's consciousness-raising masterpiece, *The Feminine Mystique*, published in 1963, Jackie recognized the dilemma of women "with the highest education, and what were they to do when the children were grown—watch the raindrops coming down the windowpane? Leave their fine minds unexercised? Of course women should work if they want to."

Friedan had once said, "It is easier to live through someone else than to become complete yourself," a challenge that Jackie was now rising to. Even Gloria Steinem noticed Jackie's change in consciousness, and put her on the cover of *Ms.* magazine. Jackie had agreed to be interviewed by the magazine because, as Steinem recalled, "it treated her as a person, instead of talking about her husbands. She asked me to remove references to them from the interview. She said, 'It has helped me to be taken seriously as an editor, for my own abilities.' "

So work, for Jackie, was an awakening. George Plimpton, who had befriended her a lifetime ago in Paris, witnessed that blossoming, realizing that at last Jackie had "come into her own."

When she was with Ari, she put aside parts of herself to pursue his
interests. I sense a change in her . . . very much more like the girl
I first knew, who had a great sense of fun and enthusiasm. It must
be an electrifying, extraordinary thing for her to be on her own—
she was always somewhat diminished by the men around her . . .

Although as a young woman she'd aspired to be a journalist
(she once said, "If I hadn't married I might have had a life very
much like Gloria Emerson's"), by embarking on a career as an editor she became closer to the idea she expressed in her Prix de Paris
essay: "a sort of Overall Art Director of the Twentieth Century,
watching everything from a chair hanging in space . . ."

Instead of becoming a writer, Jackie would now discover other
writers and bring them into print. And she loved it. At one point
she said to her friend Mabel Brandon, a fellow preservationist and
graduate of Miss Porter's, "Oh, Muffie, aren't we lucky we work?"
As William Kuhn noted in *Reading Jackie*:

Jackie's discovery in these years was that reading by herself in
a corner, sailing on a yacht, and buying couture clothes in Paris
were all a great deal less sustaining than going into the office
and drinking coffee out of a Styrofoam cup.

As part of her mandate to attract major writers and personalities to Viking, Jackie tried to convince the Duchess of Windsor,
Wallis Simpson, to write her memoirs (she offered to fly to Paris
to meet with the ailing duchess), and Princess Margaret's ex-
husband, the photographer Lord Snowdon, to write his. Neither
agreed. She tried to cajole Frank Sinatra, who had always been
interested in John Kennedy's widow, but he, too, wasn't forthcoming. After two years at Viking, Jackie jumped ship, and many at-
tributed it to her failure to lure major figures to the publishing
house. But there was another reason.

In 1977, Viking published a suspense novel by the former British Conservative MP Jeffrey Archer, titled *Shall We Tell the President?*, about a fictional attempt to assassinate Ted Kennedy. The novel had already been published in Britain, and given its subject matter, Guinzburg reportedly assured Jackie that she would not be associated with the book. But after it was roundly panned by reviewers, including a veiled reference to Jackie in *New York Times* book critic John Leonard's review ("Anyone associated with the publication of this book should be ashamed of herself"), Jackie felt that Guinzburg had left her vulnerable. In the resulting furor, Jackie suddenly resigned, complaining that Guinzburg had told the *New York Times* that "she knew all about exactly what happens in this book, and I didn't know about it at all!"

Becky Singleton, Jackie's assistant, was not alone in feeling that Jackie had been unceremonious in her sudden departure. "There was no personal discussion of the incident itself," she later said. "You do have the right as an employee to leave. But there are ways and ways to do it." Nonetheless, Jackie had met with Doubleday editor Lisa Drew—who had first turned down Archer's novel before it landed at Viking—and delicately sounded her out about a possible move to Doubleday. Her friend Tucky—Nancy Tuckerman—worked in their publicity department, and Jackie had been a personal friend of John Sargent's, who headed the publishing house. He offered her a job.

Though the much larger, more corporate publishing house didn't have as much literary cachet as Viking, Jackie was offered a decidedly better deal—$20,000 yearly for a three-day week. She accepted and began her new job on February 11, 1978. (In the gap between leaving Viking and starting at Doubleday, *Time* magazine reported that Jackie was unemployed, with the cheeky headline "Situation Wanted, References Available.") Her office was just as tiny and sunless, but when Sargent apologized to Jackie for its lack of windows, she answered, "Oh, that's alright, John. I've lots of windows in my home."

Soon Jackie would have more than just a view of east Central Park. She began building a house that year on 365 acres in Martha's Vineyard, which she would name Red Gate Farm. Sprawling between Chilmark and Menemsha, along Squibnocket Pond in Gay Head, it was on a grassy lot with scrub oaks, Scotch pines, ponds, marshes, and an old stone wall built by the original settlers, both hidden away from the prying eyes of the world and close to the ocean. It included 4,620 feet of beachfront—some of it adjacent to a nude beach. This would become Jackie's recovered version of Lasata.

In addition to the land, Jackie spent another $3 million building a 3,100-square-foot house with eight fireplaces and a guesthouse. This became Jackie's favorite home, a fulfillment of one of her lifelong goals. "I think that one of the finest things that one can do in life is to create a loved house that shelters generations and gives them memories to build on," she said about this last home she had built for herself and her children. All of the book-lined rooms faced the ocean, with spectacular views. George Plimpton described Red Gate Farm as "a dream place, a sunlit place. It's hard to explain the effect it all had on you—all the variations in color, water sparkling like diamonds everywhere you looked."

At her Martha's Vineyard summer home, Jackie indulged her desire to create a secure, *gemütlich* interior. Fires were lit every morning in her bedroom, no matter the season. She slept on pink linen bedsheets, and three linen nightgowns were pressed and laid out on her bed each evening. Jackie

rose each morning at 7 AM, ate breakfast, then covered her entire body with Pond's cold cream and swam for 2 hours in

Squibnocket Pond. After lunch, she would go biking, waterski-
ing or kayaking from 1–4 PM. Dinners were early and light and
she would often watch movies on her VCR until about 9 or 10 PM
before retiring for the night.

She was, not surprisingly, embraced by her eminent neighbors
on the Vineyard, like the singer Carly Simon and the novelist William Styron and his wife, Rose. Red Gate Farm became a beautiful refuge that would replace Hyannis as a family retreat. Given
how reckless some of their Kennedy cousins had become, Jackie
wanted to keep Caroline and John Jr. away from the Kennedy
compound and have them spend more time with their Bouvier
cousins, Anthony and Tina, described by a friend of Lee's as "really nice, well-brought-up, classy kids." She wanted her children to
know about their Kennedy legacy, but she wanted to shield them
from the Kennedy competitiveness and risk-taking behavior.

*

JACKIE WASN'T THE only sister going to work. According to DuBois,
Lee had been miffed when Jackie took a job with Viking without
telling her about it. An unnamed witness reported that Lee "reacted with red-faced ire" when she heard about Jackie going to
work: "She just lost it, she was so angry beyond all reason." If true,
her anger might have been motivated by the blatant fact that Lee
was no longer fully in Jackie's confidence, and that Jackie was now
stealing the thunder that Lee had chased and coveted throughout
much of her adult life: a meaningful career. But it might also have
been the goad that focused Lee, once again, to look for meaningful work.

In February of 1976, after the Jonas Mekas film was tabled and
Lee was edited out of *Grey Gardens* after having spearheaded the
clean-up effort, Lee put aside writing her memoir and at the age
of forty-three opened her own interior design firm in Manhattan.

She'd always had the chops—and the taste and imagination—for interior design. Why not make a profession out of it? "Decorating has always been my hobby," Lee said, "but now I'm taking it seriously. It's been cooking in my mind for 15 years. I've always been interested in art, architecture, color." It was her love of art history, after all, that had gotten her through school.

Lee first approached the highly successful designers Mark Hampton and Mario Buatta about partnering with them, but when that didn't work out, she decided she was better off going alone in her new venture. "Without a partner," she said, "I am not indebted to or irritated by anyone. I don't have to worry about disagreeing over taste or tempo." She set up shop on the second floor of her Manhattan duplex, in a room painted white, with sisal carpeting covering the floor and one large working table in the center of the room, soon laden with richly colored fabric samples, design sketches, and handwritten estimates.

Within eight months of starting her business, Lee was invited to create a model room for the Lord & Taylor department store in New York, as part of a "Celebrity-Decorated Rooms for Summer" promotion. The result was simple yet stunning, combining her love for summery rattans with cool, peachy colors, and it was featured in *House & Garden* amid much fanfare. She also landed a contract with Americana Hotels to design a VIP suite for their hotel in upscale Bal Harbour in Miami, Florida. It was a beautiful room that succeeded in combining "an aura of brightness and shine," as Lee said, with "the warmth and comfort of home . . . the quality of a residence, as opposed to a typical hotel interior." Mario Di Genova, president of the hotel chain, was pleased, commenting, "Her rooms have that touch of class, yet not with severe traditional furnishing and antiques. She's not locked into a style." For two years Lee continued to work with Di Genova, who remained impressed with her designs and her ability to attract the right kind of attention. "She was so obviously an extremely elegant woman, and she gave parties at our hotels that brought national and international attention to them," Di Genova said. He also noted that she very much wanted to make an original, artistic statement with each room she designed, and once she'd made up her mind, it was impossible to budge her. Lee was professional, but she refused to abandon her vision in the face of such mundanities as budget and durability, both of which finally became an issue for Di Genova. Lee was ultimately given just a handful of high-end suites to decorate, and when Americana Hotels was put up for sale in 1978, that association ended.

Given Lee's talent, hard work, and stellar connections, she was soon flourishing in her new profession. She moved to an office rented from architect John Carl Warnecke, who had designed the JFK memorial at Arlington National Cemetery and who was an occasional escort of Lee's. Her sleek new office was on Fifth Avenue and 59th Street across from Central Park, and with Warnecke's encouragement and mentorship Lee attracted commissions from San Francisco, Houston, and Brazil. Her success surprised even her. "It's no joke. I have been far more successful than I ever imagined!" she said. She was even making money, which made her feel more confident—she charged $500 a day for consultations and earned $25,000 to $35,000 for the rooms she designed.

One of the hallmarks of her design style was to have a fire going in the fireplace as often as possible, "like having a friend that you like to be with." She also recognized that one of her strengths was being able to design in a number of different styles, from contemporary to beach-inspired to nineteenth-century grand.

Some people sniffed at Lee's ambitions, believing that her success was a mere reflection of her exalted status, but others disagreed. An editor at *Architectural Digest*, Paige Rense, said:

I don't think people took her seriously as a decorator, though she had a lot more talent than most people decorating today. If she hadn't been Princess Radziwill, she could have been Sister Parish.

Besides Warnecke, Lee also received help and encouragement from Mark Hampton, who had become a good friend. He was able to provide her with contacts with the right contractors and tradesmen; she reciprocated by inviting him to parties where he could meet potential high-end clients. "I wanted a full-time job," she said, "and now I have really got one, and in this field I think I am as good as anybody." She relished the hard work, getting up at dawn to meet with contractors and plumbers, and she relished the confidence of being successful and recognized on her own. "I'm nobody's kid sister," she told journalist Lee Wohlfert for an interview in *People* when Jackie's name came up, as it always did.

After leaving London and her marriage to Stas, Lee had reinvented herself as a very successful Manhattan professional. That was a good thing, because when Stas died in the summer of 1976, he had nothing to leave for his children but massive debt.

*

AS HIS FORTUNES continued to dwindle, Stas Radziwill was reduced to selling their former home at 4 Buckingham Place. (It was bought by the heiress Charlotte Ford, who had been one of Stas's mistresses.) He was drinking heavily, broken by his divorce and his staggering financial losses. On June 27, 1976, Prince Stanislas Radziwill died of a heart attack, during a weekend party in Essex, England. He had returned to his room after a game of cards and, while undressing for bed, suddenly collapsed. The household was alerted several hours later when a dog brought along by another weekend guest began howling outside of Stas's room. A butler then found him lying dead on the floor. He was just sixty-two years old.

The funeral was held at St. Anna's Chapel not far from Turville Grange. His coffin was draped with the Radziwill family flag, lent to the family by a Warsaw museum. Besides Lee and her children and Jackie and Caroline, present also was Stas's longtime girlfriend, Christine Weckert, an American girl in her late twenties who was besotted with Stas and had pressured him to marry her. Friends thought that her greatest appeal was that she somewhat resembled Lee in appearance. Sadly for Christine, Stas had reportedly proposed to her just hours before his death.

Jackie was devastated when Stas suddenly died. She and Jack had always felt close to him, drawn by his warmth and lack of snobbery. His niece Countess Isabelle d'Ornano described Stas as "a great personality, someone you would not forget." The countess saw that

> Jackie loved Stas. He and Lee were so different, they had nothing in common . . . [Jackie] understood him, and whenever she spoke of him, it was with enormous affection . . . he counted in her life.

Upon his death, it was discovered that he owed 15 million pounds to his creditors, much to Lee's surprise, and by making himself personally responsible for the debts of his holding companies—which was an honorable but disastrous thing to have done—he had bankrupted his estate. Anthony left England for good, returning to live full-time with Lee in New York.

More losses were to come. Five months later, in November of 1976, Hugh D. Auchincloss, once referred to as "the first gentleman of New York," died from emphysema. Surprisingly, Auchincloss had also lost most of his fortune through bad investments. Though Janet remarried three years later, to retired investment banker Bingham Morris, she had to sell the main house and much of the land at Hammersmith Farm, moving into "the Castle," the yellow farmhouse on the property that had once served as servants' quarters.

At their stepfather's funeral, the two sisters arrived and left separately.

*

JACKIE REMAINED WORKING at Doubleday for the next sixteen years. Although there was speculation that she was involved in a romantic relationship with executive editor John Sargent Sr., a striking, bearded patrician considered one of New York's most eligible bachelors, that was a rumor never substantiated. Jackie was seeing other prominent men at the time, such as director Mike Nichols and journalist Pete Hamill, but none were serious relationships. Jackie meant it when she said she now wanted to put work above men in her life.

At first, she felt a bit lost at Doubleday, which was a much larger, much more corporate environment. Having essentially been given carte blanche at Viking to bring in writers and book ideas, she now had to run the gauntlet of weekly meetings with marketing and editorial departments to present and defend her ideas. For someone as shy as Jackie, that was a challenge. She managed to show up at editorial meetings once a month instead of weekly, and according to writer and former Doubleday editor Harriet Rubin:

> When her turn came to present her ideas, she trilled about projects that would have gotten anyone else fired for being ridiculously uncommercial: a collected Pushkin, an American "Pleiade," an illustrated children's book based on a tale in Vasari of Leonardo crafting artificial insects. She lost those battles.

Another former Doubleday editor, James Fitzgerald, described the editorial meetings as a kind of *Gong Show* in which Jackie "would go into those things and she'd get shut down and cut down on some projects . . . just like the rest of us."

One of her early successes, though, was bringing Diana Vreeland to Doubleday from Viking for the 1980 publication of *Allure*, a book of photographs. She worked closely with Vreeland, poring over photographs in the doyenne's Manhattan apartment and designing the look and scope of the collection.

Jackie lost more editorial battles than she won, but Doubleday did what it needed to keep her there as she was a considerable asset to the publishing house. For her part, Jackie wanted to be a good team player, which is why she accepted the editorial duties for bringing out Michael Jackson's memoir, *Moonwalk*, in 1988. It was a four-year undertaking, resulting in a book that Jackie felt was "a professional embarrassment," though it was her biggest commercial success as an editor. Another former colleague at Doubleday confided that Jackie was moved to discover, based on notes they exchanged, that the pop idol was barely literate.

*

IN 1976, AFTER the breakup with Peter Beard and the death of Stas, Lee began seeing Peter Tufo, a prominent Chicago-born New York lawyer involved in city politics who was also known as something of a ladies' man, having courted many socially prominent women before meeting Lee. The two had many interests in common, including theater and ballet, and Tufo seemed genuinely smitten with Lee; he was once overheard at a social gathering as saying, "Isn't she beautiful, intelligent, artistic, creative, and radiant? Lee is just so wonderful!" They took skiing vacations in Switzerland and traveled to Morocco together, and it also mattered that Tina seemed comfortable with Lee's new beau, the three of them sometimes sharing an evening out. Lee and

Tufo discussed marriage, but both were deeply caught up in their own work—by now Lee had thrown herself wholeheartedly into her interior design business. She told Klemesrud:

> In the last few years I have really learned to take care of myself. It was almost like being reborn. Before, everything was done for me. I was totally incompetent, and so was my daughter— there were endless things one could not cope with. Suddenly I was on my own with two children. It was terrifying . . . [but] I have found the most important thing is to be self-reliant. Marriage is an extremely difficult relationship . . . I am so happy on my own.

One shadow that loomed over Lee's newfound happiness with herself and her new beau was Truman Capote's disapproval—his envy, actually, as he resented the time Lee devoted to Tufo in neglect of her once closest friend. He ostensibly objected to the Manhattan lawyer's middle-class background, insisting that he was not good enough for Lee, but in truth her estrangement from him wounded his feelings and his vanity.

*

IN NOVEMBER 1976, Lee spent much of her divorce settlement from Stas to buy the beach house on Gin Lane in Southampton that she had been renting, for $329,000. There was some unpleasantness over the payment of the real estate agent's commission ("When it came to money, Lee was just impossible" he reportedly said), and Lee was obliged to occasionally rent out the house during the peak summer months, but it was a brilliant acquisition both financially and emotionally, indulging her love of the sea. The former owner, a man named Mark Goodson who had been part of Lee's social circle, greatly regretted having sold the place "in the days before properties went wild." This was when the Hamptons was still thickly populated by artists, before it became overrun with tourists, gawkers, weekenders, and the ultrawealthy—billionaires refusing to mingle with millionaires.

*

IN 1979, LEE came close to being married for a third time, but not to Tufo. She met Newton Cope, a widower and a successful restaurateur and hotelier in San Francisco, on a business trip with Mark Hampton. Lee was invited to a dinner party by a prominent rancher and vintner, Whitney Warren, who indulged in a bit of matchmaking by seating Lee next to the newly widowed, fifty-five-year-old Cope.

Cope, the father of seven children, quickly fell for Lee. They spent the entire evening in deep conversation, and when the night was over, Cope decided to ask Lee to redecorate the prestigious Huntington Hotel on Nob Hill in San Francisco, which he owned. A bicoastal romance quickly flourished, and for a while Lee was juggling her affair with Tufo in New York and her romance with Cope in San Francisco. At first she was discreet, avoiding Cope's advances and making sure to keep a door open while the two were working together on redecorating the Huntington. She wasn't yet ready to let Peter Tufo go, and as one acquaintance observed, "Lee always took her reputation quite seriously because of her sister." Nonetheless rumors abounded, and the press began asking questions about their relationship. The *Daily News* reported, "What's this hot romance between Lee and Newton Cope?" which, unfortunately, Peter Tufo saw after an evening out with Lee. Furious, he stomped out of her apartment.

Tufo was jealous, and the two spent much of their time together arguing. It had begun to dawn on Lee, anyway, that Tufo did not have the resources Lee needed to live the way she expected to

live, and she increasingly resented the time he spent at work, both
for his law practice and on his civic work such as developing and
narrating a thirteen-part television series on public education titled *Save Our Schools*. Perhaps Truman's complaint that Tufo was
"not good enough"—read "not rich enough"—for Lee had gotten
under her skin. On Tufo's part, he was still holding out the hope of
fathering children, something that held no interest for Lee, even
if that weren't impossible for her, as she had undergone a hysterectomy five years previously, when she was thirty-nine. They separated just before Christmas of 1977. (Lee would later have second
thoughts and would try to rekindle the flame, but this time it was
Tufo who made it clear that he had moved on.)

According to DuBois, Lee was left feeling restless and alone, despite her earlier claims of self-sufficiency, and she began to drink
more than usual and to take her frustration out on Tina. Seeing a
reflection of herself in her daughter, perhaps, Lee was especially
hard on Tina, wanting her to be slimmer, more outgoing, more
the image of how Lee saw herself. It had gotten so difficult for
Tina that she began spending more and more time with her aunt
Jackie, eventually moving into Jackie's Fifth Avenue apartment.
As weekends turned into months, Lee felt increasing resentment.
Was this going to be another area in which Jackie bested her, in
raising her own daughter?

Lee complained to Newton Cope, whom she was now seeing
exclusively after breaking up with Peter Tufo. Cope later told
Lee's biographer:

> It must have cooled things off between them for a while, because
> Lee never mentioned much about Jackie after that. I think she
> was hurt. She didn't say much about it, and I didn't want to pry.
> But it was quite obvious to me that Lee wasn't much of a great,
> warm mother. Tina always struck me as unhappy . . . Her father's

death must have been a terrible weight on Tina. It's too bad, because she is a very nice girl.

Lee was struggling with two seemingly intractable problems: she was hurting financially despite her design business, and she was abusing alcohol. It might have been a family disease, given her father's alcoholism, or it might have been her way of coping with her insecurities—personal and financial—and her disappointments in the men in her life. She continued to work on her design business, which helped keep her sober during the day, but she sometimes operated with clouded judgment, making grand promises to clients she couldn't fulfill. As DuBois writes, "Lee was such a perfectionist in her work that when she could not meet the demands of her unreasonable nature, she would become enraged and calm herself down with a drink."

Her drink of choice was vodka—probably introduced to her by Stas and Nureyev. Because she could go for long periods of time without drinking, and few people saw her under the influence, she continued as a high-functioning alcoholic under the radar of many of her friends and acquaintances.

At Jackie's insistence and with her help, Lee entered Alcoholics Anonymous, attending meetings twice weekly at St. Luke's Episcopal Church in East Hampton. Oddly enough, she fit in with the other recovering alcoholics, dressing down in a turtleneck and jeans, and her sincere desire to achieve sobriety impressed the group. As one member observed, "AA is a great social leveler— the road to alcoholic recovery strips away a lot of the distractions. It was probably very refreshing for her not to have to be Lee Bouvier Radziwill for once."

Her friend Ralph Rucci thought that one reason for Lee's alcoholism was that she "has absolutely no patience or tolerance for boredom—none. But Lee really took care of it—her addictions. She's quite proud of that, as she should be." But the deeper reasons emerged throughout Lee's attendance at AA meetings. A fellow member recalled that

> Lee described her life as raunchy, hard-drinking, and messy, and she confessed to how her alcoholic behavior and personality played a major role in the failure of her endeavors. She never felt that she was much of anything, that she always felt second in her family, and in truth, in every way. Her self-image was devastating and covered over with grandiosity. Alcohol gave her a false sense of confidence as a way to mask her painful shyness . . .

She admitted to sometimes picking up Anthony and Tina at school with alcohol on her breath, or forgetting to pick them up at all, and she realized that she was doing harm to them. That is probably what most alarmed Jackie, the good mother, who hated to see her nephew and niece being overlooked.

Lee carried on, traveling to San Francisco once a month to work on the Huntington Hotel commission and to continue her relationship with Cope. She was always professional, to the point that Newton Cope never saw her drink. By the end of her first year of attending meetings, Lee managed to achieve sobriety.

They spent a great deal of time together. "I had a house in Napa," Cope reminisced. "We drove up there a few times. Looked at the grapevines. What do people do? We were happy together." On his visits to see Lee in New York, he always stayed at the Carlyle Hotel, so each could maintain their privacy, even as they grew closer. Like Peter Beard and Jay Mellon before him, Cope noticed that Lee could be two different people—warm and fun-loving in private but often cold, brittle, and snobbish in public. "It's too bad she has two personalities," he said, "and her warmth isn't there all the time."

Lee ended up redecorating only five of the rooms of the Huntington Hotel—worn out from travel and the strain of fulfilling other commissions in New York—but also because her designs once again proved too lavish. She did successfully redecorate several rooms in Cope's Nob Hill apartment, however. Cope negotiated to buy the Stanhope Hotel in Manhattan, with plans to turn the penthouse into a home for Lee and himself. That deal fell through, but not the intention to live together: in April of 1979 they announced their engagement and planned a wedding for May 3.

The plan was for Lee to move to San Francisco, but keep her apartment in Manhattan and her beach house on Long Island. She would open an office of her design business in San Francisco, and they would commute between the two cities.

But an hour before the wedding was to begin, Cope called California Supreme Court Justice Stanley Bass, who was to marry them at Whitney Warren's luxurious apartment on Telegraph Hill, telling him that the marriage was off—or at least postponed. Apparently, Jackie was the catalyst.

Though they were at the lowest point in their relationship, Jackie still wanted to see her little sister well taken care of. Cope was reportedly worth around $10 million, so Jackie privately contacted him and insisted that he settle a $15,000-per-month prenuptial agreement on Lee before the marriage went through, arranged through Jackie's lawyer, Alexander Forger.

"I don't think Lee would have thought of something like that. She wasn't as money-hungry as Jackie was," a friend of both sisters believes. "Lee wanted to be taken care of, yes, but I don't think she would connive in that way." Cope ended up feeling manipulated and bullied, telling Forger, "I am not buying a cow or a celebrity the way Onassis did! I am in love with this woman!" Cope, too, was surprised to see how Lee was intimidated by her big sister.

"Why the hell are you so afraid of your sister?" Cope had asked

Lee one night, leaving a dinner party Jackie had given in honor of the couple. Cope later said, "It's too bad Lee couldn't get away from that sister of hers. Being just a few blocks away, it was like an unhealthy bond she couldn't escape from . . ."

They postponed their wedding until fall, but by then it was clear to Cope that Lee really didn't want to move her life to San Francisco. Cope, too, recognized that they had little in common. For one thing, he was a Republican who disliked the Kennedys. But mostly, Cope felt manipulated, and the dire warnings of some of his friends no doubt took their toll: that both sisters were gold diggers—"the two worst piranhas in the United States," in the words of one of Cope's friends. And on Lee's side, there was Truman reportedly whispering in her ear, "That Newton Cope out in San Francisco, that provincial little town, what's he got?"

Years later, Cope would insist that it was he who called off the marriage, wondering how much Lee had to do with insisting that he sign a $15,000-per-month prenuptial agreement: "All those articles that said I was left at the altar, and Lee called it off were wrong. I CALLED IT OFF!"

Nonetheless, they took a two-week trip, their would-be honeymoon, in St. Martin and considered marrying there—away from Jackie, and lawyers, and the press, and without the prenup. But Cope was wary by now, and the romance was soon over. Another problem awaited Lee at home: a long-simmering feud that had turned litigious between Truman Capote and Gore Vidal.

*

BY NOW JACKIE was an immensely rich woman; the $26 million settlement from Onassis grew to $150 million under the astute guidance of her trusted friend and new companion, a married Orthodox Jewish diamond broker named Maurice Tempelsman. She would additionally acquire another estimated $40 million in art, antiques, jewelry, and real estate.

Lee, on the other hand, was still struggling. With her marriage to Cope called off and her design business a success but not
enough of a success to underwrite two high-end abodes in New
York, she sold her stunning duplex apartment at 969 Park Avenue and bought a much smaller penthouse five blocks away, at
875 Park. Though smaller, it had a wraparound terrace that Lee
graced with plants in blue and silver hues, backed by a picket fence,
giving it a country air. Later she would sell that apartment and
be reduced to renting even smaller apartments in New York. She
sold many of her prized possessions: Fabergé boxes, much of her
nineteenth-century furniture, and Francis Bacon's *Figure Turning*, which sold for only $200,000. Had she waited a few years, it
would have brought her millions in the burgeoning art market of
the 1980s.

Like Lily Bart, the heroine of Edith Wharton's *House of Mirth*,
Lee was facing the prospect of a slow and steady fall, made harder
to bear by her sister's wealth. One wag even joked that since Lee
had been involved with Onassis before Jackie and had introduced
them, Jackie should have given Lee "a finder's fee" when Onassis
left her a wealthy widow.

"When you are a very, very rich girl," Truman Capote once
observed, "you don't marry the same way a real girl marries.
You marry the way another person travels in a foreign country.
You stay there until you tire of it, then you go elsewhere." That
was one area in which Truman and Gore Vidal were in agreement. "Both sisters were brought up like geishas, to get money
out of men," Vidal had waspishly said about the two sisters, whose
mother, Janet, had supplanted his own mother in the Auchincloss
household a lifetime before.

As for Jackie, she would not marry a third time. Her friendship
with Maurice Tempelsman deepened into love after they first met
in 1975, soon after Ari's death. The two attended the Broadway

musical *Chicago* and stayed up talking until 3 a.m., finding many interests in common. They both loved literature; Tempelsman introduced Jackie to Proust's masterpiece, *À la recherche du temps perdu*. From an Orthodox Jewish family in Belgium, Tempelsman had arrived in New York in 1940, having fled the Nazis. He was a supporter of Democratic causes and had been invited to the Kennedy White House on a few occasions. He was married, and he and his wife, Lily, had three children. Divorce was out of the picture, but that didn't prevent his and Jackie's relationship from blossoming over intimate dinners at Lutèce, La Côte Basque, the Four Seasons. Eventually, by 1982, Lily Tempelsman granted her husband a "get," an Orthodox Jewish divorce, and he moved in with Jackie at Ten Forty. Though rather portly and balding—certainly no peacock like Jack Kennedy or Peter Beard or even Onassis—he "worshipped the ground [Jackie] walked on," according to one of her close friends.

*

BY 1977, TRUMAN Capote was in deep decline, drinking too much, snorting cocaine, and partying at Studio 54, which had opened its doors on West 54th Street in April of that year. Truman loved the disco, describing it as "the nightclub of the future . . . Boys with boys, girls with girls, girls with boys, blacks and whites, capitalists and Marxists, Chinese and everything else—all one big mix."

Truman's weight had ballooned, drowning his once refined features in alcoholic bloat. The art collector and Picasso biographer John Richardson recalled seeing "a sort of bag lady with two enormous bags wandering around the corner of Lexington and 73rd, where I lived then. And suddenly, I realized, Christ! It's Truman!" Richardson invited the writer up for a cup of tea. He disappeared into the kitchen to make the tea, but when he returned, he noticed that "half a bottle of Vodka—or Scotch or whatever it was—was gone. I had to take him outside and gently put him into a cab."

All of Truman's celebrated swans had abandoned him after the publication in *Esquire* in November of 1975 of a salacious chapter titled "La Côte Basque 1965" from *Answered Prayers*, the book that was going to be Truman's masterpiece. Truman had boasted to Marella Agnelli that *Answered Prayers* was "going to do to America what Proust did to France." He couldn't stop talking about his planned roman à clef. He even told *People* magazine that he was constructing his book like a gun: "There's the handle, the trigger, the barrel, and finally, the bullet. And when that bullet is fired from the gun, it's going to come out with a speed and power like you've never seen: *wham!*" But he might as well have turned the gun on himself: it was nothing short of an act of social suicide.

Just ten years earlier, the 1965 publication of *In Cold Blood* had brought him international fame, sudden wealth, and literary accolades beyond anything he'd experienced before. He'd been a literary darling since the age of twenty-two, when his first novel, *Other Voices, Other Rooms*, was published, but his vivid "nonfiction novel" had created a new genre and had added gravitas to his celebrity.

In 1966, Truman had signed a contract for *Answered Prayers* for an advance of $25,000 and delivery by January 1, 1968, but no book appeared. Three years later, he renegotiated a three-book contract for an advance of $750,000, with delivery by September 1977. The contract was amended twice more, culminating in an agreement of $1 million for delivery by March 1, 1981. He missed that deadline as well.

Truman described his plan for the book to Gerald Clarke: "I always planned this book as being my principal work . . . I'm going to call it a novel, but in actual fact it's a *roman-a-clef.* Almost everything in it is true, and it has . . . every sort of person I've ever had any dealings with. I have a cast of thousands." He took his title from Saint Teresa of Avila, the sixteenth-century Carmelite nun who'd said, "More tears are shed over answered prayers than unanswered ones."

If Truman was constructing *Answered Prayers* like a gun, he pulled the trigger when "La Côte Basque 1965" appeared in *Esquire*. He had turned his narrative gifts on the haut monde of New York, his very own swans—Gloria Vanderbilt, Babe Paley, Slim Keith, Mona Harrison Williams. Just as Proust's three-thousand-page masterpiece, *À la recherche du temps perdu* (*In Search of Lost Time*), had chronicled the public and private lives of nineteenth-century Parisian aristocrats, Capote revealed the gossip, the secrets, the betrayals—even a murder—among New York society. "All literature is gossip," Truman told *Playboy* magazine when the *merde* hit the fan. "What in God's green earth is *Anna Karenina* or *War and Peace*, or *Madame Bovary*, if not gossip?"

"La Côte Basque 1965" was intended to be the fifth chapter of the finished book, and it referred to Henri Soulé's celebrated restaurant on East 55th Street, across from the St. Regis hotel. It was the elegant pond where the swans gathered to lunch.

An article by the celebrated gossip columnist Liz Smith, "Truman Capote in Hot Water" in *New York* magazine, was accompanied by an Edward Sorel caricature on the cover depicting Truman as a French poodle biting the hand of a society lady ("Capote Bites the Hands that Fed Him" read the headline). "Society's sacred monsters at the top have been in a state of shock," Smith wrote. "Never have you heard such gnashing of teeth, such cries for revenge, such shouts of betrayal and screams of outrage . . . not since Marcel Proust flattered his way into the salons of the Faubourg St. Germain . . ."

Whereas Truman had disguised many of his swans, Liz Smith outed them in her article: Lady Coolbirth was Slim Keith; Ann Hopkins was Ann Woodward; Sidney Dillon was Babe Paley's husband, William Paley. "It's one thing to tell the nastiest story in the world to all your fifty best friends," Smith wrote, "it's another to see it set down in cold, Century Expanded type."

A friend not mentioned in the story was Cecil Beaton. The two men had been close since the 1940s. It was Beaton who had introduced Truman to London literary society, and Truman had once rescued Cecil from a beating by two sailors he'd picked up in Honolulu. Though they were friends, Beaton envied Truman's success with *In Cold Blood* and the social triumph of the Black and White Ball (inspired by Beaton's black-and-white costumes for the horse-racing scene in *My Fair Lady*). If Beaton had been looking for an opportunity to break with his former protégé, this was it. Beaton had spent his entire life cultivating the rich and the royal; that's where his loyalties lay. "I hate the idea of Truman," he wrote in a letter after the notorious article was published, "how low can he sink?"

A few of Capote's friends remained loyal, however, such as the socialites Cornelia Guest and Louise Grunwald (then Louise Melhado)—though Grunwald considered herself less a swan than a "satellite."

"What's interesting about these women," Grunwald said in retrospect,

> is that they were lonely. They didn't really have anyone else to talk to, without losing face. I could have told Truman things—I had a past—but I didn't. You have to remember, these were unhappy women, and I wasn't unhappy. But he had been rebuffed by so many in that world. I didn't see much of him after that. He must have been afraid of my rejection.

Truman probably should have listened to Joe Fox, his editor, who had warned him not to publish chapters before the novel was completed. "I was against this plan, feeling that he was revealing too much of the book too soon, and said so," he later explained. But Truman felt it would be great publicity for the book—the worst decision of his professional life.

"I'd never seen anything like it," Clarke recalled.

I read "La Cote Basque" one summer day in Gloria Vanderbilt's swimming pool in the Hamptons when Gloria and her husband, Wyatt Cooper, were away. I was reading it while Truman was floating in the pool on a raft. I said, "People aren't going to be happy with this, Truman." He said, "Nah, they're too dumb. They won't know who they are." He could not have been more wrong.

How could Truman have been so blindsided by the howl of injury the story evoked? John Richardson suggested:

I wonder whether he wasn't testing the love of his friends, to see what he could get away with. We had Truman around because he paid for his supper, by being the great storyteller. Truman was a brilliant raconteur. We'd say, "Oh, do tell us what Mae West was really like," or what did he know about Doris Duke? And he'd go on in that inimitable voice for twenty minutes, and it was absolutely marvelous, one story after another. And he loved doing it—he was a show-off.

If anything, Truman was puzzled by the extreme reaction of his swans. "What did they expect?" he protested. "I'm a writer, and I used everything. Did all these people think I was there just to entertain them?" Apparently, they did.

There were many theories as to why Truman published the gossip and secrets of his society friends. Louise Grunwald believed that "surrounding himself with beauty had something to do with his own self-image. Truman wanted to *be* them." Truman had been fussed over as a young child for his beautiful blond curls, and he possessed an elfin, boyish beauty in his youth. Cooper once observed, "Truman would like to be glamorous and beautiful. He has often acted out fantasies of his own by telling his women friends how to act, who to have love affairs with, by manipulating them." Or making them over.

Unlike Truman's other swans, Lee did not break with Truman over "La Côte Basque," having been spared any mention, or betrayal of secrets, in the article. And her friendship had been deeper, more genuine, than with his other swans. But even before the publication of "La Côte Basque," she had already begun to move away from him.

What completely ended their friendship was the lawsuit for libel brought against Truman by Gore Vidal. In an interview he'd given to *Playgirl* magazine, Truman had related the story about how a drunken Gore Vidal "insulted" Jackie at a White House dinner party and was allegedly thrown out of the White House by Bobby Kennedy and Arthur Schlesinger. Gore was incensed by Truman's story, which proved to be the culmination of the smoldering feud that had gone on between the two men for decades. Besides professional jealousy, the masculine and self-contained Vidal—though gay—had contempt for overtly homosexual, feminized men like Truman. He demanded an apology and $1 million in damages.

Truman had asked Liz Smith to intervene and persuade Vidal to drop his lawsuit. Vidal refused. Truman then asked the columnist to beg Lee to give a deposition on his behalf, as he allegedly had first gotten the story from Lee. Liz asked Lee to at least say that the incident had occurred—"Otherwise, Gore is going to win this lawsuit, and it's just going to crush Truman."

Lee reportedly answered, "Oh, Liz, what does it matter? They're just a couple of fags." Liz Smith could not believe her ears. "I called Truman back and I said, 'She won't do it.'"

Lee's acid comment reflected how much she disliked being in

the middle of litigation between Gore Vidal, whom she increasingly saw as a snake, and Truman, whose alcoholism frightened her, perhaps stirring up fears about her own struggle with alcohol. In any case, it was a nasty remark, and a foolish one to make to Liz, a gossip columnist who counted Truman as a friend.

Lee stopped returning Truman's calls. "We drifted apart because of his drinking," Lee explained years later. "I never forgot about him, but we didn't see each other, because he wasn't making any sense whatsoever. It was pitiful. Heartbreaking, because there was nothing you could do. He really wanted to kill himself. It was a slow and painful suicide."

The lawsuit dragged on for seven years, until Vidal agreed to settle for a written apology and a fraction of his legal fees. He felt he had won the moral victory.

Truman escaped to Hollywood to appear in Neil Simon's crime spoof, *Murder by Death*, but he was still drinking, still angry, and still nursing his wounds. He stayed with his good friend Joanne Carson, one of Johnny Carson's ex-wives. On August 25, 1984, three days after he arrived at her house on a one-way ticket, Joanne found Truman gasping for breath, so she called the paramedics. By the time they arrived, fifty-nine-year-old Truman had died in her arms. His last words were "answered prayers," which raises the question of how much Truman welcomed his own demise.

For Lee, not seeing Truman again "was a terrible loss, because he did bring a lot of joy into my life, more than anybody I can think of, off the top of my head. He had a great sense of humor and a wonderful laugh," she wrote tenderly in *Lee*, her brief, illustrated memoir published many years later, in 2015. She had forgiven him his alcoholic excesses and his occasional venom, though she would always regret having given a deposition that favored Vidal more than it helped Capote. Lee had given a sworn affidavit to Vidal's lawyer that it was not she who had told Truman about a drunken Vidal being evicted from the White House, leaving Truman without a leg to stand on.

Why did she do it? As DuBois pointed out, to have done otherwise would have made her liable as a codefendant, vulnerable to a legal entanglement that could have cost her a fortune in attorney fees and damages—a fortune she did not have.

But she had once described Truman as her closest friend.

*

THE PREVIOUS YEAR, in March of 1983, Lee sold her penthouse at 875 Park Avenue for an especially good price because the apartment had been featured in *Architectural Digest.* From there she moved to a rented duplex apartment at 48 East 73rd Street. In downsizing, she had to shed many of her treasured objets d'art. Comparing herself to a diplomat "taking with me from place to place the pieces that I love and need and putting the rest in storage," she also said the paring down was like "going on a diet to purify yourself." But she still managed to transform the several rooms into a beautiful home. She covered the living room ceiling in gold wallpaper to complement the golden cork paper on the walls, with the effect that the entire room took on a luminous hue in evening light.

The following year, she closed down her design business.

Lee had become tired of the boring details of running a business—the endless invoices and paperwork, the waiting for materials to be delivered and being blamed by the client when they were late or didn't show up. "They think it's your fault, whereas you can do nothing whatsoever about it. You call the upholsterers, the curtain people, the carpenters, every single day, and you just repeat the same thing the next day," she complained. "I don't find decorating creative any longer. I did it until I felt boxed in."

Lee increasingly spent time in her Southampton home, wandering the beach in jeans with her hair pulled back in a ponytail, swimming almost every day the weather permitted. She hosted luncheons around the pool for her now grown children and for friends in the Hamptons, like the painter Roy Lichtenstein and his wife, Dorothy. She occasionally took on decorating jobs but only if they interested her, but she no longer looked upon it as a lucrative, full-time business.

In March of 1985 Lee began work as a roving editor-at-large for *Architectural Digest*, beginning with a story on Nureyev's sumptuous Paris apartment. She followed that up with a visit to Hammersmith Farm to report on her mother's residence in the yellow farmhouse, which she had moved into with her third husband after Hughdie's death. Though much diminished from the fairy-tale estate of Lee and Jackie's youth, it was still an impressive property.

At the end of the summer of 1986, Lee began a new job tailor-made for her interests and talents: director of special events for the influential Milanese designer Giorgio Armani, which meant that she would publicize his clothes by wearing them at important social events, appearing as Giorgio's "image-maker, aide, flag-waver, muse, and showpiece."

Lee had known the fashion designer since the late '70s, when she was on his VIP gift list and thus was the recipient of his clothes and jewelry in exchange for prominently wearing his designs among her wealthy society friends, boosting his access to new clients. She had admired his fashions from the start, saying, "His clothes suit my way of life so well. They're so effortless, so easy to wear." She also recognized Armani's modernity, his willingness to break with the past, moving from formal tweeds to unstructured jackets, rolled sleeves, understated elegance. In these ways, they were simpatico.

11

WEDDINGS AND FUNERALS

Sell everything. You'll make a lot of money.
— JACKIE

I don't do death well.
— LEE

Since 1982, Carolina Herrera—Lee's friend—had become Jackie's favorite designer, and it was she who designed Caroline Kennedy's wedding dress for her marriage to Edwin Schlossberg on July 19, 1986.

Jackie had stepped back and allowed Caroline to make her own wedding plans. Herrera recalled that Caroline wanted "to do her own wedding her own way . . . not the classic way, and Jackie was very happy about that . . . And the boys wanted to wear not morning suits, but white pants and blazers, and she was quite happy about that."

Schlossberg asked the African-American designer Willi Smith to design what the men in the wedding party would wear. He wanted a "sophisticated yet breezy effect," which was achieved by a navy blue linen suit, oversized in keeping with the fashion of the late 1980s. Ushers wore violet linen blazers with pink ties— unconventional yet somehow keeping with the casual setting at the Kennedy compound in Hyannis Port, where the reception was held. Caroline's close friend and cousin Maria Shriver, who had married Arnold Schwarzenegger three months earlier, was matron of honor, and John Jr. was best man.

Schlossberg, 41, was the scion of a wealthy Jewish family. He was thirteen years older than Caroline, but then Jack Kennedy had been twelve years older than Jackie, so that was not considered unusual. As Sarah Bradford writes in *America's Queen*:

> Like Jack, it might be said, he did not have "a steady job," nor did he have to worry too much about money. He came from a wealthy textile family with a home on Park Avenue and he himself was equipped with the regulation loft and a converted barn in the Berkshires. The only difference that might have come between them was their religion; she was from an Irish Catholic family while the Schlossbergs were practicing Jews.

Anti-Semitism, that "stupid suburban prejudice" (as Ezra Pound described it to the poet Allen Ginsberg, visiting him at St. Elizabeths Hospital in Washington, DC), ran like a vein through the Kennedy and Auchincloss families. In 1986, that no longer seemed to matter, especially since the death of Hughdie, the resident anti-Semite in the family, and certainly not to Jackie, who had unexpectedly found a soul mate in Maurice Tempelsman. Like her mother, Caroline was made truly happy by Schlossberg, an unapologetically unathletic, artistically inclined Jewish New Yorker who had once nursed an ambition to become a poet.

So Schlossberg was warmly welcomed into the family. At the rehearsal dinner, John Jr. toasted him with, "The three of us have been alone for such a long time, we welcome a fourth person." Nor did the Schlossbergs object, so on July 19, 1986, Caroline became Mrs. Edwin Schlossberg in a Catholic service at Our Lady of Victory in Centerville, Massachusetts.

As Jackie left the church after vows were exchanged, she leaned on Ted Kennedy's shoulder, tears glistening in her eyes. Tears of joy, of course, and perhaps of relief at her daughter's happiness, in a country where, just eighteen years earlier, she had felt that "they're killing Kennedys" in America.

Though she was long out of the White House, America still felt a fondness for Caroline, and many compared her wedding to Prince Andrew's marriage to Sarah Ferguson the same month. Hundreds of reporters and photographers and nearly a thousand spectators thronged the churchyard, creating such a clamor that the bride, escorted by Ted Kennedy, actually had to shush them as she entered the church.

Another of Jackie's friends, the prominent fund-raiser George Trescher, organized the lavish reception. A white tent was raised on the lawn outside matriarch Rose Kennedy's house, a puffball filled with a thousand flowers suspended above the dance floor. The New York catering firm Glorious Food planned the menu with Jackie—one area where she took full charge. Instead of "unseasonably heavy New England seafood and boiled beef," as one report mistakenly had it, the two-hour champagne reception was followed by

> a cold pea soup with mint, shrimp and apples, vegetable vinaigrette, roast chicken with rice, cold sirloin of beef, salad, raspberries and two identical wedding cakes, white inside and out—and without the traditional bride and bridegroom on top.

Jackie later joked, "I don't know how this is going to go down with those meat and potato, vanilla ice cream Kennedys."

Carly Simon, Jackie's new friend in Martha's Vineyard, sang "Chapel of Love." More tears were shed at the reception when Ted Kennedy toasted his sister-in-law as "that extraordinary gallant woman, Jack's only love." Finally, while a bank of fog rolled in from the ocean, the evening ended with a spectacular fireworks display organized by George Plimpton, which featured custom-designed fireworks for fifteen family members and friends—including "a rose for Rose Kennedy, a sailboat for Teddy, a bow tie for the professorial Arthur Schlesinger."

Tina Radziwill was reported to have been one of Caroline's bridesmaids, but though she and her mother both attended the wedding and reception, they were not included in the wedding party. Excluded from the wedding altogether were Jackie and Lee's Bouvier relatives—her first cousin and her twin aunts—because Jackie had broken off relations with her first cousin John Davis after he published his history of the Bouviers in 1969. That was the one unpardonable sin, as far as Jackie was concerned.

*

JACKIE HAD BEEN delighted at her daughter's marriage and looked forward to the prospect of grandchildren, but she was downright relieved when Lee married the Hollywood film director Herbert David Ross on September 24, 1988, at the age of fifty-five. Jackie confided in a friend, "I'm happy for Lee, because between you and me, Lee has stared into the jaws of hell."

The couple married in a civil service presided over by a judge and witnessed by Lee's close friend Rudolf Nureyev. Bob Colacello, who covered the wedding for *Vanity Fair*, noted that both bride and groom were dressed in Armani (ice blue for Lee, a tasteful gray for Ross), while Nureyev jauntily wore his trademark beret. Afterward, Jackie hosted a wedding dinner for the couple at her Fifth Avenue apartment, while a phalanx of paparazzi swarmed on the sidewalk below.

With sixty-one-year-old Ross, a radiantly happy Lee saw many of her desires and interests converge in the persona of a warm, witty, highly successful Hollywood director. He had many successful and admired films to his credit, including *Play It Again, Sam*, *The Seven-Per-Cent Solution*, *The Goodbye Girl*, and later, with Lee showing up on location in Louisiana, *Steel Magnolias*,

but it was three dance-themed movies he directed that had gotten
Lee's attention—*The Turning Point, Pennies From Heaven*, and
Nijinsky, in which Nureyev had played the title role. Lee recalled:

> I'd known all about Herbert a long, long time and had hoped
> that our paths would cross . . . When I saw *The Turning Point*,
> Herbert's name stuck in my head for a long time and then many
> years passed and I saw *Pennies from Heaven*, which I loved so
> much that I saw it three times by myself in one week.

They'd met in January at a dinner party in Bel Air given by
producer Doug Cramer, and the two immediately felt a connection. Cramer recalled, "The minute Lee and Herb met at cocktails, they started talking and didn't stop. You could almost feel
the electricity between them." Besides their love of ballet, they
shared many interests, including literature, décor, travel. Ross
called Cramer two days later to thank him for "introducing this
most enchanting woman into my life." As for Lee, she has always
loved the movies, and to this day she is one of New York's most
famous moviegoers.

They began seeing each other regularly, spending a weekend
near Santa Barbara at a ranch belonging to Ross's friend, the producer Ray Stark. Ross threw a fiftieth birthday party in Los Angeles for Nureyev, with Lee as a special guest. They traveled to the
Caribbean together in April.

In May, Lee traveled with Ross to Atlanta as he began scouting
locations for what would become the 1989 hit movie *Steel Magnolias*. He settled on the small Southern town of Natchitoches in
Louisiana—a town of moss-draped cypresses where the sweet
scent of Confederate jasmine hung in the air—a perfect place for
the romantic tear-jerker about small-town Southern women rely-
ing on their friendships to get through life. The movie provided
a breakout role for Georgia-born Julia Roberts. Shirley MacLaine,

Sally Field, Olympia Dukakis, a luminous Dolly Parton, and a somewhat miscast Daryl Hannah rounded out the cast. As a testament to Lee's affection for Ross, she flew into the humid locale over several weekends to be with the new love of her life. While the hard work of filmmaking was under way, Lee water-skied in a murky river "filled with alligators and water moccasins," as she later said. Call it love—of course it didn't hurt that Ross was worth many millions, having earned a $2 million fee for more than twenty films he directed. Which is one reason that Jackie was thrilled for her sister—not just that Lee was happy at last, but that Lee would no longer need her for the occasional rescue.

But Lee no longer needed Jackie's help because that same year, she sold her Southampton beach house on Gin Lane for $3.5 million, ten times what she had bought it for less than ten years earlier. It was bought by Frances Lear, then wife of the TV producer who created *All in the Family*, who would end up putting the property on the market in 2003, for $17 million.

Lee and Ross became engaged when Lee planned to spend the month of August in Sardinia, and Ross sent a private plane to bring her back to Natchitoches. As Nureyev remarked about them, they had both been through "difficult times." After so many disappointments in love—including an intense romance with the eminent architect Richard Meier—Lee was at loose ends. She had walked away from her design business after a decade of hard work. Her position representing Giorgio Armani's couture was satisfying but not deeply involving, and with Anthony and Tina now on their own, she was lonely—as was Ross. A year before marrying Lee, he had lost his wife of thirty years, the celebrated dancer Nora Kaye, to cancer. Her illness was a long and lingering one, and Ross had been devastated when she died.

The Brooklyn-born director, who had started his professional life as a dancer and choreographer, was a great companion for

Lee and was well liked by Anthony, Tina, and—most important, perhaps—Jackie. Though their backgrounds couldn't have been more different, Lee seemed to find an element of security and love with him. Ross was to Lee what Tempelsman was to Jackie—a cherished, charming companion whose Jewishness would have raised eyebrows among Janet Auchincloss's Newport society (and certainly with Hughdie). Perhaps that was part of their appeal.

In an aside, Gore Vidal offered up an unsubstantiated but intriguing claim that Janet Lee Auchincloss's Southern lineage might well have been Semitic.

> One should note that the first of Hughdie's three high-powered wives was Russian; the second, my mother; the third, Jackie's mother, Janet, born Lee, or as my mother used to observe thoughtfully, Levy. Apparently, Janet's father had changed his name in order to become the first Jew to be a vice president of the Morgan bank. My mother wondered how Hughdie, a quiet but sincere anti-Semite, would respond when he found out.

Lee and Ross's monthlong honeymoon in Sardinia, Milan, Verona, and Mantua had to be, in Colacello's words, "the most sophisticated month in the history of honeymoons." Much of it was spent ogling architecture, as they were looking for inspiration for the home they were planning to build on four hundred rolling acres in the Santa Ynez Valley, near Ray Stark's ranch. Their few disagreements centered on design: "He likes Tuscan, while she favors Provencal," noted Colacello. Lee was inspired by the beauty of the California acres, calling it "the most beautiful piece of property I've seen anywhere":

> As far as you can see in any direction nothing but rolling hills and the oaks that are indigenous to California. It really reminded me of Kenya, because I've never seen an expanse of land like that

in this country that wasn't dried up and barren, or anywhere in Europe either.

They certainly had the means to design and build a master-piece, given Lee's sale of her Southampton beach house and Ross's $5.6 million sale of the beautiful home he'd shared with Nora Kaye in Santa Monica, which boasted an eighty-foot-long black granite loft and a black swimming pool.

The poet Robert Lowell once wrote, "They walk the one life offered from the many chosen," and for Lee, the life offered seemed to come back to houses, homes, décor, and real estate—all of which provided her joy and a safe haven. And Ross doted on her. They spent the summer of '89 in East Hampton in a rented, oceanfront estate on Further Lane. Caroline visited with her first child, Rose, born in March of 1988, whom she'd named after her paternal grandmother, and Anthony came out every week-end from Manhattan, where he worked as a producer at the ABC newsmagazine *Day One*. Lee loved Anthony's visits and threw a lavish party for his thirtieth birthday. Her East Hampton soirees were buoyant occasions, not to be missed.

Ross's driver, John Chaney, saw how much they doted on each other. "Herbert is not prone to paying a lot of attention to any-body," he told Lee's biographer, "but he does to Lee. He gives her a lot of time, shows her a lot of love and affection and is very con-siderate. Both of them are."

Lee Bouvier Radziwill Ross, happy at last.

*

AFTER SELLING A town house she owned in Georgetown, Janet Auchincloss moved back to Hammersmith Farm to live perma-nently in the Castle. The sale brought her $650,000, which Janet put into a trust for Lee, asking Anthony to manage it. Oddly, given her relative wealth and comfort, Jackie was miffed by this and demanded to know why she'd singled out Lee to receive such a generous bequest (well over $1 million in today's dollars). "Lee needs the money," Janet told her. Jackie complained that their mother was "playing favorites," but Janet was adamant, and putting her young grandson in charge of the trust suggests that she was concerned that Lee would too quickly run through the funds.

Now settled back at Hammersmith Farm, albeit in the smaller farmhouse, Janet became increasingly confused and forgetful, showing the signs of what would later be diagnosed as Alzheimer's. She would sometimes wander into the big house that had been sold, forgetting that she no longer lived there, and rearrange the coffee-table books in the living room.

Her third husband, retired investment banker Bingham Willing "Booch" Morris, was of little help and was often irritated with her increasing confusion. They had been childhood acquaintances, and Janet had reached out to Booch on the death of his wife, which had led to their courtship and marriage.

It was not a happy union. Jackie had been horrified when she learned that Booch had melted down all of Janet's hunter trophies to sell the silver. When Janet had blissfully forgotten that her daughter with Hughdie, Janet, had died, Booch's angry response was, "You know she's dead! She died of cancer last year!" Booch hated the Kennedys and he refused to drive Janet to Boston for the dedication of the John F. Kennedy School of Government at Harvard, though he himself was a Harvard man. Her stepson Yusha drove her to Boston. Jackie was so incensed at his behavior that she managed to eventually banish him from Janet's home.

Though she grew increasingly confused, Janet continued to dress well and to look her best, remembering to wear her hat and gloves when leaving the house. She continued to spend time with her two beloved Jack Russell terriers, Victoria and Taffy. As her memory failed, she found herself dwelling more on the distant past, and often spoke about her first husband, Black Jack Bouvier, to the surprise of both Jackie and Lee.

Lee later recalled:

> It was really extraordinary . . . it was so strange to me because of the last eight, ten years of her life, she referred to him all the time . . . we had never been allowed to mention his name in her house, or her name in his house, though he mentioned it plenty—she was always referring to "Jack Bouvier and I and the horses we had and the things we did." I really thought I was hearing things . . .

Jackie called her every day and visited her every weekend toward the end, as Janet became increasingly housebound and was looked after by Yusha. Caroline visited with her young daughter, Rose, and Janet was able to rouse herself long enough to admire her first great-grandchild. The following year, in March of 1989, Janet was hospitalized for a hip fracture, and Jackie flew in from Hyannis, where she had been celebrating Rose's ninety-ninth birthday.

While Jackie held her mother's hand, Booch stayed upstairs, loudly playing a radio until Yusha told him to shut it off. Janet died in July of that year, at the age of eighty-one, and her funeral service was held at Trinity Church, attended by three hundred mourners. Lee, who had not been at her mother's bedside, attended the funeral and wept visibly as a bagpiper played "Amazing Grace." Janet's ashes, as were her daughter Janet's before her, were scattered at Hammersmith Farm.

Janet had left Hammersmith Farm to her six living children and grandchildren from her marriage to Auchincloss, and to her late daughter Janet's three children. Lee would end up selling her one-seventh ownership to her stepsister Nina, and Jackie would leave hers to Yusha, who continued to live on at the Castle. There was some resentment that Jackie and Lee inherited any part of Hammersmith Farm as they were not *Auchinclosses*, a fate that had propelled them from an early age to secure their own fortunes.

*

THE YEAR 1990 would usher in a dark decade for Lee and Jackie. In 1993, Rudolf Nureyev died after contracting AIDS and was buried at the Russian cemetery Sainte-Geneviève-des-Bois, forty minutes south of Paris. Lee attended his funeral and was struck by the sight of black-clad attendants "descending the imperial staircase of the Paris Opera," where the funeral was held. In death as in life, Nureyev knew how to make grand and memorable gestures.

Seventeen years later, Lee revisited his tomb, designed according to the dancer's wishes by the theatrical designer Ezio Frigerio, with whom he had worked on many of his ballets. In March of 2010, she described the pilgrimage to his tomb "among the shade trees and stone monuments" in a piece titled "Visiting Nureyev's Grave," for the online newsletter *Departures*.

In the brief essay, Lee muses on first seeing Nureyev dance at Covent Garden and befriending him in 1961, following his defection from the Soviet Union. She treasured his friendship to the end, thanking him for introducing her to "so much of what to this day gives me pleasure"—Scriabin's music, Mikhail Lermontov's poetry—and, finally, she describes Nureyev as "an exceptional dancer, an incredible person, and my closest friend."

*

LEE'S SADNESS OVER the passing of her longtime friend, who had added so much glamour and excitement to her life, was assuaged the following year, 1994, when her son, Anthony, became engaged to Carole Ann DiFalco, whom he met while both were working as producers at ABC News. They were covering the notorious Menendez brothers' trial at the time. Carole, an intelligent, colt-ish young woman from a colorful, working-class family in upstate New York, is currently a reality TV star on *The Real Housewives of New York City.*

Carole was very impressed with Lee, calling her "one of the most interesting women I've ever met," who, at sixty-one, still pos-sessed "a very childlike curiosity."

> When I first met her—that ravishing face!—she was oth-erworldly. I have pictures of the two of us from my life with Anthony. And I'll tell you, I don't want to stand next to Lee in a photograph again. She's too gorgeous. We'd sometimes walk through a restaurant and it would become absolutely quiet. I've been with other well-known people, but nothing like that ever happened.

Carole would often attend Lee's Sunday lunches at the East Hampton house she shared with Herbert Ross. "There was always someone interesting there," she recalled. She was impressed with the way Lee effortlessly entertained, engaging her guests in con-versations about art, literature—and gossip! "She was very enter-taining and very elegant," Carole recalled,

> but never grand. There is an elegant casualness that I don't think I've seen since. And I think that's why she really shined at those lunches and dinners in East Hampton. She was always gracious, even to her ex-lovers. And that list is massive!

Carole was also impressed by Lee's artistic talent ("She paints, she drew the orchids on our wedding invitation") and her elegant writing style: "She used to write long letters to Anthony and to her sister, in elegant, feminine, very light handwriting." When

Lee and Jackie lived just ten blocks away from each other in New York, "the letters would fly back and forth. They were like the Brontës. She was always toying with the idea of writing her story."

After marrying Anthony in 1995, Carole found herself having to "correct people when they say, 'Oh, you're married into the Kennedy family.' No, I married into the Radziwill family." It was a point of honor for her, extended to writing into her contract with *Real Housewives* a clause stating, "They are not to refer to me as a Kennedy. I just wanted it to be clear." So in marrying Anthony, she inherited one of her mother-in-law's issues, the long shadow of the Kennedys.

*

ON MAY 19, 1994, Lee was at a dinner party hosted by *Vanity Fair* editor Graydon Carter in his Greenwich Village town house when she received a phone call from her nephew. After speaking with John, she immediately left and headed for 1040 Fifth Avenue.

Jackie had been ill since the winter of 1993, having suffered a fall from her horse, named Clown, during a jump at the Piedmont Hunt Club in Virginia on November 22. She suffered an injury to her groin that became infected, eventually cured by antibiotics. The following month she and Maurice Tempelsman toured the Caribbean aboard Tempelsman's boat, the *Relemar*, when she fell ill and was rushed back to New York. Doctors at New York Hospital–Cornell Medical Center noticed her swollen lymph glands and performed a biopsy. The diagnosis: advanced non-Hodgkin's lymphoma. Yet just a few weeks earlier she had been photographed jogging in Central Park and had inspired the tabloid headline, "64 and Fit as a Fiddle. Wow! Look at Jackie Now!" She was shocked by the diagnosis, wondering why she had worked so hard at staying fit—jogging, horseback riding, even doing countless push-ups—to be struck at the age of sixty-four with so devastating a diagnosis. She finally decided to quit her two-pack-a-day cigarette habit, something that had been concealed from the public—amazingly so—for all of her adult life.

At the time, John Jr. was deeply involved in a relationship with the tall, lanky, blonde actress and heiress Daryl Hannah, whom he had met at Jackie's wedding reception for Lee and Ross. Their tempestuous off-again, on-again romance did not have Jackie's support, although she liked Daryl and was rather impressed at her family's fortune (her stepfather was the billionaire Jerrold Wexler, who had supported Democratic political candidates). Jackie felt that Daryl wasn't quite right for her son—perhaps too volatile, with a reputation for being "flaky," although that quality belied a keen intelligence. She and John fought often, in public, another violation of Jackie's insistence on privacy and public decorum for her family.

Jackie also knew that her handsome son was harboring ambitions to become an actor—an ambition she heartily disapproved of—so she might have been wary of Daryl's influence in that direction. Although she had once expressed her own theatrical ambitions, she had been skeptical of Lee's forays into that world. Having learned to cope with the gaze of the world on her every movement, she wanted nothing more than to live out her life without the intrusion of the press, and she wanted that for her children as well.

John Jr. was already attracting the wrong kind of attention, widely noticed for his masculine beauty. Andy Warhol wrote in his diary on December 20, 1980: "Vincent was having a party so cabbed there (5$). It turned out to be a really great party. I was taking pictures of this handsome kid I thought was a model and then I was embarrassed because it turned out to be John-John Kennedy."

People magazine dubbed John Jr. "America's Most Eligible Bachelor," and he appeared on the cover of their September 12,

1988, issue as "The Sexiest Man Alive," with the following admonition:

> Okay, ladies, this one's for you, but first some ground rules. GET YOUR EYES OFF THIS MAN'S CHEST! He's a serious fellow . . . Scion of the most charismatic family in American politics and heir to its most famous name.

Jackie was not pleased. She had finally persuaded her son to abandon his acting ambitions and had "wanted people to take John seriously," explained Jackie's half brother, Jamie Auchincloss. "She thought the whole sex-symbol thing was just demeaning."

Six weeks after his sister's July 19, 1986, wedding, John Jr. began classes at New York University School of Law. Jackie had won that battle. Two years later he stepped onto the podium at the 1988 Democratic National Convention in Atlanta to introduce his uncle Ted Kennedy, causing *Time* writer Walter Isaacson to worry "that the roof of the Omni Auditorium might collapse from the sudden drop in air pressure caused by the simultaneous sharp intake of so many thousands of breaths" at his appearance and "flawless performance." Jackie and Lee were present, and were impressed enough to wonder if John Jr. might well pursue "the family business—politics." All a great irony considering how carefully Jackie tried to shield her children from the public gaze, but the legacy seemed inescapable.

John Jr. would eventually attempt to meld the worlds of politics and celebrity entertainment in the short-lived magazine he founded, titled *George*, launched with much fanfare and featuring on its initial cover the model Cindy Crawford bewigged like George Washington.

The original plan, which John Jr. approved, was to depict Crawford as Jackie Kennedy. Caroline nixed that idea as tasteless.

She was far more protective of the Kennedy legacy than was her younger brother, and she had a more serious turn of mind. She aced the New York State bar exam, while John Jr. ended up having to retake the exam twice. Caroline's tastes and interests were closer to Jackie's—books, poetry, children. Her first published book, *In Our Defense: The Bill of Rights in Action*, coauthored with Ellen Alderman, became a bestseller in 1991; she followed that up with seven more books, including two poetry anthologies. One of those was compiled for children, and it bore a photograph on the cover of Caroline as a little girl reading to her teddy bear sitting next to her on a chair.

*

JACKIE WOULD NOT live long enough to get to know the woman John met at a low point in his relationship with Daryl Hannah— the stunning twenty-seven-year-old Carolyn Bessette, at the time a fashion publicist and personal shopper at Calvin Klein. Beautiful, tall, slim, poised, Carolyn had some of the same qualities as Jackie, though she didn't physically resemble her. Both women had an inner confidence and a femininity that deeply impressed people. They had a similar style sense—there are dozens of blogs devoted to Jackie and Carolyn, one which compares nearly identical camel coats the two women were photographed wearing, decades apart. And when Carolyn did become engaged to John Jr., he gave her an engagement ring that was a duplicate of the sapphire-and-emerald "swimming ring" that Maurice Tempelsman had given to Jackie, and which Jackie treasured.

Coincidentally, Carolyn was already good friends with Carole Radziwill, Anthony's wife. She described Carolyn as "quite a lovable person. She was clever, she was naughty, and she had that balance of being able to be really serious and yet funny . . . she was a great girlfriend."

. . .

When Jackie was diagnosed with cancer and instructed to begin chemotherapy, she immediately called John and Caroline to her side at Ten Forty, while her stalwart companion, Maurice, sat with her and held her hand. She told her children the diagnosis, and they all wept. But Jackie quickly pulled herself together and assured them that her doctors held out hope that she might survive.

Most people around Jackie did not know of her life-threatening illness, as she continued to work at Doubleday, though sometimes she appeared bruised as a result of her therapy. Jackie tried not to let it interfere with her editorial duties and relationships with her authors. Soon, however, the results of chemotherapy took their toll, and she hid her hair loss under a turban, joking with a colleague that it might start a trend. Once, while she was walking in Central Park, a paparazzo attempted to take her photograph. Tempelsman—usually so peaceable—angrily chased him off.

Jackie had her lawyers draft a living will instructing her children not to prolong her life by extreme measures at the end. Jackie and Lee's half sister, Janet, had died painfully in March of 1985 after a brutal struggle with lung cancer when she was just thirty-nine. Jackie had been at her half sister's bedside throughout much of the ordeal, struck by her uncomplaining stoicism. Tish Baldrige noted Jackie "was horrified at how much her sister Janet had suffered and she wasn't about to let that happen to her. Jackie always had to be in total control of her own life—that was one thing about her that never changed."

On February 11, 1994, Jackie had Tuckerman announce to the *New York Times* that she had non-Hodgkin's lymphoma.

When Lee arrived at her sister's apartment that night, Jackie was dying. Whatever dark currents had passed between the sisters over the decades, Lee only wanted Jackie to recover, to be the strong, older sister who had, from time to time, looked after Lee and tried to make sure she was well taken care of. Lee could barely imagine a world without Jackie in it. Caroline and John left Lee alone with Jackie for some time, and when Lee left Jackie's bedside, she was weeping.

A steady stream of friends and family, vetted by Caroline and John, made a pilgrimage to Ten Forty to say their farewells. Yusha, who had always loved his stepsister, drove in from Hammersmith Farm in Newport. Ted Kennedy and his new wife, Victoria Reggie, arrived. Caroline cried softly outside Jackie's bedroom, comforted by Ed Schlossberg, while John ushered in visitors for a last moment with Jackie. She and John took turns keeping vigil at their mother's bedside, reading her poems she treasured by Edna St. Vincent Millay, Robert Frost, and Emily Dickinson, and prose passages from Jean Rhys, Isak Dinesen, and Colette, Jackie's favorite writers.

Monsignor George Bardes of St. Thomas More Church arrived to administer the last rites. More friends and family members streamed into Jackie's room, two at a time—Carly Simon and Bunny Mellon, Pat Lawford and Ethel Kennedy, Eunice and Sargent Shriver. Lee went in one more time to say her final good-bye, striking at least one of the assembled mourners, John's close friend William "Billy" Noonan, as eerie:

> As the priest began the rosary which is meant to release the soul from purgatory, the surreal light caught people's bowed heads in profile . . . Then Lee Radziwill walked in. It was eerie. Jackie's sister looked so much like Jackie, and had her hair done like Jackie's, and dressed like Jackie, that for a second . . . I couldn't take my eyes off her.

Christopher Andersen notes in *The Good Son* that Jackie's presiding doctor came into her room every twenty minutes, and finally administered "enough morphine to ease her into as painless a death as possible."

Jackie passed away at 10:15 that Thursday night. John publicly announced her death, saying that she had died "surrounded by her friends and her family and her books and the people and the things that she loved. And she did it in her own way and on her own terms, and we all feel lucky for that, and now she's in God's hands." It was telling that she considered her books almost to be part of her family, among the people and things she most loved.

Once the death was announced, hordes of onlookers thronged the sidewalk in front of Jackie's building and remained there for days, leaving armfuls of flowers and memorabilia as tributes.

John said, "It's a strange procession: First come the doctors, then the lawyers, then the funeral director. It isn't simply a death, but a series of steps in death."

The funeral was held at St. Ignatius Loyola, where Jackie and Lee had both been baptized and confirmed, and the ceremony befitted a queen, with hundreds of luminaries, including Hillary Clinton and Lady Bird Johnson, in attendance. Lee arrived in a stretch limousine without Herbert Ross, who had opted to remain on location in Arizona, where he was shooting his latest film, *Boys on the Side*.

John and Caroline read poems that they selected to reflect their mother's "love of words, the bonds of home and family, and her spirit of adventure," including selections from a book of Edna St. Vincent Millay's poetry that Jackie had been given as a prize at Miss Porter's School. Mike Nichols read scripture, Jessye Norman sang "Ave Maria," and Ted Kennedy delivered the eulogy. Lee's daughter, Tina, spoke at the funeral, and Anthony was a pallbearer—but there was no place for Lee.

The family had not invited her to speak at her sister's funeral. Caroline felt that Lee had not been there for her mother during her illness, and there was probably some residual feeling that Lee had neglected Tina, who had remained close to her Kennedy cousins. If indeed Lee had shied away from visiting Jackie during her fatal illness, it was not because of a lack of feeling. If anything, it was from too much feeling. "I don't do death well," she said many years later, and the prospect of losing her sister—her best friend, her rival, her impossible role model—was too much for Lee to endure.

Jackie's body was then flown to Washington, where, accompanied by a police motorcade and a phalanx of limousines, she was transported to Arlington National Cemetery to be buried next to the grave of John F. Kennedy. Next to them were the graves of Arabella, her stillborn daughter, and her infant son, Patrick. Once again, Lee was not given a chance to speak or read a poem in her sister's memory. In a dark suit and sunglasses, she remained aloof, an onlooker, hurt and angry at being banned from speaking, while sixty-four bells rang from Washington National Cathedral to commemorate the burial of Jacqueline Kennedy Onassis, once the nation's most beloved First Lady.

Eight months after Jackie's death, Rose Kennedy passed away on January 22, 1995, having achieved the advanced age of 104—four decades longer than the life span of her famous daughter-in-law.

*

JACKIE'S FUNERAL WOULD leave Lee bitter, aware of how deep the rift between her and her sister had become. This was only exacerbated by the reading of Jackie's thirty-eight-page will the week following, leaving her nothing—not a piece of jewelry, not a trinket, not their father's writing desk, which Lee had given to Jackie after inheriting it. What was the cause of the animus? Perhaps Jackie had never gotten over her resentment when, in 1984, Janet had bequeathed the proceeds of the sale of her Georgetown town house to Lee. Perhaps Jackie felt that Lee's marriage to Herbert Ross had left her rich enough that she no longer needed any help from her. Or was there another reason that Jackie so completely snubbed Lee in her final hours? Gore Vidal had gotten to know and to admire Lee's first husband, Michael Canfield, and as part of his near obsession with Jackie and—to a lesser extent—Lee, he writes that Canfield once confided in him:

> "There were times when . . . I think [Lee] went perhaps too far, you know? Like going to bed with Jack in the room next to mine in the south of France and then . . . boasting about it."

It's hard to know if Vidal is telling a truth here, or passing on gossip, or is blinded by his eventual dislike of both sisters, especially Lee. But he had no problem assigning Jackie's omission of Lee as a kind of revenge, writing, "Now, from the grave, Jackie inserts the knife." He reports that Jackie once asked him, "Who was it who said 'Revenge is more sweet than love'?" He goes on to argue that in his opinion, "The one person [Jackie] ever loved, if indeed she was capable of such an emotion, was Bobby Kennedy. As Lee had gone to bed with Jack, symmetry required her to do so with Bobby."

If the suggestion that Lee had had a fling with Jack Kennedy is true and Gore Vidal knew about it, then perhaps that was another reason that Lee did not want to testify against Vidal in his slander suit against Truman Capote. Perhaps he held that over her, and she had more to lose siding with her dear friend than with the contentious, sometimes vicious Gore Vidal.

It seems rather churlish of Gore to have helped destroy Lee's friendship with Truman. But perhaps at the end of the day, Vidal in some sense was family, though the connection was held together by a slender thread. In patrician, well-connected families like the Auchinclosses, the Kennedys, and the Bouviers, family matters.

*

AFTER THE FUNERAL, Jackie's Fifth Avenue apartment was sold for $9.5 million and her effects were sold at Sotheby's, bringing in another $34.5 million, far exceeding the expected estimate of $5 million. Jackie's diamond ring from Onassis sold for $2.4 million, far more than its $660,000 appraisal. "Sell everything," she had told her children as she lay dying. "You'll make a lot of money." Indeed, the auction—held two years after Jackie's death—was something of a feeding frenzy, with long lines around the block. Jackie knew people would pay high prices for provenance. Even the auction catalogue brought in over $500,000. Bouvier's writing desk, which Jackie had displayed in the White House's West Wing, was appraised at $2,000 but sold for $68,000.

Caroline and John Jr. reaped more than $30 million from the auction, the rest going to charity.

*

AFTER HER MOTHER'S and her sister's deaths, more tragedies awaited Lee.

In an unforeseen twist to Anthony and Carole's fairy-tale romance, on their honeymoon Anthony discovered a testicular lump that would turn out to be cancerous. The five years of their marriage were spent in multiple surgeries and agonizing treatments for Anthony's cancer, painfully recounted in DiFalco's searing memoir, *What Remains*. As Anthony's chances of survival dwindled, John Jr. prepared a eulogy for his cousin and closest friend, whom he knew was dying.

John Jr. married Carolyn Bessette on September 21, 1996, a little over two years after Jackie's death, on Cumberland Island in Georgia, a remote hideaway perfect for a couple who had had to deal with constant prying by the public and the press.

On Friday, July 16, 1999—just three years into what many described as a tempestuous marriage—John Jr., his wife, Carolyn, and her sister, Lauren Bessette, plunged to a watery grave when John became disoriented in a heavy fog on their way to a family wedding in Hyannis.

They had planned to leave the city by 6:30 p.m. so that John Jr. still had enough light to fly by, as he had not yet mastered flying by the Piper Saratoga's instruments. Though he was a novice pilot, he expected to land in Martha's Vineyard before dark, in time to drop off Lauren and still make it to Hyannis Port. Carolyn had not been sanguine about the trip, already alarmed by John Jr.'s love of pushing the envelope, daredevilry that earned him the nickname "Master of Disaster."

Jackie had admired her son's athleticism and adventurous spirit, but she had balked at his plans to earn his pilot's license, well aware of the number of deaths by plane crash that haunted the Kennedys. Jack Kennedy's elder brother, Joseph, and his beloved sister Kathleen "Kick" Kennedy had both died young when their planes crashed. Ted Kennedy survived a plane crash that had broken his back and taken the lives of his pilot and a campaign aide. And of course Onassis had never recovered from his beloved son Alexander's death when his plane crashed on takeoff. She felt so strongly about this that she had "made John swear that he would not pursue his pilot's license," as John's biographer Christopher Andersen wrote, and on her deathbed she'd asked Tempelsman and Ted Kennedy to hold him to that promise. But it was a promise he couldn't keep. Already a risk taker, he'd loved the sense of freedom that soaring alone in the sky gave him.

Others have noted that John suffered from attention deficit disorder and thus did not have the sustained focus required in a good pilot. And that night he was flying with another handicap—he was on crutches because six weeks earlier he had broken his right ankle in a parasailing accident. Carolyn only agreed to fly to Hyannis with John because he was supposed to be copiloted with the more experienced Jay Biederman, John's flight instructor. But

Biederman canceled at the last minute, so John decided to pilot the plane on his own. It was actually Carolyn's investment banker sister, Lauren, who talked her into going. John was so confident of his abilities that he didn't bother to file a flight plan.

Already leaving too close to twilight, they then encountered an unexpected blanket of haze that settled over the coast and greatly reduced the visibility John would need to pilot the plane. At one point their Piper flew perilously close to an American Airlines jet carrying 160 passengers. The American Airlines pilot skillfully averted a collision that John and his passengers might not even have been aware of. John stayed close to the coastline where he could see the lights of the towns he knew—Greenwich, Bridgeport, Old Saybrook—but after forty minutes in the air, the dense fog blocked out their flickering lights. A more experienced pilot would have, at that point, turned on the automatic pilot and let the instruments guide the plane. John did not. When night came, visibility was zero, and John was completely disoriented. A local pilot named Tom Freeman described that sensation: "You are totally, completely in the dark—literally as well as figuratively—if you don't know how to rely on your instruments. It's a sickening, scary feeling." Without visual cues, he would not have been able to tell up from down. When the Piper Saratoga suddenly nosedived toward the blackness of the Atlantic, John apparently tried to reverse the plane's trajectory without first leveling off, resulting in a "graveyard spiral," plunging the plane with its three passengers to their deaths in the sea.

It was a blessing that Jackie did not have to live through the premature death of her son, her handsome charmer, her golden boy. But with her son, Lee would not be so blessed.

On August 10, 1999, after numerous surgeries, Anthony finally succumbed to the cancer that had robbed him and his young wife of their future. "Carolyn and John would die three weeks before

Anthony," Carole recalled, "so I was left that summer with no one that shared those memories, and no one that I could talk to about it." Ironically, Anthony outlived his cousin, so it was he who would deliver the eulogy at John's funeral.

Jackie once wrote, "This conflict with the gods is the essence of the Greek tragedy." One can look at the trajectory of Jackie's and Lee's lives and see the outline of an ancient curse: the death of the firstborn son. It began with the Kennedys, with the fatal plane crash into the sea of the firstborn Kennedy son, the charismatic Joseph Kennedy Jr., whom his father was grooming to run for president.

John and Jackie Kennedy's two sons would both be taken— Patrick, shortly after his birth, and John Jr., lost at sea. Onassis endured the death of his firstborn and only son, Alexander, and it destroyed him. Joseph, John, and Alexander were all like the Greek mythic figure Icarus, who flies too close to the sun, only to fall to a watery grave. Anthony Radziwill, another one of fate's darlings, was born the proud and loving son of a prince. He was just forty when his mother had to see him buried. She has so far outlived him by nearly twenty years.

"Did you notice that small fifth-century Roman head of a boy over the mantel?" Ralph Rucci once asked. "She's had it in her life for many, many years. It's one of her favorite things because it looks like her son, Anthony. She looks at it, and it gives her comfort."

*

LEE'S MARRIAGE TO Ross didn't survive the personal toll of those tragedies. Accompanying Lee to visit Anthony in the hospital while he endured chemotherapy treatments must have stirred up painful memories of Nora Kaye's long battle with cancer. Ross still grieved the loss of his first wife. He had created ballets for the American Ballet Theatre as a young choreographer in New York before becoming a film director, and had formed a deep, creative partnership with Nora, whom he'd married in 1959. The two had established their own ballet company, the Ballet of Two Worlds, to perform works that Ross had choreographed, including *Caprichos* (*Caprices*), inspired by Goya's etchings. They toured Europe for a year before disbanding, and the memory of their long partnership was something Ross could not let go of, to Lee's increasing resentment.

There were other issues as well. Like Stas Radziwill before him, Ross was alarmed at how quickly Lee ran through large sums of money. (It was a familiar complaint leveled at both Jackie and Lee, by all of their husbands.) Lee spent the profit from the sale of Ross and Nora's home in Los Angeles on two warehouses of furniture for the Santa Ynez Valley home they were building. She spent a fortune planting olive trees on the property, and her spending habits often put Ross in a black mood. It got so bad that he complained to a friend, who noted, "He has to do two pictures a year to break even, which is about $5 million a year. He doesn't have a lot of money put away. It's one of those odd little nightmares. All I know is, this is not a happy man."

Lee's critics point to a brouhaha over the London premiere of *Steel Magnolias* in February of 1990 as the beginning of the end for their marriage. It was a Royal Command Performance, held at the Odeon in Leicester Square, with a presentation of the film's cast to Charles and Diana, Prince and Princess of Wales.

Lee insisted that she be introduced to the royals as "Princess Radziwill," not as Lee Bouvier Ross, only to be told by Columbia Pictures that the reception line was just for those involved in the film. She would only be allowed to stand *behind* her husband. When Ross learned about that arrangement, out of deference to Lee, he refused to take part. He had to be persuaded by his friend Ray Stark. So when the grand event occurred, Lee gamely took her place in the second line of guests, behind Ross.

But when it came time to be seated for the screening, Lee balked at the seating arrangement, which had the film's principals in the front row with spouses in the second. This was unacceptable for Lee, who did, after all, still retain the (somewhat dubious) title of princess, and who had twice dined as her sister's guest of honor at the White House, and who had been hailed by thousands of Indians and Pakistanis on a state visit and had been seated next to Prime Minister Nehru—so she immediately took one of the seats in the front row, between her husband and Prince Charles. She was not going to sit behind Dolly Parton or Julia Roberts or Olympia Dukakis. Hence the clashing of two worlds: Hollywood's ever-changing hierarchy, and the time-honored protocols of state and *le haut monde*. Lee knew where she belonged—but that night belonged to Hollywood. Lee had actually stolen Julia Roberts's assigned place, and the film-industry representatives were livid. It got worse when Julia tried to take her seat, whispering to Lee that she was in the wrong place, but Lee ignored her. Finally, as DuBois reports, Ray Stark tapped her on the shoulder and asked her to leave, and when she didn't budge, he hissed, "Lee, you are a cunt."

In the end, Prince Charles and Lady Diana moved their seats to accommodate the cast of *Steel Magnolias*, amid much embarrassment all around. Olympia Dukakis and a now-tearful Julia Roberts had to find other seats. After the screening, at an elegant cast party at the Elephant, Ross tried to smooth things over with Stark, but Ray continued to fume. DuBois quotes an industry insider as saying, "It was unforgivable because it hurt him a lot with his career . . . By not standing up to Lee, Herbert jeopardized Columbia's position, jeopardized the Prince, and jeopardized his own standing in England." Ross's friends began to look upon Lee as a liability, the dominating and domineering half of the marriage.

The screenwriter and comedian Buck Henry, perhaps best

known as the writer of *The Graduate* and television's spy spoof *Get Smart*, saw that "the end of the Herb Ross marriage is when people began turning away from Lee, began to think of her as a terrible person, though I always liked Lee." Hollywood insiders certainly turned against her, but when people like the legendary director Mike Nichols—who had once seriously courted Jackie—also turned against her, it cut closer to home.

After thirteen years of marriage, the couple separated in January 2000 and divorced in May the following year. It was not a pretty sight, as the once loving couple fought over everything—every objet d'art, every dish, every stick of furniture (including a beloved antique desk Ross had bought at auction and that Lee lay claim to). They put their beautiful East Hampton home up for sale, and the comic Jerry Seinfeld offered $19 million for it. By then, Ross was dying from heart disease, and when Lee balked at selling, Ross's friends felt that she was trying to outlast him so the house and all its proceeds would be exclusively hers.

For her part, Lee had delayed the separation for the sake of Anthony, who had struggled with cancer throughout the summer of 1999, so that he and Carole would have an idyllic place to spend their weekends. She also "worked like a son of a gun to make sure [Ross] got the best treatment," according to her lawyer Stanley Pleasant, after Ross was hospitalized at Lenox Hill Hospital in Manhattan.

He died on October 11, 2001, at the age of seventy-four, having suffered with heart disease for over a year, no doubt made worse by his acrimonious divorce. His ashes were buried next to Nora Kaye's grave site in Los Angeles.

*

AFTER THE END of her marriage and the deaths of her ex-husband, her sister, her nephew, and her beloved son, Lee's outlook became darker and she became more guarded. Peter Beard and others had already noticed and commented on "the two Lees"—the warm, outgoing, adventurous Lee who thrived in the Hamptons and on Montauk, near the sea and away from New York society, and the Lee who turned brittle and aloof when she reentered the city. Many of Lee's social peers noticed how grim Lee had become, and they were highly critical of her treatment of Herb Ross throughout the divorce and through his fatal illness. The harsh, self-protective Lee seemed to have completely overtaken the carefree, game girl that Peter and others had come to love.

*

GIVEN THE AMOUNT of suffering and loss Lee endured, however, it's surprising that she was able to finally publish her long-awaited memoir in the form of a breezy, upbeat recounting of the happiest times of her life, with stunning family photographs displayed throughout. (She had learned from Peter Beard, no doubt, the life-affirming art of scrapbooking and collage.) *Happy Times* was published in 2000, and if the public expected a bitter reckoning, they would be disappointed.

In March of 2001, Lee was interviewed on the popular *Larry King Live* TV show on the occasion of her book. Larry King asked Lee, "Why this book?" and she answered:

> I did it because it was a difficult period in my life and so I was considering writing, and I thought that it would be uplifting to go back and look at some things worth remembering . . . those memories were exciting. Memories are very powerful . . .

She talked about the difficulty of growing up in a divorced household, and how much she had loved being with her father ("He was such a joy to be with, and we were the focal point of his life . . . we just adored him").

When Larry King asked Lee outright if she and Jackie had been rivals, as they were just four years apart and "both pretty,"

Lee shot back, "We really weren't . . . four years is just enough difference, I think, not to be rivals."

He pressed on with, "Your sister . . . changed America . . . the way she treated the White House, the way she was?" To which Lee responded by extolling the White House years under Jack and Jackie's stewardship, when it became a place where "music, art, science, business, philosophy" all flowed through the People's House. This had been Jackie *and* Lee's world, a place where the finest aspects of life were sought, appreciated, and flourished, where figures like Pablo Casals and André Malraux were the rock stars, then, when taste and knowledge were things to acquire and to treasure. "The idea that anything was possible was the strongest feeling all the time," Lee said.

Larry King, in his usual blunt style, then asked Lee, "Were you ever just a housewife?" Lee didn't blink at that, and she gamely explained that she did not work when her children were young, but had worked for Diana Vreeland at *Harper's Bazaar,* ran the American fashion show in Brussels for the World's Fair, and then, in the 1990s, worked for Giorgio Armani for ten years. Curiously, she didn't mention her design business—perhaps that was more a labor of love, while it lasted, than "work."

King then touched upon Lee's recent tragedies, beginning with John Jr.'s sudden death. "You had tragedy soon after John Jr., didn't you? You lost a son."

"My son died of cancer, which he had a very, very long battle with. He was just forty, by a week."

"I don't know how you—someone once said, upon losing a child, you're never the same."

Lee answered, "I think grieving is the same for everybody that lost someone you love deeply. It's the same. You know, you're really no different than anybody else who's lost somebody they adored."

Again, the talk show host pressed on: "But losing a child—just doesn't make any sense."

"No. Losing a child is a very unnatural thing."

"Where do you get the ability to bounce back from incredible tragedy?"

"It's a force of nature, and it's a determination to go forward. I guess it must be in the genes . . . how can you keep going if you don't go forward?"

*

AS MANY OF her social peers fell away after Herb Ross's death, Lee found herself befriended by a younger generation of film-makers and designers, like Sofia Coppola, Hamilton South, Marc Jacobs, and Ralph Rucci. They sought her out, and it was easier to befriend younger people who didn't hold her responsible for her history than to maintain friendships with people who had begun to describe her as cold and avaricious.

Drawn to her unerring chic, her sophistication, and her endurance, they elevated Lee to the role she was born to inhabit once Jackie's long shadow had begun to fade: style icon.

12

LEE RADZIWILL IN THE SOUTH OF FRANCE

They don't know—you don't realize—what a
punishment it can be, to be the last one left.

—LEE

*T*his in part has been a story of being and becoming, beginning in a prefeminist era when "girls who have everything are not supposed to do anything." Yet both of the Bouvier sisters achieved fame in their lifetimes. Jackie ascended to an iconic status, where she continues to reside, twenty-four years after her death. At the heart of it, Jackie was unknowable. Out of shyness, perhaps, out of a determined desire to remain private while trapped in the public gaze, she has endured as an expression of the feminine ideal, like Greta Garbo or the *Mona Lisa*—remote, mysterious, tantalizing with her Giaconda smile. When Jackie spoke publicly, it was usually on behalf of others: John Kennedy's campaign and his presidency, the decorators and curators who helped her refurbish the White House, through the many books she edited and saw published at Viking and Doubleday. Sphinx-like, she didn't seek confessional self-expression that has defined much of public discourse since the mid-twentieth century. In contrast, Lee sought to be known, to express *herself*, to have her voice, her style, her talents, her sensibilities made public. She belongs to the present, and has outlived everyone else.

. . .

In September of 2006, the late writer and journalist Christopher Hitchens reviewed five new books on the Kennedys in the *Atlantic*. In many ways, Hitchens was highly critical of the Camelot myth, in keeping with his reputation as a contrarian. In his final paragraph he wrote:

> If this vulgar hoodlum president had not been survived by a widow of exceptional bearing and grace, his reputation would probably now be dirt. Sheer discretion and consideration, exerted on her behalf (and partly demanded by her in return for "access"), conditioned many of the founding chronicles and continue to influence the successor ones. Perhaps even this spell is now not too strong to be broken . . . But all this was almost half a century ago, which is surely enough time for the dispelling of our remaining illusions.

After the review was published, Hitchens received a phone call from Lee. Hitchens had been critical of Jackie in his review, mocking her taste in using *Camelot* as the metaphor for her husband's term in office.

At the time of Lee's phone call, Hitchens was gravely ill with esophageal cancer and hospitalized at the critical care unit of the MD Anderson Cancer Center in Houston. An intimate who was with Hitchens did not want to put Lee's call through, saying, "This is ridiculous. The man's dying. He doesn't want to be criticized about something he struggled to write."

But Lee hadn't called to complain or criticize. When she finally got through, she told Hitchens, "Oh, finally someone who gets it, who's not in thrall to Camelot. I wish it had gone on for a thousand pages." She even intimated that when he got out of the hospital, they would spend time together and perhaps even work on her memoir. "Hitch had a bounce back after that, which everyone was attributing to Lee," an intimate recalled.

But that was not to be. Hitchens died on December 15, 2011, and Lee's recent book, simply called *Lee*, published by Assouline press in 2015, is not a memoir so much as a gracious and lovely trove of photographs chronicling the happiest times of her life—not very different from her earlier coffee-table book, *Happy Times*. In her reaction to Hitchens's critical review—which still manages to compliment Jackie's grace and intelligence—Lee reveals that her rival was not just her sister, but the whole Kennedy machinery that elevated Jackie to the queen of America and upset the delicate balance between them, an imbalance that was impossible for Lee to ever set right.

Agreeing with Hitchens that the Camelot myth was orchestrated with smoke and mirrors, she felt that her relationship with her sister had been tarnished by a chimera. Carole Radziwill saw that Lee was "up against sixty years of mythmaking, so I completely got it that she would appreciate Chris Hitchens's review."

But Hitchens was wrong about the "dispelling of our remaining illusions" about the Kennedys. In the more than five decades since John F. Kennedy's death, the nation continues its fascination with what is now looked upon as a golden age of civility in American politics, and its fascination with Jackie Kennedy's myth and style—and with Lee's, by extension.

Diana Vreeland was the first to publicly admire Lee's style:

> Lee has an extraordinary sense of luxury. It's real selection, real taste, *her* taste. Very, very luxurious. That doesn't mean there's a lot of *stuff.* And very, very distinctly arranged for *men.* It isn't just a woman's indulgence. Lee is a very remarkable girl. When I say remarkable I mean: *she isn't like anyone else.*

Carole Radziwill notes that Lee "has that feminine quality that's hard to put your finger on, but it has a great romantic side. Men just fell at her feet." Carole noted, too, that Lee "was always so appropriately put together for her age. She knew to stop wearing sleeveless dresses at a certain point. She just knew." Young actresses such as Abigail Spencer, who has appeared in the episodic television shows *Timeless, Mad Men,* and *Suits,* said that when preparing for the Emmy Awards recently, "All the girls took Lee as their fashion icon," loving her "ballet chic" and "barefoot elegance." It's Lee's turn, now, to be known for what her father, years ago, once said about *style*: "A habit of mind that puts quality before quantity, noble struggle before mere achievement, honor before opulence. It's what you are . . . It's what makes you a Bouvier."

In 2008, Lee managed to accomplish something never achieved by Jackie, who had adored everything French—its history, its literature, its food—since she was a young woman. Lee was awarded the Légion d'honneur by the French government, presented to her at the home of the writer and philosopher Bernard-Henri Lévy and his wife, the actress Arielle Dombasle.

"I remember when she received her Légion d'honneur in Paris in this extraordinarily beautiful, exquisite, white silk suit from Dior," recalled André Leon Talley.

> You've never seen an American woman dressed that way to go receive such a prestigious honor. We all made an effort to get there for Lee. Peter Beard came from New York. (She was in love with Peter Beard!) And Marc Jacobs was there—everyone was there to see her get her Legion d'honneur. The first thing she said to Marc was "Why have you dropped me?" Who knows where that comes from? Some fragile place of insecurity. I mean, Marc Jacobs hadn't dropped her! When she had to leave, who took her home in his car? Marc Jacobs.

In 2013, Nicky Haslam wrote an encomium to Lee that was published in the February 17, 2013, issue of *T: The New York Times*

Style Magazine, titled "The Real Lee Radziwill." She graced the cover under the rubric "True Elegance," looking regal, beautifully coifed and dressed, and cold as an ice sculpture. To accompany the issue, filmmaker Sofia Coppola (*The Virgin Suicides*, *Lost in Translation*) and Deborah Needleman, then *T*'s editor in chief, helming her first issue, interviewed Lee on camera.

They set up a small crew in Lee's apartment. In the fourteen-minute interview, Lee reminisced fondly about her Rolling Stones tour with Truman Capote and meeting Peter Beard for the first time on the island of Skorpios. She recalled the difficulties working with her aunt and cousin, the two Edie Beales, in East Hampton. But it's her time with Peter that she remembered with the most tenderness, and she credited him with opening up her mind and her spirit to undreamt-of possibilities. "When my sister asked me to come and recover after a big operation to Skorpios and have my own house there and the children," she recalled,

> it sounded like the ideal place to recuperate, and she already had asked Peter Beard, who she knew, to come and amuse her children with painting, with sculpting, with skiing, because they just adored him. His mess was everywhere in the house, of his collages, photographs, just all over every floor, and he was always on his knees gluing or rubbing a pen into his arm to get blood to put on his paintings. And then we'd go off . . . and water-ski for hours when the incredible heat had gone down . . . it was just paradise . . .

When she described Peter as "super looking [with the] body of a Greek god," he truly seems to have been the love of her life, the source of her sexual awakening, the person who made her feel most alive.

At one point, Sofia Coppola said, "I'm always struck by how incredibly strong and willful you are, and yet how you maintain this sort of childlike sense of curiosity and joy and that you're quite adventurous and naughty, and also I guess a bit vulnerable."

Lee answered, "I don't see why you can't be both."

Coppola continued admiringly, "You're just engaged with life and with people and with art and with culture," to which Lee answered, "If I wasn't curious, I wouldn't want to live. And as Luis Buñuel said in the beginning of his book . . . 'Without memory there is no life.'"

It's a charming interview, which suggests that Lee has finally found her spotlight—though on a much smaller stage than her sister's—and that she has finally found her greatest role, the part that suits her best: herself.

*

HOW DOES LEE live now? Until recently, she divided her time between New York and her three-bedroom Paris apartment on the Avenue Montaigne—with a view of the Eiffel Tower—but that apartment was recently put up for sale for $4 million. She is not giving up Paris, but she now prefers to spend her time at the Plaza Athénée. "There's a softness here that we do not find so easily at home," she told William Norwich of the *New York Times* in 2000. "Everybody isn't in such a rush. The day starts later and ends later. And when you see some sun, Paris is the most beautiful city in the world. It brings tears to your eyes."

Lee had created a minimalist, almost Zen-like refuge of order and calm in her 16th arrondissement apartment. The floor was stripped bare and left unvarnished ("A raindrop would show on it, but never mind"). She'd worked with designer Christian Liaigre to achieve an uncluttered "extraordinary sense of calm . . . I don't know what happened, but I lost the desire to acquire more things. It's very peaceful to have lost that desire."

In New York, Lee dines with longtime friends, such as Carolina and Reinaldo Herrera, Peter Beard and his wife, Nejma, Marc Jacobs, and designers Nicky Haslam and Hamilton South. As a friend related, "What she has done and will continue to do every summer is to position herself in a rented house somewhere irresistible, like Suni Agnelli's house in Porto Santo Stefano. She fills the house with friends, and that's the way she holds court these days."

Lee still loves the water, and her friend observed that she prefers "private swimming" whenever possible. "I don't swim in front of others," she explained. As Lee is still in excellent physical condition, one can speculate that her connection with the sea has now become something personal and cleansing, a refuge in a dangerous world.

"She was my mother-in-law," Carole Radziwill said about Lee, "so we didn't agree on everything, but she was very respectful of me, of my relationship with Anthony." Carole believes that Lee has made peace with the fact that she was always "overshadowed by her sister . . . But I like Lee's philosophy: you have to take ownership of your life."

That is exactly what she has done. Through it all, Lee Bouvier Canfield Radziwill Ross has managed to endure. "I don't do death well," she once said, sitting on her couch in her sun-washed living room. "There's a painting by Rubens," she mused, "in Mantua, Italy. I'd like to go back to Mantua to see this painting one more time, to say good-bye. I've always loved it. It's sad when you realize there's more life behind you than ahead of you."

Perhaps that has been Lee's greatest gift after all: to survive, and to do so with grace and courage. With her sister gone, Janet and Jack Bouvier and Hugh Auchincloss gone, Edie Beale and her daughter gone, her beloved son and nephew gone, Lee is the keeper of the Bouvier flame.

At a recent Kennedy-era event in Washington, DC, soon after

the death of Kennedy adviser and speechwriter Theodore So-
rensen in October of 2010, Lee looked around and realized that
she was the only one left. It was "alarming and shocking" to
realize that the last one standing from that time was a Bouvier
and not a Kennedy. It brought to mind Chekhov's *The Cherry
Orchard*, her favorite play, where at the end they forget to remove Firs, the old caretaker, and you can hear his lonely pounding from the locked house as workmen chop down the cherry
trees.

*

"WE'LL ALWAYS BE sisters, but we were friends once, too," Lee
confided rather wistfully that summer night, in a villa belonging to two friends, perched on the edge of a cliff overlooking the
Mediterranean. It was early July, just after Independence Day in
the States, and the sea was as blue as a Fabergé egg. Earlier that
day, somehow looking soigné in rolled-up blue jeans and sneakers,
she had held a conch shell up to her ear, to hear the sound of the
sea. It delighted her. "This could come out of a myth," she said,
happy as a girl.

The princess then boarded a yacht owned by the Agnellis.
Sailing by the small fishing village of Villefranche-sur-Mer, Lee
pointed out the Chapelle de Saint-Pierre des Pêcheurs, a fisherman's chapel as old as the Crusades, where Jean Cocteau had
painted on the ancient stone walls. "He painted John the Bap-
tist walking on water in front of the fishermen," she said. "On
another wall in the chapel, he painted Django Reinhardt," the
French gypsy guitar player of the 1920s.

The cliff-side villa had a pale, ghostly interior, which set off
the white piano in a room that opened onto a terrace with a ravishing view of the sea. Far below, one could just make out a very
tan, older man sunbathing nude, lying on his belly, like some kind

of fabulous sea creature. Lee invented a story about him—what had brought him to the Mediterranean to that particular rock by the sea—while she smoked a long, thin cigarette. Lee's two hosts teased her about her hair (the color of Veuve Clicquot), which had begun to curl in the damp sea air.

The following night, Lee attended the Grand Théâtre de Provence production of *The Magic Flute*, part of the summer's Festival d'Aix-en-Provence. Sitting in the opera house waiting for the curtain to rise, Lee commented that "when the world went mad, Provence gave the world poets—troubadours." She said that if she could have lived another life, she would have loved to have been a singer: "There's something celestial about a beautiful voice."

Even with its comedic moments, Mozart's sublime opera evoked in Lee wistful memories of her father. Despite being a bon vivant and handsome as a movie star, Bouvier had been unable to reverse his diminished circumstances. Yet the girls' early childhood at Lasata remained a treasured memory for Lee, an idyllic time before their parents' divorce, before all the wounds, the complications, the betrayals, the suffering. As her cousin John Davis has observed, however, "Not much remains of the Bouviers today and their beloved East Hampton besides their tombs."

"There's a fable or a myth—I think it's French—about a woman who survives everyone's passing," Lee mused. "And everyone says, 'She must be so strong, or so mean, to have survived it so well.' But they don't know—you don't realize—what a punishment it can be, to be the last one left."

The following twilight at the villa, as the sun turned the sea to gold, Lee was asked, "If your life was a novel, which famous writer would have written it?" She immediately answered, "Balzac." Balzac's novel *Old Goriot* came to mind. It's about a man whose daughters, to whom he was completely devoted, abandon him to die in poverty while they live rich and fashionable lives. "No, scratch that—maybe Tolstoy," she said on second thought, but considering the remarkable life she has lived—maybe both.

"I would need another lifetime," she added, "just to be able to tell this life's story."

ACKNOWLEDGMENTS
AND A NOTE ON SOURCES

The Fabulous Bouvier Sisters grew out of several interviews and subsequent articles written for *Vanity Fair*, beginning on November 11, 2011, when we first interviewed Princess Lee Radziwill for an article on Truman Capote's last, disastrous (and unfinished) novel, *Answered Prayers*. Princess Radziwill invited us into her light-filled apartment on East 72nd Street and treated us to an elegant lunch of chilled cucumber soup and a watercress salad. The interview ranged over many subjects—her friendship with Capote and its demise, the theatrical ventures they embarked upon, her response to the death of John F. Kennedy. In short, we were captivated, and the idea took root of writing a book about the relationship between Lee and her more famous sister. In May of 2016, "The Complicated Sisterhood of Jackie Kennedy and Lee Radziwill" was published in *Vanity Fair* under Sam Kashner's byline, but we still felt there was more to explore.

Once we embarked upon this book, Sam subsequently traveled to the South of France to interview Lee again and spend time with the Principessa (as Capote called her), following up with several phone conversations. Throughout it all, we found her guarded, yes, but also beguiling, witty, highly intelligent, and sometimes haunted. As always, she possessed an elegant personal style and a love for beauty reflected in every environment she inhabited.

Writing this book was like a treasure hunt, delving into the legions of articles and books written about her and Jacqueline Kennedy Onassis, sifting through the public records of two of the most written-about women of the twentieth century. Because we name the sources of our quotations throughout the book, we've dispensed with academic notes but have included a complete list of those sources used and, as follows, a list of those who kindly allowed us to interview them, either in person or by phone.

Our thanks to the late Hugh D. "Yusha" Auchincloss, Peter Beard, Harry Benson, the late Ben Bradlee, Eva Burch, the late Joanne Carson, Helen Chavchavadze, Gerald Clarke, Bob Colacello, Louise Grunwald, Buck Henry, Reinaldo Herrera, Nick Hooker, John Manchester, Jonas Mekas, the late Mike Nichols, Carole Radziwill, Diane Reverand, Frank Rich, Ralph Rucci, the late Arthur Schlesinger Jr., Allen Schwartz, the late John Seigenthaler, the late Liz Smith, James Symington, André Leon Talley, Taki Theodoracopulos, the late Robert Tracey, Matt Tyrnauer, and—before his death in 2012—the irascible, irreplaceable Gore Vidal.

Additionally, we are ever grateful to our indefatigable literary agents, David Kuhn, William LoTurco, and Alison Warren at Aevitas, for their skill and forbearance. Gratitude to our gracious and supportive editor, Gail Winston, for her scrupulous reading of this book; to the eagle-eyed copy editor, Mary Beth Constant; to associate editor, Sofia Groopman; and to HarperCollins's eminent publisher, Jonathan Burnham, for his patience and belief in us. To Mary Molineux, senior research librarian at Swem Library, College of William & Mary, and to our resourceful photo researcher, Joshua Luckenbaugh—many, many thanks!

Finally, our gratitude to Lee Radziwill, whose brilliant conversations opened a window to her past and present. It is an unpayable debt.

BIBLIOGRAPHY

Articles and Poems

Beschloss, Michael. "Five Myths About Jackie Kennedy." *Washington Post*, October 24, 2013.

Cavafy, C. P. "Ithaka." *C. P. Cavafy: Collected Poems*. Translated by Edmund Keeley and Philip Sherrard. Princeton, NJ: Princeton University Press, 1975.

Colacello, Bob. "The Last Days of Nureyev." *Vanity Fair*, March 1993.

———. "Pas de Deux." *Vanity Fair*, January 1989.

Cull, Nicholas J. "Obituary: Gloria Emerson." *Independent*, August 16, 2004. http://www.independent.co.uk/news/obituaries/gloria-emerson-550293.html.

Davidson, Guy. "Just a Couple of Fags: Truman Capote, Gore Vidal, and Celebrity Feuds." *Celebrity Studies* 7, no. 3 (2016).

Davis, Margaret Leslie. "The Two First Ladies." *Vanity Fair*, October 2008.

Emerson, Gloria. "Jacqueline Kennedy at 45." *McCall's*, July 1974: 91–116.

Hamill, Pete. "The Party." *New York Post*, November 29, 1966.

Haslam, Nicky. "The Real Lee Radziwill." *T: The New York Times Style Magazine*, February 17, 2013: 184–196.

Howard, Jane. "The Princess Goes on Stage." *Life*, July 14, 1967.

"Jackie's Summer Days at Red Gate Farm." *Ultimate Jackie*, July 12, 2009. http://ultimatejackie.blogspot.com/2009/07/jackies-summer-days-at-red-gate-farm.html.

"Jackie's White House Tour." *Time*, February 23, 1962.

Kashner, Sam. "Capote's Swan Dive." *Vanity Fair*, December 2012.

———. "A Clash of Camelots." *Vanity Fair*, October 2009.

———. "The Complicated Sisterhood of Jacqueline Kennedy and Lee Radziwill." *Vanity Fair*, May 2016.

Kennedy, Jacqueline. "Jackie's *Prix du Paris* Writing." *Vogue*, December 1960.

———. "People I Wish I Had Known." *Vogue*, February 1961: 134ff.

Klemesrud, Judy. "For Lee Radziwill, Budding Careers and New Life in New York." *New York Times*, September 1, 1974. https://nyti.ms/1Hj9FKI.

Lawrence, Greg. "Jackie O, Working Girl." *Vanity Fair*, January 2011: 97–108.

Leaming, Barbara. "The Winter of Her Despair." *Vanity Fair*, October 2014: 274–285.

Lowell, Robert. "Hospital 1." *Dolphin*. New York: Farrar, Straus & Giroux, 1973.

Luckel, Madeleine. "A Brief History of the Iconic Parisian Pied-a-Terre of Lee Radziwill—Jackie Kennedy's Younger Sister." *Vogue*, August 2017.

Mailer, Norman. "An Evening with Jackie Kennedy." *Esquire*, July 1962.

McNeil, Elizabeth. "Jackie's Secrets." *People*, December 12, 2016: 61–64.

McNeil, Liz, and Michelle Tauber. "The Carolyn No One Knew." *People*, July 10, 2017: 48–54.

Norwich, William. "Style; A New Balance." *New York Times*, October 22, 2000.

Owens, Mitchell. "Frequent Flyer: With Flowery Fabrics and Indian Accent, Lee Radziwill's Paris and Manhattan Homes Are Two of a Kind." *Elle Décor*, April 2009: 120–129.

Quinn, Sally. "In Hot Blood—and Gore." Pts. 1 and 2. *Washington Post*, June 6, 1979; June 7, 1979.

Radziwill, Lee. "Architectural Digest Visits Rudolf Nureyev." *Architectural Digest*, September 1985: 160–168.

———. "Why My Sister Married Aristotle Onassis." *Cosmopolitan*, September 1968.

Rothman, Lily. *"This is the Real* Jackie *Interview with LIFE Magazine." Time*, December 2, 2016.

Scott, Aaron. "Some Notes on *This Side of Paradise: Fragments of an Unfinished Biography* (1999)." *Senses of Cinema*, November 2011. http://sensesofcinema .com/2001/experimental-cinema-17/mekas_paradise.

Seferis, George. "The Last Day." *Collected Poems.* Translated by Edmund Keeley and Philip Sherrard. Princeton, NJ: Princeton University Press, 2014.

Steinem, Gloria. ". . . And Starring—Lee Bouvier!" *McCall's*, February 1968: 78–140.

Swanson, Kelsey. "From Saint to Sinner and Back Again: Jacqueline Kennedy Onassis Rehabilitates Her Image." *Historical Perspectives: Santa Clara University Undergraduate Journal of History, Series II*, March 2005: 70–86.

Van Zanten, Virginia. "Happy Birthday, Lee Radziwill: A Look Inside Her Stunning Homes." *Vogue*, August 2003.

Volandes, Stellene. "A Muse Suprema." *Town & Country*, November 2015: 220–224.

Walters, Barbara. "Jackie Kennedy's Performing Sister." *Good Housekeeping*, March 1963.

Warhol, Andy. "Lee by Andy Warhol." *Interview*, March 1975: 4–6.

Wohlfert, Lee. "In Style: An Ex-Princess Finds Her True Title: Lee Radziwill, Decorator." *People*, November 1, 1976: 50–57.

"Women Who Make World Fashion." *Ladies' Home Journal*, January 1973.

Books

Adler, Bill, ed. *The Eloquent Jacqueline Kennedy Onassis: A Portrait in Her Own Words.* New York: William Morrow, 2004.

Andersen, Christopher. *The Good Son: JFK Jr. and the Mother He Loved.* New York: Gallery Books, 2014.

———. *Jackie After Jack: Portrait of the Lady.* New York: William Morrow, 1998.

———. *Sweet Caroline: Last Child of Camelot.* New York: William Morrow, 2003.

Anthony, Carl Sferrazza. *As We Remember Her: Jacqueline Kennedy Onassis in the Words of Her Family and Friends.* New York: HarperCollins, 1997.

Baldrige, Letitia, with René Verdon. *In the Kennedy Style: Magical Evenings in the Kennedy White House.* New York: Doubleday, 1998.

Beaton, Cecil. *Beaton in the Sixties: The Cecil Beaton Diaries as He Wrote Them, 1965–1969.* Introduction by Hugo Vickers. New York: Alfred A. Knopf, 2004.

———. *The Unexpurgated Beaton: The Cecil Beaton Diaries as He Wrote Them, 1970–1980.* Introduction by Hugo Vickers. New York: Alfred A. Knopf, 2002.

Berman, Matt. *JFK Jr., George, & Me: A Memoir.* New York: Gallery Books, 2014.

Bouvier, Jacqueline, and Lee Bouvier. *One Special Summer.* New York: Rizzoli Books, 2006. First published 1974 by Delacorte Press (New York).

Bradford, Sarah. *America's Queen.* New York: Penguin Books, 2000.

Burton, Richard. *The Richard Burton Diaries.* Edited by Chris Williams. New Haven: Yale University Press, 2012.

Cafarakis, Christian. *The Fabulous Onassis: His Life and Loves.* New York: William Morrow, 1972.

Capote, Truman. *Too Brief a Treat: The Letters of Truman Capote.* Edited by Gerald Clarke. New York: Random House, 2004.

Clarke, Gerald. *Capote: A Biography.* New York: Simon & Schuster, 1988.

Colacello, Bob. *Holy Terror: Andy Warhol Close Up.* New York: HarperCollins, 1990.

Collier, Peter, and David Horowitz. *The Kennedys: An American Drama.* New York: Summit Books, 1984.

Corry, John. *The Manchester Affair.* New York: G. P. Putman's Sons, 1967.

Davis, John H. *The Bouviers: Portrait of an American Family.* New York: Farrar, Straus & Giroux, 1969.

DuBois, Diana. *In Her Sister's Shadow: An Intimate Biography of Lee Radziwill.* New York: Little, Brown & Co., 1995.

Evans, Peter. *Ari: The Life and Times of Aristotle Socrates Onassis.* New York: Summit Books, 1986.

———. *Nemesis: Aristotle Onassis, Jackie O, and the Love Triangle That Brought Down the Kennedys.* New York: Harper, 2004.

Hersh, Seymour M. *The Dark Side of Camelot.* Boston: Little, Brown & Co., 1997.

Hill, Clint, with Lisa McCubbin. *Mrs. Kennedy and Me.* New York: Gallery Books, 2012.

Kaplan, Alice. *Dreaming in French: The Paris Years of Jacqueline Bouvier Kennedy, Susan Sontag, and Angela Davis,* Kindle ed. University of Chicago Press, 2012.

Kavanagh, Julie. *Nureyev: The Life.* New York: Pantheon Books, 2007.

Kennedy, Jacqueline, with Arthur M. Schlesinger Jr. *Jacqueline Kennedy: Historic Conversations on Life with John F. Kennedy.* Introduction by Michael Beschloss. New York: Hyperion, 2011.

Kennedy, Robert F. *Thirteen Days: A Memoir of the Cuban Missile Crisis.* New York: W. W. Norton & Co., 1969.

Klein, Edward. *Just Jackie: Her Private Years.* New York: Ballantine Books, 1998.

Koestenbaum, Wayne. *Jackie under My Skin: Interpreting an Icon.* New York: Farrar, Straus & Giroux, 1995.

Kuhn, William. *Reading Jackie: Her Autobiography in Books.* New York: Nan A. Talese/Doubleday, 2010.

Leamer, Laurence. *The Kennedy Women: The Saga of an American Family.* New York: Villard Books, 1994.

Leaming, Barbara. *Mrs. Kennedy: The Missing History of the Kennedy Years.* New York: Free Press, 2001.

Lerman, Leo. *The Grand Surprise: The Journals of Leo Lerman.* Edited by Stephen Pascal. New York: Alfred A. Knopf, 2007.

Manchester, William. *Controversy: And Other Essays in Journalism, 1950–1975.* Boston: Little, Brown & Co., 1976.

———. *The Death of a President: November 1963.* New York: Harper & Row, 1967.

Noonan, William Sylvester, with Robert Huber. *Forever Young: My Friendship with John F. Kennedy, Jr.* New York: Viking, 2006.

Onassis, Jacqueline, ed. *In the Russian Style.* New York: Viking Press, 1976.

Pottker, Jan. *Janet & Jackie: The Story of a Mother and Her Daughter, Jacqueline Kennedy Onassis.* New York: St. Martin's Press, 2001.

Radziwill, Carole. *What Remains: A Memoir of Fate, Friendship, and Love.* New York: Scribner, 2005.

Radziwill, Lee. *Happy Times.* New York: Assouline, 2000.

———. *Lee.* New York: Assouline, 2015.

Reeves, Richard. *President Kennedy: Profile of Power.* New York: Simon & Schuster, 1993.

Richards, Keith, with James Fox. *Life.* New York and Boston: Little, Brown & Co., 2010.

Salinger, Pierre. *With Kennedy.* New York: Doubleday & Co., 1966.

Schlesinger, Arthur M., Jr. *Journals, 1952–2000.* New York: Penguin Press, 2007.

———. *A Thousand Days: John F. Kennedy in the White House.* Boston: Houghton Mifflin Co., 1965.

Smith, Sally Bedell. *Grace and Power: The Private World of the Kennedy White House.* New York: Random House, 2004.

Solway, Diane. *Nureyev: His Life.* New York: William Morrow, 1998.

Strong, Roy. *The Roy Strong Diaries, 1967–1987.* London: Weidenfeld & Nicolson, 1997.

Terenzio, RoseMarie. *Fairy Tale Interrupted: A Memoir of Life, Love, and Loss.* New York: Gallery Books, 2012.

Theodoracopulos, Taki. *Princes, Playboys, & High-Class Tarts.* Princeton, NJ: Karz-Cohl Publishing, 1984.

Thomas, Evan. *Robert Kennedy: His Life.* New York: Simon & Schuster, 2000.

Vidal, Gore. *Palimpsest: A Memoir.* New York: Random House, 1995.

Warhol, Andy. *The Andy Warhol Diaries.* Edited by Pat Hackett. New York: Warner Books, 1989.

Wilson, Edmund. *The Sixties: The Last Journal, 1960–1972.* New York: Farrar, Straus & Giroux, 1993.

Retrievals, Online Interviews, Blogs, and Documentaries

Capote, Truman. Interview by Stanley Siegel, *The Stanley Siegel Show*, June 1979.

"Jackie Kennedy Onassis: In a Class of Her Own." *Biography*, A&E, 1996.

Radziwill, Lee. Interview by Larry King, *Larry King Live*, March 27, 2001.

———. Interview by Sofia Coppola and Deborah Needleman, *T: The New York Times Style Magazine*, February 17, 2013. https://tmagazine.blogs.nytimes.com/2013/02/07/the-real-lee-radziwill/.

INDEX

ABOUT THE AUTHORS

SAM KASHNER is the author of the comic novel *Sinatra-land* and four nonfiction books, including the acclaimed memoir *When I Was Cool*. He has written extensively for *Vanity Fair.*

NANCY SCHOENBERGER is the author of *Dangerous Muse: The Life of Lady Caroline Blackwood*; *Wayne and Ford: The Films, the Friendship, and the Forging of an American Hero*; and coauthor with Sam Kashner of *Furious Love: Elizabeth Taylor, Richard Burton, and the Marriage of the Century.* She has published three award-winning books of poetry and directs the creative writing program at the College of William & Mary.